Teaching
in Counselor
Education:
Engaging Students
in Learning

Edited by John D. West, Ed.D.
Donald L. Bubenzer, Ph.D.
Jane A. Cox, Ph.D.
Jason M. McGlothlin, Ph.D.

A Product of the
Association for Counselor Education and Supervision
6101 Stevenson Avenue, Suite 600
Alexandria, Virginia 22304

Teaching in Counselor Education: Engaging Students in Learning

Association for Counselor Education and Supervision
6101 Stevenson Avenue, Suite 600
Alexandria, VA 22304

Library of Congress Cataloging-in-Publication Data

Teaching in counselor education : engaging students in learning / edited by John D. West, Ed.D., Donald L. Bubenzer, Ph.D., Jane A. Cox, Ph.D., Jason M. McGlothlin, Ph.D.
    pages cm
Includes bibliographical references and index.
ISBN 978-1-55620-329-9
    1. Mental health counseling—Study and teaching. 2. Mental health counselors—Education. I. West, John D., editor of compilation. II. Bubenzer, Donald L., editor of compilation. III. Cox, Jane A., editor of compilation. IV. McGlothlin, Jason M., editor of compilation.
RA790.8.T37 2013
362.2′0425—dc23   2012048846

To Order

Mail
American Counseling Association
6101 Stevenson Avenue, Suite 600
Alexandria, VA 22304

Phone
800-422-2648 x222
703-823-9800 x222
M–F, 8 am – 6 pm, ET

Fax
703-370-4833

Web
www.counseling.org/publications

Acknowledgments and Note to the Reader

This book is dedicated to all our teachers, colleagues, and students who have taught us about the practices of teaching in counselor education. We, like many of you, have been profoundly influenced by teachers and, as a result, teaching has gained a special place in our lives as counselor educators. It is our hope that this book will serve as a means for helping some to initially consider perspectives on teaching while helping others to continue thoughtful reflection on teaching.

Part of our stories as counselor educators includes an investment in "life-long learning" with regard to counseling and counselor education. For us, writing and editing this book has created an additional place in time to think about the practice of teaching along with considering future possibilities for our teaching. This, in turn, will hopefully open further opportunities for students to become engaged in learning. For this continued reflection on teaching, we are indeed indebted to authors in this text for their time and talent in conveying perspectives on various aspects of teaching.

Of course, one of the ways the counseling profession can show commitment to the practice of teaching is by subjecting it to scholarly inquiry and discussion. It is our hope that a number of high quality manuscripts and professional presentations around teaching will continue to be valued. Ideally, these scholarly products will be generative in character so that the study of teaching in counselor education might be a "life-long learning" process for all of us and for future generations of counselor educators.

Because we are invested in practices of teaching in counselor education, we invite readers to share with us their thoughts on teaching. These thoughts might pertain to any number of teaching practices in counselor education as well as processes for evaluating one's practice. In part, it is through conversations with colleagues and students that our understandings of teaching will continue to develop. The opportunity to serve as a teacher is a special privilege that can result in great professional pleasure, and requires continuous curiosity, dedication, and an ability to connect with others. We wish for all those who decide to step into this role, a professionally fulfilling life as a teacher.

Best wishes,
John, Don, Jane, and Jason
Counseling and Human Development Services Program
Kent State University

Table of Contents

Contributors

Annette C. Albrecht, Ph.D., N.C.C., L.P.C.-S., is a Professor at Tarleton State University. Ann has previously served as co-chair of the ACES Distance Learning task force and has provided leadership to SACES in a number of positions. She co-authored *High Tech High Touch: Distance Learning in Counselor Education* for ACES and is a lifetime member of the Association.

Janine M. Bernard, Ph.D., is Professor and Doctoral Program Coordinator in the Counseling and Human Services Department at Syracuse University. Janine is an ACA Fellow and a recipient of ACA's Arthur A. Hitchcock Distinguished Professional Services Award. She is a past NARACES President and a former board member and chair of the NBCC Board of Directors. She has also been active as a site team member and site team leader for CACREP.

Loretta J. Bradley, a Ph.D. graduate from Purdue University, is a Paul Whitfield Horn Professor in the College of Education at Texas Tech University. Loretta is a former president of the Association for Counselor Education and Supervision and the American Counseling Association. She received the TTU Chancellor's Distinguished Teaching Award and President's Excellence in Teaching Award and research awards from ACES, ACA, and The British Counselling Association for Counselling and Psychotherapy.

Donald L. Bubenzer, Ph.D., is Professor Emeritus in Counseling and Human Development Services at Kent State University where he also served in different administrative capacities. Don has been a member of the American Counseling Association and the Association for Counselor Education and Supervision and he has served as President of the Ohio Counselors Association and the Ohio Association for Counselor Education and Supervision.

JoLynn V. Carney, Ph.D., L.P.C.C.-S., N.C.C., is Associate Professor of Counselor Education at Penn State University. JoLynn's extensive service to professional organizations includes being President of Chi Sigma Iota, chair of ACES regional committees, as well as an editorial board member on several prominent ACA journals.

Jane A. Cox, Ph.D., is Associate Professor and Doctoral Coordinator in Kent State University's Counseling and Human Development Services program. She has served as president, secretary, and program chair for the North Central Association for Counselor Education and Supervision, program chair for the 2007 Association for Counselor Education and Supervision national conference, and reviewer on the editorial board for *Counselor Education and Supervision*. Jane also served as the president of the Ohio Association for Counselor Education and Supervision.

Norma L. Day-Vines, Ph.D., is Professor of Counseling and Human Services at Johns Hopkins University. Her research focuses on strategies and interventions for working more effectively with culturally and linguistically diverse clients and has appeared in the *Journal of Counseling & Development* and *Counselor Education and Supervision*.

Janet Froeschle, Ph.D., is an Associate Professor of Counselor Education in the Educational Psychology and Leadership Department at Texas Tech University. She received her Ph.D. in Counselor Education from Texas A & M University-Corpus Christi and is both a licensed professional counselor and certified school counselor in Texas. Janet has membership in both the American Counseling Association and the Association for Counselor Education and Supervision.

Kelsey George, M.Ed., is currently a doctoral student and Teaching Fellow in the Counseling and Human Development Services program at Kent State University. She is an active member in ACA, ACES, CSI, and OCA and holds Professional Counselor (P.C.) licensure in Ohio.

Richard J. Hazler, Ph.D., L.P.C.C.-S., N.C.C. is Professor of Counselor Education at Penn State University. Richard's extensive experience in professional organizations includes being President of a number of associations including the Association for Humanistic Education and Development (now Association for Humanistic Counseling), Chi Sigma Iota, two state branches of ACA and ACES, and he has served as chair of numerous national committees including Strategic Planning and Professional Development for ACA.

Bret Hendricks, Ed.D., is an Associate Professor and Clinical Director of Counselor Education at Texas Tech University. His major research interests are substance abuse and professional counselor ethics. He is a former president of the International Association for Marriage and Family Counselors and a frequent presenter at counseling conferences.

Michelle S. Gimenez Hinkle, Ph.D., is an Assistant Professor in the Department of Special Education and Counseling at William Paterson University. She has also taught in the Counseling and Human Development Services program at Kent State University and is a member of the American Counseling Association and the Association for Counselor Education and Supervision.

Cheryl Holcomb-McCoy, Ph.D., is the Vice Dean of Academic Affairs and Professor of Counseling and Human Services at Johns Hopkins University. Her areas of research specialization include the measurement of multicultural self-efficacy and cultural competence in school counseling, best practices in urban school counselor preparation, and the examination of school counseling programs that influence students' college readiness. Cheryl has authored over 50 articles in refereed national journals and is the author of the best-selling book entitled, *School Counseling to Close the Achievement Gap: A Social Justice Framework for Success* (Corwin Press). Currently she is an Associate Editor for the *Journal of Counseling & Development.* In 2009, she was awarded the prestigious Mary Smith Arnold Anti-Oppression Award at the American Counseling Association conference in Charlotte, NC. And in 2007, the Association for Multicultural Counseling and Development (AMCD) selected her for the Exemplary Diversity Leadership Award.

Gulnora Hundley, M.D., Ph.D., L.M.H.C. is Director of the Community Counseling Clinic, College of Education, at the University of Central Florida where she also teaches graduate courses in Mental Health Counseling. She has been a member of the American Counseling Association for ten years and has made a number of presentations at both national and international ACA conferences. Gulnora has worked as a counselor in community mental health clinics in Central Florida and has a private practice in Winter Park.

Marty Jencius, Ph.D., is Associate Professor in the Counseling and Human Development Services Program at Kent State University. He has served as the ACA Cybertechnology Taskforce Chair and as the Technology Interest Network Chair for ACES. He is the creator of CESNET-L listserv, the *Journal of Technology in Counseling,* CounselorAudioSource.net, Counselor Education in Second Life, and other counselor education technology resources.

Dennis G. Jones, Ph.D., is a Professor and Dean at Tarleton State University. Dennis has previously served as co-chair of the ACES Distance Learning task force and has provided leadership to SACES in a number of positions. He co-authored *High Tech High Touch: Distance Learning in Counselor Education* for ACES and is a lifetime member of the Association.

Courtland C. Lee, Ph.D., is Professor of Counselor Education at the University of Maryland at College Park. He is a Fellow and past president of the American

Counseling Association. He has held numerous leadership positions in the Association for Counselor Education and Supervision (ACES), including ACES representative to the CACREP Board and National Awards Committee Chair.

Melissa Luke, Ph.D., is Assistant Professor and Coordinator of the School Counseling program in the Counseling and Human Services Department at Syracuse University. Melissa has over 15 years experience working as both a teacher and counselor in K-12 public schools. She co-chairs the New Faculty Interest Network and is a member of the Awards Committee within ACES. In addition, Melissa is a member of the editorial boards of the *Journal of Counseling and Development* and *Professional School Counseling,* as well as serves as the NARACES Regional Chapter Facilitator for Chi Sigma Iota.

Jason McGlothlin, Ph.D., is currently an Associate Professor in the Counseling and Human Development Services Program and coordinates the Clinical Mental Health Counseling and School Counseling programs at Kent State University. He earned his Ph.D. in Counselor Education and Supervision from Ohio University and is a Professional Clinical Counselor with Supervisory endorsement (P.C.C.-S.) in Ohio. Jason has been an active member in ACA and ACES since 1996 and served in various roles such as editorial board member for *Counselor Education and Supervision,* publicity and promotion committee chair for the 2007 ACES national conference, technology chair for the ACA Midwest region, and president of the Ohio ACES.

GoEun Na, M.A., is a doctoral student in Counselor Education at the University of Maryland, College Park. She has presented at a number of local and national conferences on cross-cultural counseling and supervision. She was awarded a 2011 Leadership Fellowship from Chi Sigma Iota and has served as the Webmaster of the Maryland Association for Counseling and Development.

Gerald Parr, Ph.D., is a Professor in the College of Education at Texas Tech University. A past president of the West Texas Counseling Association, he received a Writing Award from the Texas Counseling Association in 1988. He has received the President's Excellence in Teaching Award at Texas Tech University twice.

Roxanna N. Pebdani, M.A., is a doctoral candidate in Counselor Education at the University of Maryland at College Park. She has presented at ACA conferences on multicultural counseling, sexuality and disability, the reasonable accommodation process for people with disabilities, and the transition process for youth with disabilities to work or to post-secondary education. She is a past president of the Rho Beta Chapter of Chi Sigma Iota.

Mark L. Savickas, Ph.D., is Professor of Family and Community Medicine at the Northeastern Ohio Medical University and Adjunct Professor in the Counseling and Human Development Services Program at Kent State University. Mark is a Fellow of the American Counseling Association and editor of the *Journal of Vocational Behavior*. He has made over 500 presentations to professional organizations and groups in 15 countries.

Diana L. VanWinkle, M.Ed., is currently a doctoral candidate in the Counseling and Human Development Services program at Kent State University. She has taught several graduate level counseling courses and is an active member of ACA and ACES.

John D. West, Ed.D., is Professor of Counseling and Human Development Services at Kent State University. John is a member of the Association for Counselor Education and Supervision and the American Counseling Association, and he has been grateful for opportunities to learn about counselor education from teachers, colleagues, and students.

Mark E. Young, Ph.D., is Professor of Counselor Education at the University of Central Florida and is the Coordinator of the Marriage and Family Therapy Program and Director of Faculty Development for the UCF Marriage and Family Research Institute. He is recipient of ACA's David K. Brooks Distinguished Mentor Award and is currently President of the Association for Spiritual, Ethical and Religious Values in Counseling, an ACA Division. For more than 15 years, Mark worked as a counselor in community mental health, corrections, and private practice and has been a counselor educator for the past 25 years.

Preface

Overview of Teaching in Counselor Education: Engaging Students in Learning

DONALD L. BUBENZER
JOHN D. WEST
JANE A. COX
JASON McGLOTHLIN

ften through our years together as counselor educators we have sat as colleagues at Kent State and at times with more distant colleagues, pondering teachers, teaching, and student engagement in learning. Those conversations might have gone like this, "I (Don) remember Dr. Richard Fisch once saying, 'So the question is, did Columbus discover America or did he create it?'" The question stuck and Don was puzzled by that catchy turn of a phrase. A few years later two of us sat interviewing Dr. Ken Gergen and he said in effect, "We create reality by the language we choose to describe it." Again, at the time the idea was novel to us, novel enough to stick in our minds and yet too novel, at the moment, to incorporate into a coherent story that would broaden our lives and guide our thinking. But along the way Don pondered comments by Drs. Fisch and Gergen and he began to think about Mr. Warren Moon, and the Art History course he took in 1963; you know, the one we all took where we memorized paintings and artists. At the time Don was so busy with the memorization that the instructor's point of the course did not sink in, or maybe it did. At least the pictures were there and perhaps so were Mr. Moon's lectures, which held meaning waiting to be released as suggested by comments from Drs. Fisch and Gergen. Art has suggested different realities at different times to different people based on the context in which it was inspired and based on conversations among those who view it. Yet there has to be enough commonness among the perspectives of some viewers for the art to gain traction and hold significance over time. Both the artist and the viewers share their perspectives, resulting in a landscape of created realities.

Well, of course what has been described is one perspective and others might have had similar experiences and come to different perspectives or no perspective depending on their own experiences and understandings. Obviously, Don has been drawn to the narrativist-constructionist perspectives, at least for now. But, behind this narrative of constructed realities, there were three teachers mentioned, and many more recalled, who by lecture, discussion, demonstration, media, activity, and feedback provided the context for learning.

One in our group (John) has on many occasions lauded the teaching efforts of instructors he had in graduate school. For example, one faculty member had an uncommon ability to move students to a more thoughtful place, as an opportunity was opened for thinking during quiet moments of listening and note taking and reflecting on presentations. This individual moved students to additional thought and interest in the presentation and was a masterful lecturer. Another seemed to always be available to students who wanted to talk about counseling theories. With a genuine interest in the subject, even out-of-class discussions easily turned into role plays in the professor's office. There were few things more exciting than taking the role of the counselor as the faculty member role played the part of the client. And yet another faculty member had an ability to facilitate a seminar in such a way that the students felt compelled to be prepared in order to offer an informed contribution. This individual was able to combine a welcoming manner with a clear expectation that students should be prepared. In each of these cases, there was an affirming style on the part of the faculty member. Stephenson (2001) seemed to be writing to the importance of an affirming style when he noted that "extraordinary teachers" have an "exceptional ability to connect with students" (p. xxxi).

Don remembers a rather quiet and demure professor, who gave excellent feedback on written work. This individual circled subject-verb agreement issues, noted formatting issues by number according to the most recent edition of the *Publication Manual of the American Psychological Association* (currently the 2010 edition), so that they had to be looked up, while also providing grades for both content and writing style, and this professor allowed students additional opportunities to improve on their work. He remembers being so embarrassed by his errors, and the time it had required this professor to correct his paper, that he vowed to take the mechanics of writing much more seriously. The faculty member's use of feedback as a teaching mechanism certainly impacted the time Don takes and the nature of feedback he gives students today. These thoughts seem similar to comments made by Stephenson (2001) when he wrote, "One of the biggest misconceptions about highly rated teachers is that they are easy. Far from it —extraordinary teachers are demanding instructors who teach rigorous courses" (p. xxxii). In turn, Bain (2004) asked, "Why do some teachers expect more and get students to produce it . . . while others fail miserably with what they regard as 'higher' standards?" (p. 71). After considering data from his own research as well as literature on "stereotypes" (pp. 72-76), Bain, in part, noted exemplary teachers

> took all their students seriously, and treated each one with respect. . . .
> [and] they could convince their students through . . . sincerity . . . [that the

suggestions they offered were] based on the high standards of the best . . . scholarly . . . thinking, and [a belief by the professor that the] student had the capacity to benefit from the advice. (pp. 76-77)

Jane spoke of the time faculty members took with her on Saturday mornings to work with her on her dissertation. It was time given at least monthly, sometimes weekly, for over a year. That time together included general discussions of literature related to "reflective" practices and to her experiences in implementing those practices, as well as the research she was conducting on the use of "reflecting teams" stimulated by the work of Tom Andersen (1991). It included critiques of writing and thinking, and Jane mentioned, "We were discovering how to work together and growing together in our understandings of the theory and practice of using 'reflection' as a way of learning, maybe even as a way of life." Stephenson (2001) wrote, "Extraordinary teachers have a passion for four things—learning, their fields, their students, and teaching. In other words, they believe deeply in their work, the people they serve, and their mission" (p. xxii). It has been our experience that these beliefs are often evident in time and commitment given to students during their studies.

Jason has fondly recalled relationships he developed with faculty members and how each of these relationships was unique. He was caught by the notion that faculty members who inspired him also challenged him to think for himself, and encouraged Jason to be comfortable with the unknown. During the oral portion of his doctoral comprehensive examinations, Jason remembers feeling confident and yet nervous in front of the five members of his committee. One committee member asked a question that Jason interpreted as abstract and unclear and he politely noted, "I am not sure if I am following your question, can you tell me more?" The response was, "No, I want you to wrestle with my question." In that moment Jason remembers feeling frustrated by the comment; however, he posed a few responses that he thought addressed the question. The individual replied with a smile and said something to the effect of, "Good response, not what I was looking for, but your thinking is sound." Allowing Jason to think through the question and sift through the ambiguity was the faculty member's goal. Jason mentions having carried this experience with him and having remembered the individual's intent during his own teaching. Struggling with meaning can cultivate even richer understandings. Herbert Tucker (2003), a professor of poetry, suggested that having students wrestle with ambiguity can lead to broader and clearer understandings. In counseling, our clients can at times experience a lack of clarity around their difficulties. It is up to us as counselors to help them work through their ambiguity and gain helpful perspectives. Being clear with students is important in many situations; however, working with ambiguity can lead to useful understandings and it also mirrors efforts found in the counselor-client relationship. A great amount of learning can come from working with the unknown.

In a final example of the effect a teacher might have on a student, Don recalls sitting in the Jolly Roger Doughnut Shop in Lancaster, Ohio, late at night with two faculty members discussing the effort to get legislation passed that would license counselors in Ohio. They had dropped him off in Lancaster to teach a class for one of them while they went on to Columbus to speak with legislators and legislative committees about what counselors had to offer the citizens. On the way back from their duties, Don was picked up in Lancaster and he recalls how "we all sat, talked, and enjoyed the doughnuts." He remembers how the two faculty members were invested in the legislative effort both as a way of serving citizens and as a way of establishing the counseling profession. They had been at work on the issue for several years but were especially hopeful that progress was being made. They spoke specifically and respectfully of legislators and the kind of information that was needed to help individuals see the merit of licensure. Don recalls being struck by the confidence they had in him to teach, by their commitment to counselors, citizens, and the legislative effort, and by the respect they had for those who served the public as legislators. He still looks back on that time as making a difference in the emergence of the counseling profession and in the eventual realization that "in many ways, their work made it possible for me to have a 35 year career in counselor education. It was a lesson in vision, strategy, and commitment that I will never forget." These comments remind us of Bain's (2004) remarks that, "Highly effective teachers tend to reflect a strong trust in students. They usually believe that students want to learn, and they assume, until proven otherwise, that they can" (p. 18). Each of the above memories also brings to mind comments from *The Art of Teaching* by Parini (2005),

> Nobody who has taught for very long has not experienced the strange allure and intimacy of the teacher-student relationship. . . . It moves beyond what psychologists refer to as transference. There is true love in the passing on of knowledge, and this involves understanding: the teacher must really know the student, on some deep level, for teaching of the most intense kind to happen. The student must have real love for the teacher. We have all experienced this, from first grade through graduate school, and beyond. I have loved my best teachers. (p. 124)

For us these teaching-mentoring moments came as gifts; gifts we did not receive and open at the time and gifts given by teachers who assumed they were just doing their jobs; trying to help society to be more inclusive, more skillfully caring, and to move our knowledge base in ways that were more responsive to human and environmental needs. But now in our careers, we understand their involvements with us to have been gifts. They were teaching us not only about the content of counselor education but also about the caring lifestyle of being a counselor educator. They had accepted a sacred responsibility, that is an essential trust (see Kittredge, 1999, p. 42), to care deeply about the well-being of the world in which they lived and as teachers they had accepted the challenge of engaging others in the caring and learning process. Through their involvements they passed that trust onto us. We hope we are good stewards of the gifts we have been given. As you read the chapters in this book we trust you will be touched by the generosity and caring of these author-teachers who themselves seem to see teaching as a sacred trust; an opportunity to live generous lives.

FOCUS OF THE BOOK

The idea for this book grew then from discussions we had about teaching and from our own experiences as teachers. Some of us were inclined, as learners, to have an appreciation for the spoken word via lectures, some liked class discussions, others appreciated applied work in field settings, and some thought they grew from classroom activities and processing. Instructor and student feedback encouraged rethinking and improvement in our teaching. Each of us thought that exposure to the critical issues of the time, as formal students and later in life, helped us realize that social justice, inclusion, and environmental concern, that is, values, were always critical components of the teaching-learning process.

With time, we each gained further clarity around the complexities of the teaching-learning process. Although we might each prefer some teaching modalities, for example, lecturing, there were often different aspects of the modality that held the appeal. For one it might be the turn of phrases and for someone else it might be connections the instructor made between concepts and life as experienced by the student. The appeal was often a part of a larger context or narrative on teaching and learning that we perceived as having its origins in earlier life experiences, and in our histories as educators, which were expressed in involvements with students, colleagues, and professional issues, as well as our professional dreams and commitments for the future.

We decided to delve further into the practices of teaching by contacting colleagues who we thought held a particular aspect of teaching close to their heart and who we thought had special insights and knowledge about the use of that particular component of teaching. We asked these counselor educators to address four facets of working with a specified teaching modality or issue. Authors first discussed a rationale for their particular modality and reviewed literature related to the modality. For example, they might have noted why they thought the use of the seminar was a valuable learning activity and reviewed literature about the use of the seminar format. Secondly, they noted practices of implementing the teaching modality that they found useful. Either integrated into this discussion or in a separate section they described experiences or examples they had in using the modality. Finally, they offered their thoughts on evaluating the effectiveness of the particular approach that was the topic of their discussion. These discussions of the engagement of students in meaningful learning, using specific modalities or issues, comprise chapters 2–12 of the text and are further described below. Chapter 1 has an intentionally different structure and discusses literature illustrating assumptions and beliefs about teaching and how beliefs about teaching are associated with practices by means of a teaching philosophy statement, whereas the closing chapter, 13, reviews ideas from the authors and addresses the need to be a reflective teacher.

TEACHING MODALITIES AND ISSUES

In Chapter 2, *Creating a Syllabus and Course Anticipation: Early Engagement of Students,* Jane Cox addresses three functions that syllabi might serve: communication, organization, and agreement (Eberly, Newton, & Wiggins, 2001). A syllabus communicates not only the goals and objectives for a course but also the instructor's preferred tone for the course. Organization is about conveying the flow of the course and developing teaching strategies to accompany the flow. Agreement notes the more specific expectations for assignments, class participation expectations, and grading criteria. Jane also shares thought on a pre-course teaching practice designed to encourage students to become engaged in the process of learning. Finally, evaluation of syllabi both by colleagues and students is addressed.

Mark Savickas (*Preparing and Presenting Lectures That Exemplify the Ideals of Counselor Education,* Chapter 3) addresses the historical context of lecturing in education. His chapter models how a scholar might think about the lecturing process. Mark notes that counselor educators who lecture have an advantage of bringing their counseling skills to the process. He provides ideas about purposes that lectures might serve, as well as ideas about lecture preparation and delivery. We would have a particular appreciation for an underlying theme of Mark's lecture preparation; that is, engaging students with the larger world in which they live via art, music, prose, media, daily events, and active learning.

In Chapter 4, *Making Use of the Seminar,* JoLynn Carney and Richard Hazler tackle the teaching methodology of the seminar as a means of engaging students in learning. They note that a value of the seminar is in connecting knowledge to experience. With the presupposition of students possessing knowledge, they focus on what are sometimes termed "higher order" thinking skills including: analysis, synthesis, application, and evaluation (Bloom, Engelhart, Furst, Hill, & Krathwohl, 1956). The authors note that an attribute of the seminar is the stimulation of a diversity of ideas. Our own experience is that in leading seminars one must often wade through a wilderness of ideas to arrive at the promised land of well-formulated thought. JoLynn and Richard guide the reader through instructional practices, useful to seminars, that offer roads to the promised land.

Mark Young and Gulnora Hundley (*Connecting Experiential Education and Reflection in the Counselor Education Classroom*, Chapter 5) posit that experiential learning is a preferred approach to use with adult learners. The mode connects experience with new learning often through the medium of reflective practices. With an emphasis on the importance of critical reflection, the authors discuss four types of experiential exercises: experiments, simulations, case study and critical incident analysis, and problem-based learning that they think have particular utility to counselor educators. Finally, they discuss some of the pitfalls of the evaluation of students who are involved in experiential learning and offer suggestions for avoiding these problems.

Chapter 6, *Using Out-of-Class Learning Activities*, explores, from both an instructor's and students' perspective, the practices and value of using what has been historically thought of as homework to increase students' engagement and learning. Jason McGlothlin, Diana VanWinkle, and Kelsey George suggest that for out-of-class assignments to have the greatest impact they must address course objectives and be prescribed in ways so that students can understand the relevance of the assignment to their own professional growth. The authors suggest further criteria to be used in developing out-of-class learning assignments and provide examples of such assignments and methods for evaluating them.

Marty Jencius (*Using Technology in Teaching*, Chapter 7) provides a brief historic review of the advances made in technology that have pertinence to education over the past 20 years. He then, given a focus on pedagogical purpose, provides criteria (e.g., cost, sustainability, ease of use, etc.) to help the counselor educator decide which technologies are worthy of investment. Specific technological applications for the classroom are also discussed, for example, microblogging, news feeds, virtual worlds, and so forth.

Annette Albrecht and Dennis Jones (*Using Distance Learning in Teaching*, Chapter 8) provide a glossary of terms used in the distance learning arena. They use these terms to describe some of the "best" practices of distance learning. The practices convey the need for thoughtful organization of distance learning courses. The authors also suggest practices for evaluating the distance learning process and outcomes. Their comments on distance learning are timely in light of the interest shown by counselor education programs in the practice of distance learning.

One might posit that professions are judged by how well they are perceived to serve a public good. In serving that public good, professions must insure their viability by developing professionals capable of providing excellent services to the public and to the profession that supports them. Most of the chapters in this book address the preparation of professionals to deliver services to the public. In Chapter 9, *Teaching to Encourage Professional Involvement*, Courtland Lee, GoEun

Na, and Roxanna Pebdani explore ideas related to the preparation of individuals to provide service to the profession. Courtland, GoEun, and Roxanna give particular attention in the chapter to instruction that encourages meaningful professional involvement among counselor trainees.

Janine Bernard and Melissa Luke (*Reflecting on Student-Teacher Relationships Within Counselor Education*, Chapter 10) address teacher-student relationships that encourage student learning. Although they address inappropriate faculty-student relationships, their primary focus is on using relational skills common to counselors and counselor educators to enhance teacher-student relationships focused on learning. Janine and Melissa discuss the use of boundary maintenance, challenging, empathy, modeling, and self-disclosure with students as well as enhancement of student-to-student interactions. They also address topics such as social networking and experience levels of students as considerations in developing relationships focused on learning. Similar to the counselor-client relationship, we have come to believe that the teacher-student relationship is a meaningful component in the student's educational experience.

Loretta Bradley, Janet Froeschle, Gerald Parr, and Bret Hendricks (*Using Solution Focused Evaluation to Engage Students in the Learning Process*, Chapter 11) address the issue of how one makes student evaluations a learning process as well as an evaluation process. More specifically they discuss ways of using solution focused evaluation as a source for student engagement in learning. The authors stress the importance of having students involved in their own evaluation and draw from writings on solution focused techniques. Finally, they suggest the use of Student Evaluations of Teaching (SETs) in assessing the helpfulness of solution focused evaluations in counselor education courses.

In Chapter 12 (*Broaching the Subjects of Race, Ethnicity, and Culture as a Tool for Addressing Diversity in Counselor Education Classes*), Norma Day-Vines and Cheryl Holcomb-McCoy introduce conceptual frameworks, the *Continuum of Broaching Behavior* (Day-Vines et al., 2007) and the *Multidimensional Model of Broaching Behavior*, as tools that counselor educators and counselors-in-training might use in advancing their ability to hold conversations concerning race, ethnicity, and culture. These frameworks are viewed as potential resources for counselor education and for engaging others in a multiculturally sensitive manner.

CONCLUSION

The Council for Accreditation of Counseling and Related Educational Programs (CACREP, 2009) notes in its doctoral standards (Section IV.C.2.) students are to receive preparation in "instructional theory and methods relevant to counselor education." It would appear that teaching about theory and method might be a rather straightforward endeavor, yet, as noted by Parker Palmer (2007), we find that "writing about teaching" is done with a good deal of "humility" (p. xi). For us, this is because, much like walking on a forest trail, there can be an endless series of noteworthy, absorbing, and inspiring images to investigate, from those that lie right at one's feet to those that remain further up the trail. With regard to teaching, these images can include an array of narratives about instruction with some focusing on methods used by the instructor and others focusing on the self or selves one chooses for company in the classroom. So while reading this book and considering methods of teaching, we would ask that you also reflect on personal stories about what it means to be a teacher in counselor education, for this will be taken up again later in the Epilogue.

REFERENCES

American Psychological Association. (2010). *Publication manual of the American Psychological Association* (6th ed.). Washington, DC: Author.

Andersen, T. (Ed.). (1991). *The reflecting team: Dialogues and dialogues about the dialogues.* New York, NY: Norton.

Bain, K. (2004). *What the best college teachers do.* Cambridge, MA: Harvard University Press.

Bloom, B. S., Engelhart, M. D., Furst, F. J., Hill, W. H., & Krathwohl, D. R. (1956). *Taxonomy of educational objectives: Cognitive domain.* New York, NY: McKay.

Council for Accreditation of Counseling and Related Educational Programs. (2009). *2009 standards.* Retrieved from http://www.cacrep.org/doc/2009%20Standards.pdf

Day-Vines, N. L., Wood, S. M., Grothaus, T., Craigen, L., Holman, A., Dotson-Blake, K., & Douglass, M. J. (2007). Broaching the subjects of race, ethnicity, and culture during the counseling process. *Journal of Counseling & Development, 85*(4), 401–409.

Eberly, M. B., Newton, S. E., & Wiggins, R. A. (2001). The syllabus as a tool for student-centered learning. *The Journal of General Education, 50,* 56–74.

Kittredge, W. (1999). *Taking care: Thoughts on storytelling and belief.* Minneapolis, MN: Milkwood Editions.

Palmer, P. J. (2007). *The courage to teach: Exploring the inner landscape of a teacher's life* (10th ed.). San Francisco, CA: Jossey-Bass.

Parini, J. (2005). *The art of teaching.* New York, NY: Oxford University Press.

Stephenson, F. (Ed.). (2001). *Extraordinary teachers: The essence of excellent teaching.* Kansas City, MO: Andrews McMeel.

Tucker, H. G. (2003). Teaching ambiguity. *Pedagogy: Critical Approaches to Literature, Language, Composition, and Culture, 3*(3), 441–450.

CHAPTER 1

Considering and Articulating One's Beliefs About Teaching

JOHN D. WEST

DONALD L. BUBENZER

MICHELLE S. GIMENEZ HINKLE

ordon Gee, President of The Ohio State University, mentioned in an October 7, 2009 address to the faculty that "if we are to live up to our noble callings . . . there are substantial changes we must make. . . . Changing the way we define scholarship, appreciate new forms of engagement, and properly reward superb teaching can be this University's signal differential" (The essay, para. 51 and 53). Gee, in part, appeared to be calling attention to the importance of teaching in a university community. Ernest Boyer (1990), approximately two decades earlier, sought to give a renewed definition to scholarship by providing a more integrated view of traditional research and teaching in an engaged environment. Boyer's view was partly intended to raise the status of instruction by establishing an integrated view of scholarship. Within counselor education, Davis, Levitt, Mc-Glothlin, and Hill (2006) surveyed CACREP-accredited program liaisons (from master's and doctoral degree granting programs as well as master's degree only programs) and found, with regard to importance for tenure and promotion decisions, no significant difference between the valuing of the domains of teaching, scholarship, and service. Comments by Davis et al. also seem to signal a perceived level of importance given to teaching and an integration of the roles of faculty members in counselor education.

1

Although the importance of teaching in higher education can almost be assumed, the relationship between teaching and the outcomes of learning are vastly complex and include teaching, learning, and contextual variables. For example, conversations on and off campus might signal differing views on the nature and goals of education held by faculty members, students, and what we might term society at large. Regarding views on teaching, there is a plurality of methods of instruction, with underlying variables including beliefs and thoughts about teaching, and it is the manifestation of these beliefs in practices of teaching that is the focus of this book. In this chapter, however, we would like to highlight the importance of one's beliefs about teaching, and so we will take a moment to review—for illustrative purposes—six examples of literature pertaining to beliefs about teaching. Then, we will present how counselor educators might make their beliefs about teaching more transparent through the development of a teaching philosophy statement.

BELIEFS ABOUT TEACHING

Beliefs about pedagogy suggest methodologies for the practice of teaching; for example, it may be proposed that students learn best when they apply their knowledge to real world problems. Such a belief might lead to the use of case studies, problem focused learning, or simulations in counselor education. On the other hand, there may be some who believe in the importance of conceptual understanding and who think lecture is the best method of teaching. Through a review of related literature, we identified a number of beliefs that appear relevant to the practice of teaching. Ginsberg (2007), for example, used interviews and observations to identify characteristics of college and university faculty members who were identified as good communicators. She presented narratives from faculty members and described them as sharing two characteristics: a "humanistic" perspective of students and an appreciation of "reflection" in teaching (p. 4). It was mentioned that, in part, humanism might be characterized by demonstrations of "care and concern for . . . students" (p. 5), and she referenced Shulman (1987) and mentioned that reflection might include an "ability to consider the teaching process as it . . . [relates] to the students' learning" (p. 11).

In addition, Fitzmaurice (2008) conducted a qualitative study with data coming from teaching philosophy statements constructed by individuals who finished "a postgraduate certificate in teaching and learning in higher education" (p. 344). Five themes about good teaching emerged from analysis of these statements. "A deep obligation to help students learn" was mentioned (p. 345). "A desire to create a space for learning and encourage student voice" was identified and, in part, consisted of helping students develop an analytic style in relation to their studies (p. 346). Third, "Caring for students and developing the whole person" was also noted from the analysis (p. 347). Fourth, "Reflection on practice" was identified as a theme descriptive of high quality teaching (p. 347). Finally, "Professional values and morality" was recognized and it was noted that "there is evidence in the statements of a clear commitment to values such as care, responsibility, respect and trust and the relevance of virtue ethics can be seen" (p. 348). In commenting on these beliefs about teaching, Fitzmaurice appeared to indicate that consideration has been directed towards results of teaching and "little attention has been given to the moral and ethical dimensions of teaching, to those features that make teaching responsible as well as effective . . . . The challenge is to integrate the two concepts" (p. 350).

Earlier, Pratt (1992) studied 253 individuals, with 218 described as educators of adult learners, in five countries, with regard to their "conceptions of teaching" (pp. 205-206). Pratt described conceptions as, in part, including beliefs about teaching (p. 205). He used phenomenography as a method of research (p. 204) and, from interviews, found five conceptions pertaining to teaching. One conception was described as the "Engineering Conception: Delivering Content" and emphasized the presentation of content (p. 210). Another conception was described as the "Apprenticeship Conception: Modeling Ways of Being" where teachers demonstrated certain "values and knowledge" in their work (p. 211). As Pratt suggested, this conception of teaching might be observed at an internship site, where a less experienced person works under the tutelage and supervision of a more experienced professional (p. 213). The "Developmental Conception: Cultivating the Intellect" was described as helping students move past current ways of reasoning to more developed ways of contemplating (p. 213). The "Nurturing Conception: Facilitating Personal Agency" focused on providing "emotional support" while also offering problems or dilemmas as well as instruction for consideration (p. 214). Finally, the "Social Reform Conception: Seeking A Better Society" described teaching that was characterized by noticeable standards or values connected to an image of an improved civilization which informed one's instruction (p. 216). Here Pratt provided the example of a person working with women on career development and "expressed a feminist perspective wherein knowledge and authority were socially constructed" (p. 216). It would seem that this 1992 study identified five conceptions that, in part, included beliefs about teaching, and that these conceptions might be easily recognized today.

A fourth example of literature related to beliefs about teaching comes from a study by Hativa, Barak, and Simhi (2001). They mentioned a view of teachers being thoughtfully engaged in their work (p. 699), and the teachers in their study were those who received elevated evaluations of undergraduate-level instruction at a university in Israel (p. 704). As part of the study, the authors interviewed four faculty members about four identified dimensions of teaching, specifically, "Lesson organization," "Lesson clarity," "Making a lesson interesting/engaging," and "Classroom climate" (p. 707). It was noted that two interviewees indicated "Lesson organization" to have "importance" or to be "important" (p. 709). Regarding "Lesson clarity," each of the participants was familiar with "the importance of clear teaching, of posing questions during the lesson to check for student understanding, and of giving good examples and illustrations" (p. 709). Each of the four participants had an appreciation for "the importance of maintaining student attention throughout the lesson" (p. 709). And, finally, regarding "Classroom climate," the four interviewees acknowledged "the need to create a pleasant classroom climate that is conducive to learning" (p. 709).

In another case, Herron, Beedle, and King (2006) used qualitative methodology and investigated "perceptions" (p. 78) of seven female College of Education faculty members in an educational leadership program regarding their teaching. With regard to one of the themes that was listed as a finding from the study ("Perceptions of Faculty Role"; p. 78), the researchers noted that participants supported empowering students, with prominence given to involvement in one's studies, and many viewed themselves as facilitators of knowledge acquisition which, at times, included helping students find individual or personal understandings of one's studies. Participants thought students' requirements for learning should be acknowledged in selecting teaching procedures. "Planning" was prioritized as important, however, it was mentioned that, "Faculty did allow flexibility in planning for the class, developing strategies as the class progressed and allowing more flexibility for graduate students" (p.78). These were some of the views or beliefs participants held about their own teaching and they were associated with the theme, "Perceptions of Faculty Role." These views and beliefs seemed to speak to an interest in working with students, affirming their active involvement in learning, and responding to their requirements for learning.

Finally, in the book titled, *What the Best College Teachers Do*, Bain (2004) described his study of teachers in higher education and their work relative to good teaching (p. 4). In soliciting teachers for the study, he mentioned criteria that included, in part, support for the idea that students had been pleased with the teaching they received "and inspired by it to continue to learn" (p. 7), and support for the idea that "the [teacher's] learning objectives . . . [were] worthy and substantial" (p. 8). Various methods were used to collect data for the study; for example, observations and interviews were utilized and items used by instructors were reviewed (p. 11). Conclusions included, but were not limited to, the following: (a) exemplary instructors are very familiar with information pertaining to their course(s), they can consider the merit of their ideas relative to course content, and they clearly present their thoughts (pp. 15–16); (b) they regard teaching as a valuable undertaking (p. 17); (c) they have high standards for students and promote productivity with expectations that exemplify "the kind of thinking and acting [that is] expected for life" (pp. 17–18); (d) they try to create an analytic atmosphere where students "learn by confronting intriguing . . . important problems

... that will challenge them to ... examine their mental models of reality" (p. 18); (e) they show a "trust in students" and generally assume that they have a desire to study (p. 18); and (f) these instructors have a plan for judging their teaching and implementing helpful modifications (p. 19).

From the foregoing it appears clear that teachers viewed their beliefs about teaching as important. For example, some beliefs from the highlighted studies revealed the importance of encouraging students to establish individual and personal understandings of their schoolwork, assisting them with more involved ways of reasoning, having supportive relationships with students, teaching in an explicit and unambiguous manner, using methodologies that maintain student interest, maintaining familiarity with information pertaining to one's courses(s) and considering the merit of one's thoughts relative to course content, as well as creating opportunities for students to work with professionally relevant issues while also evaluating their understandings. Certain of these beliefs may hold almost universal acclaim by teachers while others may be reflective of segments of the teaching population. How these beliefs are manifested, whether they are universal or segmented, depends upon the characteristics of the teacher, the learner, and the context and thus there are diverse ways in which they may be displayed. For instance, although there may be a near universal belief that caring about students' learning is important for effective teaching, how the caring is manifested may differ substantially depending upon the teacher, the student, and the learning context. As an example, caring about students' learning might result in providing individual homework assignments or in refraining from individual assignments with an inclination towards group work.

In line with this idea of differential practices, the authors of this chapter consider it important for teachers to be aware of their beliefs and the connection between their beliefs and instructional behavior. Counselor educators may be interested in studying how teachers put their beliefs about teaching into practice (e.g., see Hativa et al., 2001) as well as the impact their beliefs have on student learning. Such intentionality requires counselor educators to find meaningful and revealing ways to surface assumptions and beliefs about teaching. To that end we will now comment on the practice of developing a teaching philosophy statement as a way of making one's beliefs about teaching more transparent to oneself and to students.

TRANSPARENCY OF ONE'S BELIEFS: DEVELOPING A TEACHING PHILOSOPHY STATEMENT

Brookfield (2006) wrote about the importance of faculty members developing their own truths (beliefs) about teaching. He mentioned that we may as faculty ignore our own thoughts pertaining to pedagogy, "Many of us are so cowed by the presumed wisdom of authorities in our field ... that we dismiss our private ... [understandings] as fantasies until an expert legitimizes them by voicing them" (p. 13). He suggested that teachers might more often listen to their own voices. As a caveat, however, he also noted, "Of course, experience can sometimes be a terrible teacher. Simply having experiences does not imply that they are reflected on, understood, or analyzed critically" (p. 15). In spite of this warning, Brookfield commented, "If you don't already do so, then, you should begin to trust your inner voice a little more and accept the possibility that your . . . insights might possess as much validity as those of experts in the field" (p. 16).

Another writer who has encouraged the surfacing of assumptions and the examination of beliefs is Kenneth Gergen. For example, Gergen (2009) mentioned that while "empirical research strives to reveal the one true answer to any question [e.g., What is good teaching?] . . . there is no single array of words . . . that is uniquely suited to [the one true answer]" (p. 61). Mary and Kenneth Gergen (2003) noted that, "By usual scientific standards, knowledge [e.g., knowledge about teaching] is an accurate and unbiased representation of the world as it is" (p. 60), however, they went on to comment,

> every community shares certain values [beliefs], and these will inevitably be reflected in the results of inquiry. Research that studies the differences between 'men' and 'women,' for example, sustains a way of life in which it is important to notice differences of this kind. (p. 60)

Instead of maintaining the beliefs of one certain community, Gergen and Gergen supported lifting up or making transparent various beliefs and research practices. Brookfield (2006) also mentioned, "There are no seven habits of effective teaching, no five rules for pedagogic success" (p. 1). And we, in turn, would support Gergen's (2009) and Brookfield's (1995, 2006) position and suggest that taking a reflective stance can serve to bring understanding to one's actions.

Indeed, some have advocated for investigating beliefs held by individual faculty members, and have written about the development of "teaching philosophy statements," and it is to teaching philosophy statements that we now turn as a way of making one's beliefs about teaching more transparent. Peters (2009) noted, "A 'teaching philosophy'" is a "personal belief, style and statement designed to encourage professional reflection" (p. 112). Schönwetter, Sokal, Friesen, and Taylor (2002), after conducting a literature review, wrote "a teaching philosophy statement has been assigned many purposes" and, in part, they noted that these include "clarifying what good teaching is [perceived to be]," assisting in the "evaluation of teaching," and "promoting . . . professional development" (p. 85). Lang (2010) commented on the writing of teaching philosophy statements, and indicated that providing references for ideas suggests that the author views teaching as deserving of deliberate and thoughtful investigation (Cite your sources, para. 4). Lang also suggested bringing clarity of expression to the teaching philosophy statement by, for example, describing an instructional procedure that captured the students' attention (Be specific, para. 1). Pratt (2005), however, included a cautionary note and mentioned that no specific view encompasses all of what might be considered effective instruction (p. 35).

In an often referenced manuscript by Chism (1997–98), she commented on how teaching philosophy statements are frequently short, a couple of pages in length, and that they may be written in the "first person" (The Format of the Statement, para. 1). She listed five components of a teaching philosophy statement and mentioned that they provide an understanding of the way in which learning is thought to happen, that is, what teachers think happens during an instructional-learning episode based on earlier incidents or readings (Conceptualization of learning, para. 3). Secondly, she indicated that such statements of belief might contain thoughts the teacher has about what one does to encourage understanding (Conceptualization of teaching, para. 1). Teaching philosophy statements can include "content goals" from one's field of study, "process goals" related to skill based learning, and "career and lifelong goals" that might relate to issues like adopting a supportive and collaborative stance when working with others (Goals for students, para. 1). Further, she noted that the teaching philosophy statement can include an account of how beliefs about instruction are integrated into a plan for teaching (Implementation of the philosophy, para. 1). Finally, she indicated that the teaching philosophy statement can conclude with remarks about the journey one has taken as a teacher, the current edges of one's growth as a teacher, as well as one's ideas for growth into the future (Personal growth plan, para. 1).

We present the following questions to possibly assist readers in surfacing some of their own beliefs about teaching, relative to the five components of a teaching philosophy statement suggested by Chism (1997–98). These questions are illustrative and not intended to limit inquiry into one's teaching:

1. Conceptualization of learning
    - From your experiences, what student variables are critical in accounting for learning?
    - From your professional readings, what student variables are critical in accounting for learning?
2. Conceptualization of teaching
    - What characteristics do you possess that most influence your classroom teaching; for example, being organized, employing humor, applying a thoughtful and reflective style?
    - What characteristics are you seeking to cultivate as part of your classroom teaching?
3. Goals for students
    - With regard to the courses you teach, what content do you think is most important for students to learn and why?

- What skills and professional behaviors do you want to see students obtain as a result of taking courses you teach and why?
4. Strategy for implementation of teaching philosophy
   - In planning a course, what teaching strategies do you consider helpful to students in meeting goals of the course and why?
   - What methods of receiving feedback about teaching do you believe are most useful and why?
5. Personal journey as a teacher
   - What classroom experiences have occurred in your recent past that could influence your teaching?
   - How do you see yourself developing in the relatively near future as a teacher who engages students in learning?

AN ILLUSTRATIVE TEACHING PHILOSOPHY STATEMENT

The following is constructed as a possible teaching philosophy statement for a particular course (Theories of Counseling) and utilizes ideas from Peters (2009), Schönwetter et al. (2002), Lang (2010), and Chism (1997–98); however, one might also construct a teaching philosophy statement that is more general in nature and suited for multiple courses. Lang (2010) mentioned that faculty members may find themselves teaching courses for "majors in . . . [their] discipline" and "courses that . . . fulfill core requirements for graduation" (Make distinctions, para. 1) and because these "two types of classes" might be taught in a dissimilar fashion, the teaching philosophy statement can "describe . . . differences in the way I teach [each of] them" (Make distinctions, para. 2). This comment by Lang led us to think that a faculty member might also construct a teaching philosophy statement for a particular course, such as Theories of Counseling.

> As you enter this course you might be wondering about our work together during the semester. I am sharing this teaching philosophy statement with the hope that it will bring some clarity to your questions.
>
> As with any adventure, an appropriate starting place would seem to include consideration of the purpose for the journey. In the case of our time together, in this course, the goal is to increase your familiarity with major theories of counseling used in conceptualizing clients and their presenting problems as well as familiarity with methods of intervention consistent with these theories of counseling. A limited amount of practice with skills will occur in this course through experiential exercises (e.g., role plays); however, skill acquisition will be emphasized in other courses that come later in your master's degree program, that is, Pre-Practicum in Counseling, Practicum in Counseling, and Internship in Counseling.
>
> It has been my experience and belief that it is helpful for students to familiarize themselves with theories and methods of intervention prior to

supervised practice. Since having an understanding of theories and methods of intervention are the main aims of the course, your understandings will be evaluated, in part, through objective and short answer items on examinations. The objective items will require familiarity with concepts associated with counseling theories and the short answer items will ask students to conceptualize a counseling case and articulate possible counseling interventions. It is hoped that together we can bring a component of knowledge (pertaining to counseling theory) into your professional life and it is hoped that we can initiate the process of thinking about intervening with clients. I have intentionally used the pronoun "we" since enrollment in this course carries with it the expectation and belief that teaching and learning involve relational responsibility.

From literature (e.g., Kolb, 1984; Kolb, Boyatzis, & Mainemelis, 2001) and my own experiences, I have come to believe that it is important to consider what might be thought of as formats for learning and I will contemplate their possible utility during our time together in this course. That is, opportunities for learning will occur through a blending of reading assignments and opportunities for writing about counseling theories, along with listening to lectures and taking notes, as well as engaging in classroom discussions, and participating in experiential activities where students make use of theoretical concepts through analysis of fictional case studies and role plays. It is thought to be important for students to give themselves to each of the learning activities in order to take advantage of opportunities presented in the course.

I also believe that teaching is embedded in notions of instructor preparedness and treating students with respect. Preparedness is, in some ways, similar to Brookfield's (2006) description of "credibility" which he notes as being valued by students (p. 56). With regard to preparedness, I need to be prepared with worthwhile content for students and prepared with a variety of teaching procedures that will hopefully open opportunities for students to consider the usefulness of counseling theories. My general style is to take our time in exploring ideas in the classroom. I assume, by slowing the process down, students can thoughtfully consider counseling theories, for example, this might occur by posing questions or brief assignments at the beginning of class related to one's eventual practice, such as, "Take a moment and write down your thoughts on conditions under which you might find yourself using Behavior Therapy." This, of course, requires that students stay actively engaged by remaining up to date with assigned readings and participating in class. I also try to respect your (the students') commitment to the course by, from time to time, asking for feedback on how the course is progressing, that is, how well you understand concepts presented in class and whether the procedures used in teaching are facilitating your involvement with the content. For me, this appears similar to Brookfield's (1995) use of the "learning journal" and "critical incident questionnaire."

With regard to teaching, for the past few years I have been working to help students find the usefulness of counseling theories in professional practice. In the counseling profession, I believe that application of theory to practice is vital. In part, this familiarity with counseling theory is demonstrated in the ability to speak to case studies from various perspectives and to plan interventions utilizing methodology consistent with those perspectives. Consequently, when considering fictional case studies, I might ask questions to hopefully assist students in applying theory to their work with clients, such as, "From Client-Centered Therapy and Behavior Therapy, what might a counselor consider in building a therapeutic relationship?" "From Cognitive Therapy and Behavior Therapy, what might a counselor consider when conceptualizing a client's presenting problem?" "From Cognitive Therapy and Solution-Focused Therapy, what might a counselor consider when intervening with a client?" When addressing these or other questions pertaining to theories of counseling, we will consider a variety of cultural contexts such as client ethnicity, race, age, sexual orientation, and abilities. I am also interested in helping you develop an initial view of yourself as a practitioner and may use questions like, "With this fictional case study in mind, which theory or theories of counseling might you see yourself using?" "For what reasons have you selected this particular theory or these theories?" "What limitations might this theory or these theories present in working with the case study?" Searching for relevance in learning is a task faced by teachers and students alike. I plan to continue to work at this as a teacher and it is my hope that the course becomes a meaningful professional experience for you, an experience that stimulates active involvement in the continued study of counseling theories even after our time together has ended.

It is with an understanding of our beliefs about teaching that we might expect to effectively communicate with colleagues about our practice, evaluate our work, reconsider our positions, and redesign our efforts. It would also seem that, as instructors, we might anticipate our teaching philosophy statements will go through revisions as we engage in continued professional development (Chism, 1997–98; Schönwetter et al., 2002). Because of the reflection needed to develop a teaching philosophy statement, some educators might choose to begin writing such statements for individual courses—as we have done above—and later attempt to formulate a statement of beliefs that is applicable to the whole of one's teaching. Such a statement might be appended to one's syllabus (Schönwetter et al., 2002). This process of articulating and intentionally applying our beliefs to teaching is part of the essence of who we are as counselor educators. As in counseling, counselor education faculty members need to be familiar with professional literature associated with their practice, which includes considering beliefs about teaching.

REFERENCES

Bain, K. (2002). *What the best college teachers do.* Cambridge, MA: Harvard University Press.
Boyer, E. L. (1990). *Scholarship reconsidered: Priorities of the professoriate.* New York, NY: Carnegie Foundation for the Advancement of Teaching.

Brookfield, S. D. (1995). *Becoming a critically reflective teacher.* San Francisco, CA: Jossey-Bass.

Brookfield, S. D. (2006). *The skillful teacher: On technique, trust, and responsiveness in the classroom* (2nd ed.). San Francisco, CA: Jossey-Bass.

Chism, N. V. N. (1997–98). Developing a philosophy of teaching statement. *Essays on Teaching Excellence: Towards the Best in the Academy, 9*(3). Retrieved from http://www.podnetwork.org/publications/teachingexcellence/97-98/V9,%20N3%20Chism.pdf

Davis, T. E., Levitt, D. H., McGlothlin, J. M., & Hill, N. R. (2006). Perceived expectations related to promotion and tenure: A national survey of CACREP program liaisons. *Counselor Education and Supervision, 46,* 146–156.

Fitzmaurice, M. (2008). Voices from within: Teaching in higher education as a moral practice. *Teaching in Higher Education, 13,* 341–352. doi: 0.1080/13562510802045386

Gee, G. (2009). Right here, right now: A crystallization of response. Retrieved from http://president.osu.edu/speeches/fac_10072009.php

Gergen, K. J. (2009). *An invitation to social construction.* Los Angeles, CA: Sage.

Gergen, M., & Gergen, K. J. (2003). Horizons of inquiry: Introduction. In M. Gergen & K. J. Gergen (Eds.), *Social construction: A reader* (pp. 60–64). Thousand Oaks, CA: Sage.

Ginsberg, S. M. (2007). Shared characteristics of college faculty who are effective communicators. *The Journal of Effective Teaching, 7,* 1–3.

Hativa, N., Barak, R., & Simhi, E. (2001). Exemplary university teachers: Knowledge and beliefs regarding effective teaching dimensions and strategies. *The Journal of Higher Education, 72,* 699–729.

Herron, J. F., Beedle, J., & King, S. B. (2006). Making pedagogical decisions: Reasons female faculty in educational leadership select instructional methods. *International Journal of Teaching and Learning in Higher Education, 17,* 75–85.

Kolb, D. A. (1984). *Experiential learning: Experience as the source of learning and development.* Englewood Cliffs, NJ: Prentice Hall.

Kolb, D. A., Boyatzis, R. E., & Mainemelis, C. (2001). Experiential learning theory: Previous research and new directions. In R. J. Sternberg & L. Zhang (Eds.), *Perspectives on thinking, learning, and cognitive styles* (pp. 227-247). Mahwah, NJ: Lawrence Erlbaum.

Lang, J. M. (2010). 5 steps to a memorable teaching philosophy. Retrieved from http://www.Chronicle.com

Peters, M. A. (2009). Editorial: A teaching philosophy or philosophy of teaching? *Educational Philosophy and Theory, 41,* 111–113. doi:10.1111/j.1469-812.2009.00526.x

Pratt, D. D. (1992). Conceptions of teaching. *Adult Education Quarterly, 42,* 203–220.

Pratt, D. D. (2005). Personal philosophies of teaching: A false promise? *Academe, 91*(1), 32–35. doi: 10.2307/40252734

Schönwetter, D. J., Sokal, L., Friesen, M., & Taylor, K. L. (2002). Teaching philosophies reconsidered: A conceptual model for the development and evaluation of teaching philosophy statements. *The International Journal for Academic Development, 7,* 83–97. doi: 10.1080/1360144210156501

Shulman, L. S. (1987). Knowledge and teaching: Foundations of the new reform. *Harvard Educational Review, 57*(1), 1–22.

CHAPTER 2

Creating a Syllabus and Course Anticipation: Early Engagement of Students

JANE A. COX

Recently a colleague of mine was joking about how his syllabus for a particular course has doubled in length since he began teaching this course 10 years ago. He attributed this expansion to the addition of required university statements, accreditation evidence, and his continual efforts to make course expectations more explicit. Although this last reason, providing clearer expectations, may be helpful, the flip side might be Singham's (2007) caution against "'syllabus creep' whereby faculty keep adding new rules to combat each student excuse for not meeting existing rules" (p. 55). Singham went so far as to call for "death to the syllabus" (p. 55), at least for syllabi that were rigid, rule-bound documents that attempt to cover every possible student problem that might arise. He lamented the fact that some faculty create rule-bound syllabi chiefly to avoid using judgment in ambiguous situations and to defend themselves against grade disputes. Though Singham is a physics professor, his advice to consider carefully how to construct syllabi that most fully engage students at the beginning of a term applies to all disciplines, including counselor education.

FUNCTIONS OF SYLLABI:
COMMUNICATION, ORGANIZATION, AND AGREEMENT

In light of Singham's (2007) cautions, and in our efforts to provide an environment in which students will engage in active learning, it is important to consider the reasons why we should have course syllabi and how best to construct them. In their review of literature, Eberly, Newton, and Wiggins (2001) noted three general functions of syllabi: syllabi are a means to communicate with students; syllabi promote course organization; and syllabi serve as agreements between faculty and students (p. 59). Regarding communication with students, syllabi typically convey a wealth of information, such as course objectives, weekly course schedule, assignments, grading policies, and so forth. Faculty and students are perhaps most familiar with this type of syllabi communication, much of which centers on faculty expectations of students. Perhaps there is not as much familiarity with the potential for syllabi to communicate less concrete information, such as the instructor's philosophy of teaching and learning, or the tone of the course. For example, syllabus creation can offer instructors an opportunity to invite students to be collaborators in the learning process, to invite them on an "educational adventure" (Matejka & Kurke, 1994, p. 117).

It is important to consider not only *what* is communicated to students through syllabi (the content), but also *how* it is communicated (i.e., the tone; Harnish et al., 2011; Matejka & Kurke, 1994). The tone of a syllabus conveys information about the instructor's teaching style and sets the stage for student engagement. Slattery and Carlson (2005) noted that there is variety in tone, some possibilities being "warm and friendly, formal, condescending, or confrontational" (p. 159). Harnish et al. (2011) advocated for the development of a "warm" syllabus, one that "provides a sense of belonging and community . . . [and] removes unnecessary and unhelpful barriers between instructors and students, making the classroom a comfortable and safe place for discovery" (p. 23). These authors suggested several strategies for creation of a warm syllabus, including use of "positive language," explanation of the purpose of assignments, "humor," "compassion" (for example, flexibility in attendance when students have family emergencies), and "enthusiasm" (pp. 23–24). The examples they provided are evidence of a learner-centered environment. For instance, they suggested that instructors creating a warm syllabus may choose student-centered language, even in simple, practical items, such as listing "student hours" rather than "office hours" (p. 26). As another example, for items such as optional readings, instead of simply stating that optional readings are on reserve in the library, instructors could note how they chose the optional readings and why they find them important (p. 27). Instructors using such language, and creating warm syllabi, hope to motivate students to engage more fully in their learning. Counselor educators should be especially skilled at creating warm syllabi, since in their clinical training and practice they have learned the rapport building skills and attention to language that are required.

The creation of syllabi also serves the purpose of providing structure and organization to a course. If our goal is to produce syllabi that engage students in active learning from the outset of a course, considerable thought and planning must go into both the design of a new course syllabus and revision of existing syllabi. Instructors consider the purpose of the course, what content will be shared in the course, how students will be involved in that content (activities and assignments), what they hope students will gain from the course (outcomes), and how they will measure student outcomes (O'Brien, Millis, & Cohen, 2008).

Much has been written on what components instructors should include in their syllabi (e.g., Matejka & Kurke, 1994; O'Brien et al., 2008; Slattery & Carlson, 2005, Weimer, 2002). In their comprehensive book on course syllabi, O'Brien et al. (2008) offered a checklist of possible items for inclusion in a syllabus, including common elements such as course description, required readings, weekly schedule, and policies. In addition to these familiar items, O'Brien et al. also suggested that instructors include their philosophy of teaching in the syllabus, which might take the form of a letter to students. Their example of this is a list entitled "my rules of the road" which includes such "rules" as "I believe too many classroom rules get in the way of good teaching and good learning" (p. 47) and "Teaching is something I do *with* students, not something I do *to* them" (p. 48). This relates back to the communication of a warm tone in a syllabus. O'Brien et al. also suggested including information in the syllabus about how students can be successful in the class, such as suggestions on how to study for the course (p. 103). This conveys a tone that reflects the instructor's investment in helping students succeed.

Finally, a commonly cited purpose of syllabi is that they serve as an agreement or contract between instructors and students (Eberly et al., 2001; Hudd, 2003; Matejka & Kurke, 1994). Syllabi convey both what an instructor expects of students, and what students can expect of the instructor and course. This is not unlike our use of informed consent statements with clients in counseling; we want clients (and students) to know what we are willing and able to offer, and what we expect of them in return. As contracts, syllabi can be viewed as protective, in that they may protect students by holding an instructor accountable to cover the material and facilitate the activities noted in the syllabi. They also protect faculty in the event of a student complaint, such as a grade grievance or lawsuit. Slattery and Carlson (2005) described this as an "evidentiary function" of a syllabus (p. 160). For example, in the event of a grade grievance, the syllabus can provide evidence of the course expectations and grading procedures.

The use of syllabi to protect faculty from potential actions taken against them by students carries with it the risk of the protective factor overriding the other functions of syllabi (e.g., communication). If this happens, then syllabi become the rule-bound documents that Singham (2007) cautioned us against. Therefore, one challenge that faculty face is how to balance the implementation of the various functions of syllabi.

Often what is missing in the syllabus "contract" is the other party's (students') input into the creation of the syllabus. When I began my career as a counselor educator, I attended a lecture for new faculty presented by a Full Professor in the English department who discussed how he and his students constructed components of the syllabus together, such as the course goals and evaluation methods. He acknowledged that this activity was time consuming and somewhat delayed the start of the course, but noted that students were highly invested in the course, taking ownership for what they learned rather than overly relying on him to fill them with course content. Many authors have suggested that students be involved in the planning of a course (Benjamin, 2005; Hudd, 2003; McDevitt, 2004; Singham, 2007). For example, Hudd (2003) described how she worked collaboratively with students to create their course assignments for a sociology class. She gave students guidance regarding the types of issues they should consider when making suggestions for assignments, such as what types of assignments to include (projects, exams, etc.) and when assignments should be due (p. 197). Hudd asserted that students more actively participated in their learning when she shared the power of syllabus creation with them.

In addition to its use as a communication and organizational tool, and as a means to "contract" with students, syllabi can also serve other purposes. For instance, syllabi present evidence of meeting accreditation standards; they are included in self-studies for the Council for Accreditation of Counseling and Related Educational Programs (CACREP) and are reviewed by CACREP site team members during site visits. Syllabi are also reviewed when faculty are trying to determine proof of equivalency requirements for transferred courses (Eberly et al., 2001; Wasley, 2008) and they can be used to evaluate an instructor's "scholarship of teaching" (Albers, 2003), as discussed later in this chapter.

Other Means of Course Anticipation

The syllabus may be thought of as students' first introduction to a course, yet there are other means to engage students even before the course begins. For instance, I recently sent an email to the doctoral students enrolled in an upcoming Supervision of Counseling course. In addition to previewing some of the practical issues, such as possible assignments, I attempted to convey anticipation of and enthusiasm for the course, and expressed a warm tone, by writing,

> Though time consuming, the supervision course is a fun course (at least I think it is!) and very hands-on. It's one of the courses I enjoy teaching the most. I look

forward to working with all of you this fall and will send more information about the course in the next week or so (e.g., I'll post the syllabus to Vista).

Contacting students before a course begins serves as a "welcoming strategy" (Thompson, 2007), is an additional way to communicate information, begins to set the tone for the course, and hopefully elicits their anticipation.

The first day of class is another opportunity to motivate students to become engaged and excited about a course. Too often that first day is viewed by students and faculty alike as a chance to have a "short" class, one in which the only activity is to review the syllabus. Matejka and Kurke (1994) encouraged instructors to consider what type of impression they wish to leave with students on that first day, knowing that the first day "set[s] the tone" (p. 115) for the course. Therefore these authors suggested that instructors over-prepare for that first day, having enough material ready to immediately begin actively involving students in their learning, including a brief "memorable" (p. 155) activity which helps students become engaged in the course.

Considerations for Enhancing Course Anticipation and Syllabus Creation

There are no doubt innumerable ways to construct a syllabus and to invite students into a learning experience; syllabi are as varied as (and reflective of) our teaching styles. The following are a few suggestions to consider as you create new or revise existing syllabi.

▶ *Keep student engagement in the forefront.* From the initial development of a course and its syllabus, think about how to best motivate and empower students to invest in their learning. Consider how your syllabus might either intimidate students or encourage them to be active participants in the course. Think about how you might motivate students to be engaged through all that you write in the syllabus, from course objectives to grading policies. One component of this might be how we invite students to become learners with us, or our "hospitality." O'Reilley (1998) noted that

> Hospitality defines a space for the visitor—the student—to be herself, because she is received graciously. . . . I mention this hospitality space, too, in the syllabus. I tell the students that I expect them to attend class regularly, and that I will try to receive them with unconditional presence. (p. 8)

▶ *Make planning and organization a priority.* Time spent in the planning phase can save time later. Matejka and Kurke (1994) viewed syllabi as "preventive medicine" (p. 116), in that a well thought out syllabus (e.g., one which considers potential questions that students may have) will save time and prevent possible future problems. In his book on designing college courses, Fink (2003) recommended 10 steps for instructors to move through before creating the syllabus. For example, in his first step of "[identifying] important situational factors" (p. 69), Fink suggested that instructors consider factors such as the expectations of potential stakeholders or evaluators (e.g., accreditation bodies, state licensure boards, society as a whole) and the students' situation and attributes (e.g., students' learning styles, probable goals for the course, and status as full or part-time).

▶ *Find ways to connect with students before the start of the term.* Technology has made this easy to do, since I can simply look up my class roster online and email all students as a group. As mentioned previously, communicating with students before the start of the course is one way to welcome them and inspire them to get excited about investing their time and energy in the course. When I email students before the semester starts, I give them a preview of the course and let them know of my excitement earlier than I might have otherwise. If I plan early enough to do a thorough review and update of the course, and then post the syllabus online a week or two before the start of the term, I'm not scurrying around at the last minute to revise course material and copy syllabi. So not only does pre-term communication with students help prepare them for the course, it helps me better prepare as well.

▶ *Carefully consider what components you want to include in your syllabus.* In addition to the previously mentioned traditional components (e.g., course description, course outline) and more creative elements (e.g., letter to students), consider other items that might be of use to students. Where might they find help with writing on campus? What are policies of the university (e.g., attendance policies) and the program (e.g., for professional behavior) that would be important to include on a syllabus? New faculty can look to experienced instructors for assistance, as well as explore the literature that discusses in detail possible components of syllabi (for example, O'Brien et al., 2008; Slattery & Carlson, 2005).

▶ *Take care in the presentation of your syllabi.* As with all printed material, the reader gets a quick first impression by how the material appears on the page. Matejka and Kurke (1994) suggested using a variety of fonts and layouts to make a syllabus look professional, though it is important not to overdo the formatting and distract the reader (Slattery & Carlson, 2005). Consider the order in which you want to present the various elements of your syllabus, perhaps putting what is most important and what students need to access most often on the first pages (Slattery & Carlson, 2005, p. 163). Make your syllabi as readable as possible, assessing this by asking for input from colleagues and students.

▶ *Explore ways to use the syllabus to send "motivational messages"* (Slattery & Carlson, 2005). Find ways to invite students to the "feast" by creating a "promising syllabus" (Bain, 2004, p. 75), one which articulates the opportunities that await students enrolled in your course. As mentioned previously, one way to send such a message is the inclusion of a letter in your syllabus. Below is an excerpt from a letter that one of my colleagues includes in his *College Teaching in Counseling and Human Development Services* syllabus. I believe this is a good example of both a motivation message to students, and an invitation to actively and collaboratively engage in learning:

> Welcome to *College Teaching in Counseling and Human Development Services.* I am excited about your enrollment in the course and look forward to having you as an active member of the class. I think everything that we teach in your doctoral program is important but this course has special meaning for me. Fundamentally this course is an opportunity for doctoral students to gain experience in teaching and reflect on their process of teaching. . . . This may be your one opportunity to fully explore your teaching during your academic career. With the pressure of research and publication in higher education, a counselor educator can easily forget the importance of the "educator" part of your role. I am hoping that you will engage the material fully and be prepared for class. Just doing the reading and being in class is half of the effort. Each week every student should bring in reflections and questions about the material you have been responsible for reading. Please come ready to stimulate discussion, present your point of view, and ask questions when necessary. The most exciting classes I teach are ones where the group takes responsibility for the learning and they become a learning entity, using me not for initiation or expertise but for guidance. . . . The group is small enough that we can all proceed with the learning process without it being teacher centered, respecting the rights of others to speak and the responsibility of ourselves to contribute. If in the class we can model the best of what we would expect of our students, we can maximize the potential for us to be the best of who we are as teachers. (Jencius, 2011)

▶ *Make use of existing resources.* The American Counseling Association (ACA) and the Association for Counselor Education and Supervision (ACES) joined together to create the ACA/ACES Syllabus Clearinghouse, which members can access at http://www.acesonline.net/. Counselor educators can post their syllabi to the clearinghouse so that others can get ideas for course activities and assignments, textbooks, and so forth. As of October 2010, approximately 300 syllabi were available in a variety of courses, such as counseling theories, professional orientation, and practicum (ACA, 2011).

▶ *Make the syllabus your own.* While it is useful to draw on existing resources, such as the ACA/ACES Syllabus Clearinghouse or existing syllabi at one's institution, it is important that instructors craft syllabi that reflect their ideas and values, rather than simply having them "handed down from generation to generation" (Eberly et al., 2001, p. 56). I made this mistake once when I inherited a syllabus for a couples counseling course. Though I was not required to use the syllabus, I stuck closely to its content, out of respect and appreciation for the former instructor and knowing that it had worked well for him. The first few times I taught the course, I struggled with presenting some of the material, not knowing how to "bring it alive" as he had. When I finally gave myself permission to make changes that reflected my strengths (e.g., more processing and less lecture), I was more confident and genuine in my teaching and believe that my students gained more information and skills as a result.

▶ *Ensure that assignments are related to course goals.* We teach our students that when they write treatment plans for/with clients in counseling, the objectives and strategies have to relate back to the treatment goals. Similarly, when writing syllabi, course assignments should relate directly back to goals for the course. If there is an assignment that does not clearly relate to a course goal, consider revising or eliminating the assignment, or revising the goals (Slattery & Carlson, 2005). A review for such consistency will help instructors ensure that assignments are meaningful ways to accomplish course goals and help students see the relevance of assignments.

▶ *Explain the rationale for course activities and assignments.* As with most undertakings in life, people engage more if they find meaning in what they are doing. Instructors can use the syllabus as one vehicle that not only articulates the expectations of students, but also explains why the instructor has those expectations (Slattery & Carlson, 2005; Stark, 2000). For instance, one assignment I have for students in a couples counseling class is to interview a diverse, underrepresented couple (e.g., mixed race couple, gay or lesbian couple). I explain in the syllabus that interviewing such couples will help students gain more appreciation for the issues that these couples face (that "majority" couples do not face), and how this will ultimately help when they counsel underrepresented individuals and couples. Though a few students worry about locating such couples, they take the extra effort (and find the extra courage they may require) to interview underrepresented couples, and often discover this to be the most rewarding and enlightening activity of the course.

▶ *Routinely revise your syllabus.* Perhaps one of the greatest challenges we face as educators is staying current. Keeping up with the counseling literature can be a daunting but necessary task; we are responsible for conveying up-to-date information to students. We are also responsible for being constantly creative in how we present this information to our students, so hopefully our method of presentation changes over our years of teaching. By continually updating our syllabi, we not only present fresh material and methods to students, but we can stay refreshed ourselves as we remain learners. We may also revise our syllabi based on past experiences with a course (Matejka & Kurke, 1994; Slattery & Carlson, 2005), for example, to clarify a confusing assignment or more deeply address an important topic (e.g., by adding new readings).

▶ *Model being a counselor through use of syllabi.* In all of our activities as instructors, we have the potential to model aspects of being an effective counselor. Though counseling and instruction are different, there are some similarities. When considering these similarities, we might ask ourselves "What do I hope to model for students?" Through our syllabi, we may consider how to model good communication, effective collaboration, shared responsibility, and appropriate boundary setting, all the while being transparent regarding the power differential between student and instructor. Done effectively, this may help students consider how to carry out these same types of behaviors with their clients.

EVALUATION OF THE EFFECTIVENESS OF SYLLABI

When considering how to evaluate the effectiveness of syllabi, we have to first decide what it is we wish to evaluate. Reconsidering the purposes for syllabi (communication, organization, and agreement) can guide us in determining what we want to assess. Concrete communication (the content of a syllabus) is probably the easiest function to evaluate. Raymark and Connor-Greene (2002) proposed giving students a take-home quiz on the syllabus, as a simple method to determine if instructors conveyed the intended content. These authors constructed items for a quiz based on their experience of the questions that students typically asked and whose answers could be found on the syllabus. While a quiz encourages students to carefully review syllabi, it can also inform the instructor about possible areas of confusion; if students consistently "miss" items on the quiz, this would signal the need for the instructor to review those areas on the syllabi that students are misunderstanding.

The remaining areas of organization and agreement or contract (as well as communication) might be best evaluated by one's colleagues; just as we may have peers observe our teaching to give us suggestions for improvement, peers can also review our syllabi to offer helpful tips. Bain (2004) noted a preference for this type of peer evaluation rather than a one-time observation of teaching, because he believed observers tend to give positive teaching evaluations to their colleagues who teach as they do (pp. 168–169). Also, a single teaching observation may not give an adequate indication of the instructor's teaching ability. Rather, Bain contended that

> Peers can . . . provide essential comments on the qualities of the learning objectives. They can look at the syllabus, the way students are assessed, the nature of assignments, reports from the teacher, and even examples of student work to understand the nature of those objectives. (p. 169)

I found this type of peer review particularly valuable when creating my portfolio for tenure and promotion. I was fortunate enough to have an experienced colleague in Educational Psychology who was willing to share his expertise in educational effectiveness and he reviewed seven of my syllabi. This colleague reviewed all components of these syllabi, including structure, organization, readings, assignments, and outcome measures. His feedback from such a thorough review helped me reflect on how to strengthen my syllabi and helped reviewers assess my abilities as an instructor. Similarly, Albers (2003) confirmed that syllabi review can be used to assess faculty during the renewal, tenure, and promotion process.

Colleagues who are willing to not only review syllabi, but also observe our teaching can give us feedback on the consistency between the two. They can comment on the clarity of our communication and organization, as delivered both in our syllabi and in our classroom teaching. As Slattery and Carlson (2005) suggested, "Tone and proposed process articulated in the syllabus should match. Professors who expect to take an expert role should clearly communicate this in their syllabi, just as those who adopt a more student-centered approach should communicate this" (p. 163).

Counselor education programs that are accredited by CACREP are presented with another opportunity for peer review and feedback. Accreditation site teams review syllabi and ask questions about items that are not clear. Having such outside evaluators assess our syllabi offers us another chance to reconsider what we want and need to communicate through our syllabi and how best to do so.

CLOSING THOUGHTS

A gift that has come to me from reading literature about syllabi (in preparation for writing this chapter) is that it has caused me to think more deeply about how I develop syllabi and about teaching in general. So I leave you with a few of the thoughts on which I continue to reflect, in hopes that they may in some small way help you also to think about syllabi and the messages we hope to convey through them.

One of my greatest challenges when creating syllabi is thinking through how to simultaneously establish authority and be collaborative with students. Though I do not particularly like to think that I need to establish authority, or want to view myself as an instructor who has this as a goal, I know that I do indeed use the syllabus to convey my role as instructor. Though this certainly can be appropriate, I can get too caught up in firmly laying out expectations of students, in order to forewarn those few who may be tempted to underachieve, miss class, turn assignments in late, and so forth. Thompson (2007) articulated this challenge well by stating,

> teachers must balance the tension between showing students that they are caring, warm and friendly individuals while simultaneously demonstrating that they are serious, task-oriented and evaluative. . . . Whereas teachers often strive to create a hospitable environment to make students feel welcome the first day of class, they must also establish rules and procedures that illustrate their authority. (p. 55)

I do not want to be so authoritative with students that I convey "learning, like medicine, is good for you but not enjoyable" (Singham, 2007, p .55). Singham wondered if students are so conditioned to believe this (from past educational experiences) that we can not change their perspective. But he also noted that "students act the way they do because we treat them the way we do" (p. 55). So I hope to keep contemplating how to treat counselor education students in ways that convey my presumption that they are excited about their learning and just waiting for me to set the stage for their engagement, beginning with the syllabus. I imagine that I will continue to work with this tension between collaboration and authority throughout the rest of my teaching career, continuing to realize that it does not have to be an either/or debate. I am grateful for these types of challenges, as they encourage me to continue to be a reflective and engaged instructor.

Another challenge I hope to continue to wrestle with is how to use syllabi (and all other aspects of teaching) to open up space for student learning. Mary Rose O'Reilley (1998), in her book *Radical Presence: Teaching as Contemplative Practice*, influenced me greatly with her thoughts about the teaching and learning processes. She wrote about creating space for student learning (giving credit to Parker Palmer for this notion), rather than simply aiming to fill students up with our knowledge and wisdom (p. 1). I am left thinking about her ideas about hospitality and how to better use syllabi to welcome students into an active, engaged learning community.

REFERENCES

Albers, C. (2003). Using the syllabus to document the scholarship of teaching. *Teaching Sociology, 31*, 60–72.

American Counseling Association. (2011). *ACA-ACES syllabus clearinghouse submission*. Retrieved from http://www.counseling.org/Resources/TP/SyllabusClearinghouse Submission/CT2.aspx

Bain, K. (2004). *What the best college teachers do*. Cambridge, MA: Harvard Press.

Benjamin, Jr., L. T. (2005). Setting course goals: Privileges and responsibilities in a world of ideas. *Teaching of Psychology, 32*, 147–149.

Eberly, M. B., Newton, S. E., & Wiggins, R. A. (2001). The syllabus as a tool for student-centered learning. *The Journal of General Education, 50*, 56–74.

Fink, L. D. (2003). *Creating significant learning experiences*. San Francisco, CA: Jossey-Bass.

Harnish, R. J., O'Brien McElwee, R., Slattery, J. M., Frantz, S., Haney, M. R., Chore, C. M., & Penley, J. (2011). Creating the foundation for a warm classroom climate: Best practices in syllabus tone. *Observer, 24*(1), 23–27.

Hudd, S. S. (2003). Syllabus under construction: Involving students in the creation of class assignments. *Teaching Sociology, 31*, 195–202.

Jencius, M. (2011). CHDS 88294: College Teaching in Counseling and Human Development Services [Syllabus]. Kent State University, Kent, OH.

Matejka, K., & Kurke, L. G. (1994). Designing a great syllabus. *College Teaching, 42,* 115–118.

McDevitt, B. (2004). Negotiating the syllabus: A win-win situation? *ELT Journal, 58,* 3–9.

O'Brien, J. G., Millis, B. J., & Cohen, M. W. (2008). *The course syllabus: A learning-centered approach* (2nd ed.). San Francisco, CA: Jossey-Bass.

O'Reilley, M. R. (1998). *Radical presence: Teaching as contemplative practice.* Portsmouth, NH: Boynton/Cook.

Raymark, P. H., & Connor-Greene, P. A. (2002). The syllabus quiz. *Teaching of Psychology, 29,* 286–288.

Singham, M. (2007). Death to the syllabus! *Liberal Education, 93*(4), 52–56.

Slattery, J. M., & Carlson, J. F. (2005). Preparing an effective syllabus: Current best practices. *College Teaching, 53,* 159–164.

Stark, J. S. (2000). Planning introductory college courses: Content, context and form. *Instructional Science, 28,* 413–438.

Thompson, B. (2007). The syllabus as a communication document: Constructing and presenting the syllabus. *Communication Education, 56,* 54–74.

Wasley, P. (2008). Research yields tips on crafting better syllabi. *The Chronicle of Higher Education, 54*(27), A11.

Weimer, M. (2002). *Learner-centered teaching.* San Francisco, CA: Jossey-Bass.

CHAPTER 3

Preparing and Presenting Lectures That Exemplify the Ideals of Counselor Education

MARK L. SAVICKAS

A chapter about the lecture in counselor education provides both readers and the writer an opportunity to reflect upon and improve their instructional methods and habits. In preparing to write this chapter, I quickly found numerous books, articles, and websites about lecturing. Initially I questioned whether professors needed another one. Then I began to find books and articles devoted to lecturing in particular disciplines such as history, English, physics, and sociology. Next, I looked for a book about effective lecturing in counselor education. I found none but the search crystallized a question, "What is the purpose of and procedures for an effective lecture in counselor education?" And, I thought of a simple answer. In addition to presenting content, counselor education lecturers should model good counseling practices. That is the unique advice offered in this chapter, namely *take your counseling skills to the lectern*.

In elaborating this main point, I describe the lecture, its rationale, and my experience with lecturing. In so doing, I agree with an analogy offered by Donald Bligh (2000) in the fifth edition of his classic book, *What's the Use of Lectures?* Bligh compared lecturing to musical composition and performance. He explained that if individuals want to write a symphony, they should first study the symphonic form. After learning the general form, a composer writes in a particular musical style that she or he prefers, while realizing that listeners will have their own preferences. So this chapter discusses the form of the lecture to prompt readers to reflect on their preferences.

THE LECTURE

Readers of this book may have more than once wondered why they attend or give lectures. This question caught my attention when I began my first teaching position. The previous occupant of my new office had left behind several books on educational psychology. Thumbing through the books, one article caught my attention. It was entitled something like "The Purpose of the Lecture." The first paragraph asked a question that remains with me today, "What is the purpose of the lecture since the invention of the printing press?"

A lecture serves to orally communicate important information to a large group of people. In a formal lecture, the presenter typically reads a written document or at least follows a detailed outline. The word "lecture" comes from the Latin *lectus* meaning to read. Lectern denotes the reading desk used by lecturers. Instructors read a lecture. However, this response to the query about the lecture's purpose ignores the second part of the question, "since the invention of the printing press."

The mechanical printing press, starting late in the 15th century, turned books into a media for mass communication. Until then, lecturers typically possessed the only book. They transmitted the knowledge in the book by reading aloud important passages as students took notes (Dyer, 2009). However, today students have their own books. They may acquire the information in the book quickly and accurately, and at their own pace. Reading a book may be a better way of gaining information than listening to a formal lecture on the same material. Obviously this article on educational psychology left me wondering about how I should lecture. I did not want to read a book to graduate students in counselor education yet I was assigned 2.5-hour class periods in which to lecture to large groups of students. I wondered what I could do instead of lecture. In due course, I came to understand that a lecture does not have to be a formal presentation that repeats the material in the book. The presentation may be an informal lecture, sometimes called a lecture demonstration or lecture discussion that concentrates not on the information but rather explains why the information matters, elaborates its meaning, and discusses how to use it. The informal lecture may be used to clarify the material in the readings and increase student understanding of it. That is why the informal lecture remains the dominant instructional method in higher education.

LECTURE PROS AND CONS

There are several additional reasons for the lecture's predominance. The first is efficiency. The time saved by lecturing rather than tutoring or problem-based instruction may be used for research and advising. A second reason is ease of preparation. Once a lecture is prepared, it is easy to revise it for a second use. A third reason is that counselor education departments use lecture courses with large enrollments to balance small enrollments in practica and doctoral seminars, thereby making delivery of the program economically feasible.

From a pedagogical perspective, a lecture is an excellent instructional method for presenting new information and an orientation to important material before engaging students in more active learning. The lecture is a time-efficient means to introduce students to the information that they will apply in practica and internships. Large-group lectures on counseling theories, tests and measurement, diagnosis, human development, career development, learning theory, substance abuse, and multiculturalism provide an overview for studying the subjects in-depth and offer guiding frameworks for using the material in practice. In the phrase "present a lecture," the word "present" even implies introduction because it means introduce or bring before the public. And, the lecture is a structured way to introduce students to difficult ideas and potentially disturbing topics. Of course a lecturer prompts further study and application of a subject by igniting students' curiosity about the new material. A sparkling lecture may even recruit students to specialize in a particular area of counseling practice or doctoral study.

Although the lecture possesses many positive features as a method of instruction, it has negative features as well. The main criticisms of the lecture format arise from it being teacher-centered rather than learner-centered. Recall that the word *lectus* is defined by what the teacher does. It goes without saying that in preparing a lecture, an instructor learns more than the students will learn.

Defining the lecture as something done by the instructor is particularly problematic in the discipline of counseling. Counselor educators concentrate on relationships between clients and counselors. The working alliance and interpersonal reciprocity that defines these relationships is central to counseling practice. For the lecturer, the partner is not the personal student but an impersonal audience. The lecturer gives a performance. One of my colleagues describes a good lecture as science and show business. Recall that the word "present" may mean introduce, yet it may also mean a gift; in this case, a gift that the lecturer gives to the audience. In presenting a lecture, an instructor thinks more of the audience than of the individual student. This is in contrast to small group classes in which there is a stronger relationship between the students and teachers. The instructor teaches the students rather than presents the material. Teaching is not a performance; it is an interaction between teacher and learner. The role of reciprocity is between individuals; the professor even knows the students' names. This lack of reciprocity between lecturer and audience pertains particularly to a free-standing lecture. When an instructor presents a series of lectures to the same students during the course of a semester, however, that teacher does learn the students' names and forms relationships that will influence subsequent lectures.

Teachers can allow for students who learn at different paces. A lecturer cannot. The lecture is geared to the middle of the audience, not to the curious and prepared nor to the indifferent and unprepared. Exceptional students at both ends of the distribution may be somewhat ignored. Because lecturers do not have a personal interaction with individual students, lecturers cannot easily assess students' attitudes during a presentation, although an effective lecture may shape or even change students' attitudes. They also do not teach skills. Graduate students are adults who want to apply what they learn, and do so soon. They do not want to memorize facts. Instead, they seek to learn principles, concepts, and applications. They also would benefit from critical thinking about the material and being actively engaged with it.

STUDYING HOW TO LECTURE

Despite these limitations, lectures may be a superb instructional method if a lecturer works at it. Returning to Bligh's (2000) analogy to writing a symphony, the lecturer may master the form by studying it. Part of studying the lecture should concentrate on the quality materials available in books, journals, and websites. Based on my review of the literature on lecturing, I recommend a few places to start. First one might consult a classic article by Murray and Murray (1992) that provides an orientation to effective lecturing in terms of anticipation, preparation, execution, and support. Anticipation means considering the students' place in the curriculum, prior learning, and level of preparation as they enter the lecture hall. Preparation means making decisions about what material to include based on the objectives and then constructing a structured and organized lecture. Execution means using performance skills (e.g., timing, body movements, eye contact) to effectively present the lecture. Support means evaluating the lecture through self-reflection, peer feedback, and student evaluations. A good follow-up to Murray and Murray's article is Sullivan and McIntosh's (1996) 14-page outline of effective lecturing that includes when to lecture, planning the lecture, lecture components, presenting the lecture, reducing presentation anxiety, and evaluating the lecture.

Further study of micro-skills and strategies for lecturing may be easily done on the World Wide Web, starting with the resources on your own university's web pages. You might then move to the web pages produced by the Center for

Teaching Excellence and Faculty Development at the University of Medicine and Dentistry of New Jersey. In particular, review the pages on *Traditional Teaching: Web Resources* (Cook & Scanlan, 2003) that present 10 topics on lecturing with a total of 210 links to other websites.

PREPARING AN EFFECTIVE LECTURE

Lecture implies that you have prepared a presentation before you enter the classroom. Thus, an effective lecture is prepared first and delivered later—the better the preparation, the better the lecture. However, it is not enough to concentrate on the content of a lecture. The effective lecturer balances preparation of content with equal attention to the process of delivering that content. Most counselor educators have a set of personal guidelines that they follow in constructing the content and process of a lecture. Consider the following guidelines about preparing a lecture.

▶ *Be intentional in what you choose to teach.* It is wise to begin lecture preparations with the end in mind. Ask yourself what outcomes you seek. Answer this question by identifying the big ideas that you wish to impress on students. The answer should focus on student needs, not your own needs. This is particularly important when you are lecturing on topics about which you research or write. You know a great deal about these topics and care deeply about them. Remind yourself that students do not need all the details.

▶ *State big ideas succinctly.* After identifying the big ideas, try to state them succinctly. Challenge yourself to state each big idea from a lecture in one sentence and then one paragraph. You may even try reducing the ideas to a few key terms. For practice, try to craft a single sentence that explains your favorite counseling theory. Maybe Adlerians believe that increasing social interest will solve life's difficulties or Rogerians assume that reflection of feeling and meaning helps clients discover their authentic self. Now you can conceive how each of these sentences may be elaborated in a "two-minute elevator speech," a one-hour lecture, or a six-hour workshop.

▶ *Spiral through big ideas three times.* At any point during a lecture, not everyone will be listening to you. Thus the big ideas need to be repeated. For maximal effectiveness, you should use a variety of approaches each time you repeat the big idea. It is also useful to begin the lecture with the end in mind. Use your two-minute elevator speech to capture the interest and attention of students. The speech should serve as an advanced organizer to introduce the key concepts and summarize the important information that the students will learn. And, at the conclusion of the lecture, summarize succinctly what they have learned. You might even begin by saying, "If anyone asks you what we did in class today, this is what you could tell them."

▶ **Contextualize the ideas.** The big ideas should be related to other material that the students already know or will soon learn. In addition to placing the ideas into contemporary context, they should be considered in historical context. For example, in teaching counseling theories, it is important to mention the historical era and cultural context in which a theory emerged. Students need to understand that counseling theories and techniques develop to respond to the questions asked and needs felt by certain types of clients in particular contexts. The repression of Freud's turn of the century Vienna evoked psychoanalysis while the disillusionment with authorities following World War II evoked client-centered and Gestalt therapies. The bustle of life in high modernity produced brief therapies while 21st century post-modernity has produced narrative therapy.

▶ **Offer alternative views.** In addition to contextualizing ideas and practices, counselor educators conscientiously offer alternative perspectives. They realize that individuals may take multiple perspectives on any issue and that where they stand shapes what they see. For example, when teaching the measurement of individual differences, a lecturer might mention that the logical positivist viewpoint of inherent traits differs radically from the social constructionist viewpoint of traits as interpersonal reputation. Or, that the two epistemic positions differ on their views of working with "the self" during counseling; one helps a client to actualize the self while the other helps a client to construct the self. Providing students with alternative positions or lenses for looking opens their eyes to new visions and insights.

▶ **Organize the material differently than in the textbook.** Students who study different organizations of the same material achieve higher levels of mastery. Gestalt learning theory (Bigge & Shermis, 1992) recommends that lecturers help students recognize a problem, learn its elements and concepts, and then keep reorganizing them. Rather than preparing lectures directly from the students' textbook, consider slightly reorganizing the material. Ideas for different organizations of the same material may be found in other textbooks. This does not mean the languid practice of assigning the students one textbook while lecturing from another textbook. It does mean restructuring the material in the book and mentioning additional points, examples, and illustrations.

▶ **Prompt critical thinking.** It is useful to invite students to practice thinking like a counselor, especially by having them apply what you have just presented. You may do so by intermittently asking rhetorical questions and also by having them process case studies and simulation problems that require critical thinking. Occasionally, you might work through a case yourself by thinking aloud so students can hear you process information.

▶ **Include active learning.** It is important to provide opportunities for active learning during the lecture. These activities are best inserted at key junctures in the lecture material. Consider using 10–15 minutes of activities for every 45 minutes

of lecture, and be sure to keep the activities directly relevant. There are two popular activities that engage students and prompt interaction. The first is called "think,
write, pair, and share" (Johnson, Johnson, & Smith, 1991). You ask students to
think in some particular manner about a big idea that you have just presented.
Then they write their thoughts down, pair up with a partner, and read their notes
to each other. This is followed by discussion between the partners, then discussion
among pairs of partners or the whole class, and finally debriefing by the lecturer.
A second activity involves students in discussion by projecting a few examination
questions, especially application-type questions, for each block of the lecture.

▶ **Include aesthetics.** An outstanding lecture illustrates core ideas with ex-
emplars from a variety of cultural forms including literature, art, poetry, and myth.
With regard to literature, lectures may use classic or popular books to illustrate
their points. For example, a colleague uses the chapters in Sherwood Anderson's
(1919) *Winesburg, Ohio* to teach psychopathology. Each chapter in that first modern novel tells the story of a "grotesque" adaptation to life that illustrates personality disorders. Some lecturers play songs that express the key ideas. While words
depict thoughts and music evokes feelings, a song helps students feel a thought.
Consider for example Paul Simon's (1965) song *I am a Rock*. Listening to that song,
students may feel the meaning of schizoid personality disorder as well as four rules
(Becker, 1991) followed by adult children of alcoholics (i.e., don't say, don't trust,
don't feel, and don't tell). Poems may also add feeling to key ideas. For example
Wallace Stevens' (1990) *The Idea of Order at Key West* elicits feelings about the
narrative construction of reality and Emily Dickinson's (1960) *The Province of the
Saved* summons sentiments about becoming a counselor.

▶ **Develop skill at storytelling.** As noted earlier, lectures should combine science with storytelling. Myths, parables, and fairy tales contain wisdom and make
points memorable. For example, Cinderella is an appropriate fairy tale to tell before teaching Erik Erikson's (1968) psychosocial stages because she experiences
the first five stages, beginning with mistrust of caregivers and ending with identity
achievement. Myths, legends, and folktales engage students as they discuss difficult
topics in a safe space. A rich source of myths for the counselor education curriculum appears in a series of books by the mythologist and storyteller Michael Meade
(2010; http://www.mosaicvoices.org). Also, consider sharing stories about your
own experiences as a counselor. You may wish to further develop your skill at storytelling by studying Lipman's (1999) *Improving Your Storytelling* and Goodman's
(2010) *Storytelling as Best Practice*.

▶ **Use professional media.** Lectures should not be just auditory; they should
include pertinent and engaging slides and media to liven things up. Of course,
there are many professional films produced for classroom use beginning with the
famous videotape entitled *Three Approaches to Psychotherapy* (Shostrom, 1986) in
which Perls, Rogers, and Ellis interview a woman named Gloria. Jon Carlson has

produced a particularly useful *Psychotherapy Video Series* (http://www.apa.org/pubs/videos/about-videos.aspx).

Short clips from motion pictures have long been used by counselor educators to animate core principles and prompt discussion. Best practices and suggested clips appear in an article by Toman and Rak (2000) on the use of cinema in the counselor education curriculum. Also, consider browsing two books about using movie clips to teach about positive psychology (Niemiec & Wedding, 2008) and mental illness (Wedding, Boyd, & Niemiec, 2009).

▶ *Accommodate diverse learning styles.* The lecture is best for auditory learners and linear thinkers. Help students with other learning styles by using visuals and multimedia. Sometimes a picture is worth a thousand words. My best example of this is Holland's (1997) RIASEC hexagon. While I can explain orally the construct of type consistency, showing a picture of the hexagon communicates to students in a different way. Also, be sensitive to the needs of students with disabilities. For example, if a visually-impaired student attends your lecture, then be sure that you or the person sitting next to the student reads aloud all the information on slides.

▶ *Include social justice issues.* Counselor educators are concerned in every lecture with teaching for diversity and social justice. They discuss the meaning of the material across all groups as well as whose voices are being left out of the discussion and what actions might be taken to foster social equality. For example, when lecturing about a psychometric inventory, they address bias in the items and norms as well as whether the key studies on the inventory included a representative sample. Useful ideas about teaching for diversity and social justice appear in sourcebooks by Adams, Bell, and Griffin (2007) and by Enns and Sinacore (2004).

▶ *Discuss epistemology and philosophy.* When they lecture, counselor educators model how ideas should not be taken for granted. They encourage students to consider the assumptions that underlie the material. As a simple example, almost every major concept in the counselor education curriculum may be examined from the epistemic position of logical positivism or social constructionism and most research questions may be approached with quantitative or qualitative methods. Discussions of meta-cognition help students realize that their own philosophy of science will shape their practice.

DELIVERING AN EFFECTIVE LECTURE

When I first began working at a medical school, a few of the senior faculty wanted to preserve the tradition in which assistant and associate professors could write a lecture but only a full professor could present it. They asserted that preparing a lecture is one thing, whereas presenting it is another thing. We have all witnessed how poor delivery—whether due to anxiety or carelessness—can ruin a well-prepared lecture. Effective lecturers invest as much effort into delivering a lecture as they do in crafting it. Consider whether any of the following advice about this effort might be useful to you in presenting your own lectures.

▶ *Rehearse.* Recall the old joke about a visitor who asked a native New Yorker how to get to Carnegie Hall. Of course, the answer was "practice, practice, practice!" Similar to a Carnegie Hall performer, the effective lecturer rehearses before performing. And, this rehearsal is not just for the premiere presentation of a lecture, it needs to be ongoing and occur before every repeat performance. For a new lecture, it is advisable to rehearse the lecture with an audio or video recorder and then review the results. Immediately before going to the lecture hall, prepare yourself physically and mentally. Some counselor educators take a walk or nap or meditate. Whatever works for you, be sure to create a transitional space between other work tasks and entering the lecture hall.

▶ *Arrive early.* If you arrive at the classroom well in advance of the scheduled start time you may circulate among the students and get to know them personally. It helps to learn about their current academic circumstances: Do they have a big test coming up in another class or did they just get the results from one? How are things going for them?

▶ *Welcome the students.* Counselor educators use their professional skills to create a sense of community and belongingness in the lecture hall. This includes encouraging students to connect with each other and feel at home in the lecture hall. It may be useful to think of how the working alliance in therapy may be transferred to the lecture hall. This "educational alliance" between students and lecturer may include agreement on the goals of the lecture, consideration of the students' ability and responsibility in working toward those goals, the lecturer's empathy toward students, and a respectful connection between students and lecturer that enhances students' commitment to a career in counseling.

▶ *Begin with conversation.* I always begin by asking students to share an interesting experience or significant accomplishment during the last week. Did anyone have a birthday, anniversary, buy a car, start a new job, and so on? Sometimes students will talk about a bad event such as a car accident or death of loved one. Model your counseling skills as you process the bad news with the students. You may choose to share something about your own week but a little self-disclosure goes a long way. If you do choose to share something, it is best to directly relate it to the material for that lecture. For example, in beginning a lecture on early recollections as a projective technique, I mentioned that my wife and I had just seen a movie entitled *The King's Speech* (Hooper, 2010) in which the therapist began the first session by asking the King about his earliest recollection. I also make a habit of beginning each lecture with a relevant story from that day's newspaper as a means of grounding the material in real world experiences.

▶ *Increase motivation to learn.* Lecturers should attempt to cultivate students' existing motivation. This may include mentioning how the lecture material relates to their development as counselors. Relating the material to their career development and future jobs lends practical meaning to the lecture. It explains what the material may do for them and what opportunities it might eventually provide. Also when possible, connect lecture material to workshops, conferences, and journals of the American Counseling Association and its Divisions. For example, when lecturing on career counseling, a faculty member may mention the meetings and publications of the National Career Development Association and its State Branches.

▶ *Model ethical behavior.* It is important that faculty model the values of the counseling profession during the lecture. Ethical principles and behavior become more credible when every faculty member displays them while delivering their lectures. It is important the lecturer use non-sexist language and draw appropriate examples and illustrations from a range of cultures, ethnic groups, and religions. When the occasion arises, the lecturer may describe an ethical issue and how she or he dealt with it.

▶ *Use platform skills.* It almost goes without saying that delivery of the material counts. Lecturers are the "sage on the stage" so they need to attend to their performance. In gaining the audience's attention and earning their respect, everything from clothing to speaking voice matters. They must begin and end on time. As they speak, they avoid jargon and use simple language to communicate complex ideas. Effective lecturers are in tune with the emotional content of their material and use their counseling skills to process strong feelings elicited in the students. They always remember that they are there for the audience.

EVALUATE THE LECTURE

Improving lecture preparation and presentation skills requires evaluation and constructive feedback. This feedback differs from course evaluations. Before each lecture, an instructor may recruit a dozen volunteers to later submit anonymous answers to two questions: "What did you find useful in this lecture?" and "How could the lecture have been more useful to you?" I realize that these questions elicit positive responses, yet I also realize that this is the type of feedback that instructors can accept, process, and use. If you are fortunate enough to have willing colleagues, then invite them to your lectures and solicit their feedback. If they attend multiple lectures, then just sit down with them after each presentation and request feedback about one thing you did well and one thing you could improve. Over time, this simple procedure will markedly improve your lectures. If they can only attend one lecture, then ask them to evaluate your lecture on 29 micro-skills by completing "A Lecture Skills Checklist" (Appendix A in Sullivan & McIntosh, 1996).

CONCLUSION

This chapter on the lecture began by offering the unique advice of taking your counseling skills to the lectern. While lecturers in counselor education should follow the generic principles for presenting effective lectures, they may go further by exemplifying the ideals of the counseling profession in their lecture preparations and presentations. This includes forming a relationship with the audience by negotiating shared goals, acknowledging the students' place in the curriculum, deliberately processing emotional components of the material and students reactions to it, and forging a working alliance that enhances students' commitment to the profession of counseling. As they do so, counselor educators should demonstrate ethical behavior, sensitivity to student needs, and compassionate response to student concerns. They also should display a commitment to social justice and an openness to diverse ideas. Standing at the lectern, counselor education faculty present themselves as counselors first and lecturers second. They model a relationship with their students that exemplifies the best practices in counseling while at the same time presenting lectures that advance students' professional development.

REFERENCES

Adams, M., Bell, L. A., & Griffin, P. (2007). *Teaching for diversity and social justice* (2nd ed). New York, NY: Routledge/Taylor & Francis Group.

Anderson, S. (1919). *Winesburg, Ohio.* New York, NY: B. W. Huebsch.

Becker, R. A. (1991). *Don't talk, don't trust, don't feel: Our family secrets.* Deerfield Beach, FL: HCI Books.

Bigge, M. L., & Shermis, S. S. (1992). *Learning theories for teachers* (5th ed.). New York, NY: Harper Collins.

Bligh, D. A. (2000). *What's the use of lectures?* (5th ed.). San Francisco, CA: Jossey-Bass.

Carlson, J. *Psychotherapy Video Series* [Videos]. Washington, DC: American Psychological Association. Available from http://www.apa.org/pubs/videos/about-videos.aspx

Cook, S. D., & Scanlan, C. L. (2003). *Traditional teaching: Web resources.* University of Medicine and Dentistry of New Jersey: Center for Teaching Excellence. Retrieved from http://cte.umdnj.edu/traditional_teaching/index.cfm

Dickinson, E. (1960). *The complete poems of Emily Dickenson.* New York, NY: Little, Brown & Co.

Dyer, J. (2009). Speculative "musica" and the medieval university of Paris. *Music and Letters, 90,* 177–204. doi: 10.1093/ml/gcn089

Enns, C. Z., & Sinacore, A. L. (Eds.). (2004). *Teaching and social justice: Integrating multicultural and feminist theories in the classroom.* Washington, DC: American Psychological Association.

Erikson, E. H. (1968). *Identity: Youth and crisis.* New York, NY: Norton.

Goodman, A. (2010). *Storytelling as best practice.* Los Angeles, CA: Author.

Holland, J. L. (1997). *Making vocational choices: A theory of vocational personalities and work environments* (3rd ed.). Odessa, FL: Psychological Assessment Resources.

Hooper, T. (Director). (2010). *The king's speech.* Paddington, NSW, Australia: See-saw Films.

Johnson, D. W., Johnson, R. T., & Smith, K. A. (1991). *Cooperative learning: Increasing college faculty instructional productivity.* Washington, DC: ASHE/ERIC Higher Education.

Lipman, D. (1999). *Improving your storytelling.* Atlanta, GA: August House.

Meade, M. (2010). *Fate and destiny: The two agreements of the soul.* Baraboo, WI: Greenfire Press.

Murray, J. P., & Murray, J. I. (1992). How do I lecture thee? *College Teaching, 40*(3), 109–113.

Niemiec, R., & Wedding, D. (2008). *Positive psychology at the movies: Using films to build virtues and character strengths.* Gottingen, Germany: Hogrefe & Huber.

Shostrom, E. (1986). *Three approaches to psychotherapy* (VHS Videotape). Corona del Mar, CA: Psychological and Educational Films.

Simon, P. (1965). I am a rock [Recorded by P. Simon & A. Garfunkel]. On *Sounds of Silence* (Record album). New York, NY: Columbia Records.

Stevens, W. (1990). *Opus posthumous* (Rev. ed.). London, England: Faber and Faber.

Sullivan, R., & McIntosh, N. (December, 1996). *Delivering effective lectures.* U. S. Agency for International Development (Johns Hopkins University). Retrieved from http://www.reproline.jhu.edu/english/6read/6training/lecture/delivering_lecture.htm

Toman S. M., & Rak, C. F. (2000) The use of cinema in the counselor education curriculum: Strategies and outcomes. *Counselor Education & Supervision, 40*, 105–114.

Wedding, D., Boyd, M. A., & Niemiec, R. M. (2009). *Movies and mental illness: Using films to understand psychopathology.* Gottingen, Germany: Hogrefe & Huber.

CHAPTER 4

Making Use of the Seminar

JOLYNN V. CARNEY

RICHARD J. HAZLER

T he seminar teaching format is based more on participant discussion of significant issues rather than an instructor lecturing on relevant topics. It requires a more collegial approach to learning and demands more investment of students than some other teaching methods. What this process entails and how to make it work is the focus of this chapter.

THE LECTURE, SEMINAR, AND STATS EXPERIENCE

Attending to the Lecture

I (Richard) entered a doctoral program having always been a poor math student, so my greatest worry was statistics. On the first day of class, I entered the lecture hall with the professor down below back-grounded by four huge blackboards. He began explaining the chapter assignment and writing on the first board. I had read the chapters with minimal understanding, so I furiously wrote the formulas he was using on the board as he spoke. By the start of the second blackboard, I was lost, hopeless.

Discussing in Seminar

My doctoral program had a separate research class for new Ph.D. students. There was content to read, but the class was based on discussions around selected topics and how we might find ways to answer difficult research questions of interest to us. These discussions could be exciting at times when ideas came together and frustrating when we struggled with questions or disagreed on answers. Eventually the discussions led to conceptualizing research designs that began to make practical sense of how to collect needed information, how we could use it to demonstrate results, and how much value we should place on the results. To my great surprise, I found myself conceptualizing the need for specific kinds of statistics that would help me make a case for the results. I did not need to become a statistician. All I needed to know was how to utilize certain ones to answer my questions.

Thinking During the Lecture

Back in the statistics lecture hall midway through the semester, I was no longer taking down all the professor was writing on the board. I could not keep up and listen at the same time. Now I was listening some, but mostly thinking about how the professor's comments would fit into my own research questions and potential data. I missed lots of what was being said because of the thinking and jotting down notes about my ideas, but that did not matter. Content was also in the book. Now this class was exciting, useful, and moving me forward in ways no math class had ever done. Praise was coming from several sources including myself for doing so well, and I still could not remember the formulas.

RATIONALE FOR THE SEMINAR FORMAT IN COUNSELOR EDUCATION

Describing Seminar

A constructivist approach to teaching and learning in adults emphasizes the integration of past and present experiences with new knowledge and skills (Smith & McCormick, 1992). Professors like the one in the statistics course often are great at explaining new knowledge, but in many cases that new knowledge has minimal value because it lacks significant connections to student experiences and no opportunity to explore the issues through discussion. The information could potentially be memorized and recalled, but knowing alone does not produce effective application especially when the content is not connected to a broader context such as how statistics fit into the larger world of research methodologies.

Counseling is above all an application field of study, so students must go well beyond the lowest of Bloom's Taxonomy (Bloom, Engelhart, Furst, Hill, & Krathwohl, 1956) levels of knowledge and comprehension to the more complex levels of application with clients, analysis and synthesis of various types of information, and appropriately evaluating clients and oneself as the counselor. Bloom's Taxonomy has been emphasized in the counselor education literature as a basis for improving supervision (Granello, 2000), student writing (Granello, 2001), and organizing the master's program course sequence (Granello & Hazler, 1998). The lower levels of knowledge and comprehension provide valuable foundation information that emphasizes memory, but does not translate clearly into practice. Application is the next level where information is now applied to specific situations such as counseling practice. Analysis and synthesis are the two levels that break situations down into component parts (analysis) and then put parts together in new wholes (synthesis), as one must do in working with the complexity of client situations. A final level of the Taxonomy is evaluation where judgments are made based on defined criteria. This stage is critical in how counselors change and adapt based on learning gained from previous stages. The lecture hall can provide the knowledge base, but it is the seminar format that offers much more in the way of integrating information into the actual experience of the trainee, counselor, supervisor, or counselor educator.

Dictionaries are consistent in their definition of a seminar by describing it in terms specific or similar to "a group of advanced students studying under a professor with each doing original research and all exchanging results through reports and discussions." Second and third definitions expand this to "2) an advanced or graduate course often featuring informality and discussion ... 3) a meeting for giving and discussing information" (Merriam-Webster, 2012). These definitions lack a research line in any profession and authors describing their specific use of the term use any one or combination of the three definitions.

The definitions do make it clear that a true seminar is much more than a small number of students in a class. It is more than a small group discussion and is definitely not group counseling focused on personal problems. Seminar teaching is grounded in a group to which each member brings specific knowledge and experiences to a discussion around a given topic in order to actively provide the diversity of ideas, information, and perceptions that promote student-led inquiry, creative thinking, and conceptual development (Tsui & Gao, 2006). The group also has a leader or leaders who bring additional expertise about the topic and importantly must have the ability to facilitate small group discussion that promotes active exploration for new learning through both sharing individual perspectives and seeking the perspectives of others. This interactive and reciprocal teaching and learning process creates a learning community, but it does not happen easily or automatically. Several essential concepts that provide the foundation for the seminar format are discussed below.

Critical Seminar Concepts

Depth of discussion. The seminar is a time for spending significant energy on a specific issue, topic, situation, or client. Expectations of outcomes should revolve around gaining depth of understanding rather than large amounts of specific information. Seminar can be conceptualized as similar to qualitative research which emphasizes depth of understanding of a few research participants or focused situation versus the generalized details that appear to be true across large populations and situations (quantitative research; Creswell, 2009). Information that is available from assignments, readings, or experiences, both professional and personal, are examined and explored in ways designed to create new conceptualizations and abilities that promote more personally and professionally integrated performance.

Critical thinking. The higher-order thinking processes described in the advanced levels of Bloom's Taxonomy (Bloom et al., 1956) are where critical thinking occurs. It can be broadly conceptualized as students' abilities to identify the issues, recognize relationships among the issues, make inferences, draw conclusions, and evaluate those conclusions based on the evidence (Tsui, 2006). Purposeful instruction methods enhance critical thinking skills (Pascarella & Terenzini, 2005) when utilized within a seminar format, which researchers propose teaches students how to think, not what to think (Tsui, 2002).

Shared knowledge and experience. The seminar emphasizes the shared knowledge and experiences of students participating in the learning with a reduced focus on the seminar leader's greater expertise. Members of a successful seminar must invest themselves in ways that provide input for others while also seeking input for themselves. No single brilliant idea is what makes a seminar work. It is the diversity of experiences and information that helps create common understandings of problems and solutions for the issues at hand. Seminar leaders must control their desire to tell all they know or they will reduce the time for participant exploration. Too much instructor control also communicates the message that real knowledge comes not from the integration of ideas, but only from the most knowledgeable, powerful person in the room.

Exposure to the topic. Important discussion must have some basis for participant involvement so the students must have some exposure to the seminar discussion topic. This exposure may come through assigned readings, personal experiences, or personally held beliefs and values. The stronger the basis of all the members, the more potential there is for significant learning and growth. Seminar leaders clarify for participants what the topic is and what aspects of their study, experience, or self-examination are needed to form the basis of their participation.

Student developmental level. Students with less exposure to a profession or course of study naturally have less information, skills, and experience than they will after further involvement. The seminar is built around the level of student development (Moore, 1994) and level of expertise (Benner, 1984). The thinking and work expected at an entry level will be very different from that of more advanced levels. Bloom's Taxonomy of Learning (Bloom et al., 1956) also reflects development, in that information and understanding serve as necessary foundations for more advanced levels of cognitively complex learning. A quality counseling seminar focused on ethics, for example, requires some level of knowledge and understanding of the issues, so new students with less knowledge and experience will view ethics much more simplistically than advanced students or professionals who have additional knowledge and exposure to the complexities of these issues with clients.

Group process. We have found that seminar groups, like all groups, have a natural evolution that requires more leader direction in the earliest stages and less as the group members take more ownership of the discussion. There will be stages when discussions run smoothly and other times when they break down leading to frustration because of group members' lack of knowledge, understanding, or hesitancies to engage. Excitement will be present at times and frustration at others. Frustrated students at these times want us to fix the problem or provide the right answers, but doing so defeats the student-led learning principle that underlies the seminar. Frustration, in addition to excitement, is an important component in learning to be a critical thinker. Perceiving what is influencing the group process and learning to understand it, recognizing its different stages, and taking appropriate facilitative actions are critical factors in the effectiveness of such a group effort (Corey, Corey, & Corey, 2010).

PROCESS FOR CONDUCTING SEMINARS

The seminar format can be viewed as more complex due to the various dynamics created from the engaged, interactive learning model as compared to the more passive learning style created by the lecture format. The complexity of ideas and the process involved in a true seminar require instructors to be more process oriented and flexible in both their thinking and running of the course. Important seminar considerations to address are: various leader interventions, class size, stages in the process, and essential leader characteristics.

▶ *Leader intervention to advance the discussion.* Seminar leaders (instructor or peer-leader) must identify times when it is appropriate to intervene in the discussions of seminar participants. One of these times is when the leader can call attention to similarities or differences in the discussion in order to focus attention on where those might have arisen or how they might change the focus of the discussion. This is not simply identifying similarities and differences, but doing so in ways that promote additional understanding or development of the discussion which promote critical thinking skills (Bloom et al., 1956; Tsui, 2001).

A common occurrence in my (Richard) child counseling course is how students discuss and conceptualize children versus adults. A given case will have students expressing how important it is to listen closely and observe children in order to promote a therapeutic alliance. Then they will often go on to simply describe what teachers, administrators, or parents are not doing or should be doing. Inevitably the discussion focuses on how to help the child, while adults are simply expected to "do their job."

This situation calls for an intervention to advance the discussion and learning. I begin by confirming the various students' accurate identification of significant parts of the case (analysis), but then ask, "How do the adults feel and what do they need?" This causes students to place themselves in a situation where they can recognize how the situation and emotions of the adults are ignored. I might then say, "In which model would you be more likely to feel support; being cared about or urged to do your job?" Of course, we all respond better when someone cares about us, so the students begin to discuss how they feel about the adults and how they might form more supportive relationships with them. This is an example of Bloom's evaluation level (noting how people feel when judged versus supported) and then synthesis can occur where the analyzed components are integrated in a more productive counseling and consultation model.

▶ *Leader intervention to advance topic understanding.* Another point for intervention is when the facilitator (peer-leader or instructor) uses personal or professional knowledge or experience to demonstrate how to integrate pieces of the discussion for greater understanding of the issue at hand (Bloom et al., 1956; Tsui, 2001). Much discussion in my (JoLynn's) doctoral supervision seminar focuses on developing a supervisor identity including what theory or model will guide the supervision process. Students can struggle with understanding how to choose between theoretical orientations (e.g., cognitive; Liese & Beck, 1997), developmental approaches (e.g., integrated developmental model; Stoltenberg, McNeill, & Delworth, 1998) and social role models (e.g., discrimination model; Bernard, 1979).

Eventually they gain a sense of the differences and similarities between these models, but become frustrated with how to integrate them successfully into a working supervisory style (Bloom's analysis and synthesis levels). This is a good time to use a supervisee and supervisor narrative from a recorded supervision session. Asking students to categorize actual statements into theoretical models and justify the reasoning underlying those decisions, forces students to more closely examine how they and colleagues intentionally or unintentionally use different supervisory approaches and how they evaluate the effectiveness in given situations.

▶ *Maximizing investment: Sufficient opportunity to connect.* You can have a large class and divide them into small groups for discussion, but is this truly a seminar? The answer is probably no because the instructor/facilitator cannot be invested in the same way with each group. The seminar format requires a facilitator who plays a unique role in organizing and maintaining the progress of the group. Seminars must be small enough for leaders to help each member share his or her thinking, question his or her understanding, and revise beliefs based on peer-critiques/input. Regular meetings of adults should ideally be small enough for ample opportunity to interact, but also large enough for a variety of opinions and experiences to emerge. Research does not identify exact optimal numbers of participants for seminars, but a common recommended range that allows for group process to occur is around 8 participants (Corey et al., 2010) not to exceed 12 (CACREP, 2009).

When I (JoLynn) have a seminar group that is larger than five or six, I need to be more active at inviting input from quiet members and reducing the dominance of others. It is very common for me to interrupt a person to say, "If I can stop you for a minute, Jill, I'd like to emphasize the important point you are making and see how it resonates with others." The quiet participant may require a different type of invitation such as: "Your face seems to be indicating that you have some thoughts on this issue and I'd like to invite you to share them with us."

Smaller seminar groups most often need the instructor to increase the diversity of ideas brought to the discussion that would more commonly arise with the additional members in a larger group. In these situations, it is my broader experience that allows me to present ideas and experiences that are different from those being expressed by the small number of seminar participants. Simply offering content that confirms their limited ideas would not help increase the creativity and advanced levels of thinking that are the best applications of a seminar.

▶ *Various actions for various points in the process.* In order for useful group process to occur in a successful seminar, attention must be given to unique needs during different stages of group process as proposed by Corey et al. (2010): the initial stage, transition stage, working stage, and termination. Before the class begins, the instructor needs to assess the readiness level of potential participants in order to determine how the seminar can be organized and what reasonable expectations are for the course.

Initial stage—Participants new to the seminar format may exhibit hesitancy about engaging in this interactive, self-reflective learning experience. They may have questions about how the course will work. Important first steps clarify the rules, responsibilities, expectations, and evaluation components of the class. Students should be encouraged to discuss these issues and not simply to ask questions of the instructor.

Each new group of students in my (JoLynn's) suicide seminar fills me with wonder about their openness to engaging in the class versus the didactic classes I teach. Inevitably there are students who would rather I lecture so they can sit passively in the room as they have been trained to do over years of schooling. They want to know how to assess and intervene with a suicidal client, but they do not want to feel the personal emotions and reactions that are involved. I need to resist my desire to move immediately into these areas, but instead explain the course content and the importance of their active involvement to fully understand what motivates a person to commit suicide rather than reject the option, as well as dealing with the aftermath of a suicide attempt. I must deal patiently with their hesitancy to explore the topic, provide rationale behind the need to be involved, and not demand immediate equal involvement from everyone. The task is to give some of the structure the students desire and begin the process of encouraging discussion of issues that are likely to be uncomfortable.

Transition stage—As simple surface discussions move to more complex and personalized ones, additional tension results that has students increase pressures on the leader to take more control and reduce anxieties about what to do and how they are doing. Instructors must fight this press to do more with a balance of support and not giving into the pressure in order to enable students to remain engaged in the discussion.

I (Richard) have gotten things started in a multicultural seminar so that students seem pleased with the content, objectives, and assignments. But as the emphasis moves from my explanations, to their easy politically correct talk about knowledge and into the areas of their personal privilege and biases, they become increasingly uncomfortable. Resistance begins to occur as I say things like, "Why don't you tell us more?" Or students will become quiet, hoping a peer or I will take the lead. This is a time of trial for the instructor, because all the pressure is on me to provide them with information so they will all be appreciative and relax. Unfortunately, this will also short circuit the best benefits of the group discussion where students work through the anxiety to explore more difficult issues and take more leadership for which they do not feel fully prepared. So I need to be patient, encourage discussion, assure them that I know why it is difficult, support those willing to risk being wrong or seen in a poor light, and allow for silences and frustrations to be part of the experience. I communicate confidence in their ability to deal with important difficult issues often with a statement like, "It is difficult to take this step out of the PC (politically correct) world and look at the not so correct side of ourselves, but it is only in these difficult efforts where major gains in understanding the issues and the impact on those who suffer most from them can be found."

Working stage—Students deal with critical issues in high quality and personalized ways that promote maximum learning at some points. Seminars do not always get to or remain at this stage, but at the working stage the learning is much more in depth and personally meaningful. It is also the most rewarding for instructors who appreciate the value of the seminar format.

When the students really engage by exploring complexities and depth of ideas, evaluating effectively, and making appropriate changes in their thinking and actions, it is time for the leader/facilitator to focus on the group's process.

Once students in my (JoLynn) suicide seminar begin to deal with their actual emotions and experiences, my role becomes that of supporting their courage to risk reacting in ways not expected in traditional classes, emphasizing key points, and highlighting connections with the research and comments of others. The key task is to pay attention to the flow of the discussion and involvement of members so that I can see when to stay quiet and when I can promote growth through their comments.

Termination – Courses come to an end and the key questions are what did the students gain from the course and what will they do to continue this growth? The key is to begin ending the course before the semester is over. "We have this week and next, so everyone needs to be thinking about what you need to do to make the best use of these final sessions. Let's take a few minutes to see how well we have met course goals and your personal goals." A reworded, but similar statement works for individual class sessions just as they do for counseling sessions.

All too often a great discussion with important points, significant learning, and lots of excitement gets lost simply because *time is up*. Individuals can walk away pleased, excited, frustrated, or disappointed, but the most important aspect is that they recognize what they learned and what they can do with it. As the end of a session or course approaches, the seminar session(s) should be pulled together, to highlight the findings and successes everyone has recognized, and set any agendas such as what students will do differently between sessions or how students will utilize what was learned from the classes overall. We like the starting place to include student input with a go-around activity asking people to react to their learning, growth, future actions, or other issues that are core to their development. Once we have this information, we can make our own assessment that connects student input with our learning objectives for them.

▶ *Treat each class as a new adventure.* Seminar instructors and students who have experienced a highly interactive, in-depth, and meaningful session will be excited about the next session and expecting that they will begin right where they left off. This never really happens. The heightened mental, emotional, and even physical states from a very strong session will seldom be present to start the next one. Each session brings new questions of "What will I do?" and "What will others do?" Instructors have to build the group process again, recognizing the need for some form of beginning stage, transitioning to more difficult issues, and potentially into a working stage. The danger is that the initial disappointment on the part of instructor and/or students will promote less discussion or move the instructor to do more presenting than supporting the seminar process.

The times I (Richard) am worst at running a seminar are when I become too confident: "Last week was great, the students were really taking it to heart, they were fully involved, and raring to go out and implement their new knowledge. This week it will be great to see them and to hear about what has happened. I can just sit back and relax." Students can feel the same way so the class often starts slowly and everyone feels some disappointment that things are not the same as the last session. The feeling is like the day after finishing a major research study when you celebrate that day, but the next day you wonder, "Can I duplicate that success now that I have to start again?" Only if you recognize that a letdown will come and that you must do your homework in preparation for next steps in the process, can you take advantage of the seminar.

The multicultural seminar provides an excellent example. There will be sessions where students gain great trust in each other, explore their own sensitive issues in ways they have not done before, and deal with difficult reactions from others. We leave class on a high, but by the next session it doesn't feel the same and everyone is uncomfortable about how to get the experience going again. My job is to let them know that this is normal and then we often start with trying to get in touch with what was so good about the last session, how did it feel when you were outside the class for awhile, how are you feeling about it now, and what can we do to move ourselves forward based on what we learned last time? I know I, just like the students, will feel challenged about getting the class going again but I need to help them face the questions rather than take the easy way out and do more of the talking myself.

▶ *Instructor characteristics.* The instructor's flexibility may be called upon to a greater extent than in a more traditional course. A standard presentation with some discussion format will provide most instructors with confidence that things will go well as long as they know the information to be presented, have planned reasonably well for the session, organized their technology, and offered opportunities for students to ask or answer questions. A seminar format does not offer such security. Instructional self-efficacy is important because participant involvement and investment can take the topic into areas in which the instructor is not prepared or knowledgeable and a process may evolve that can at times be frustrating, uncomfortable, and complex (Tsui, 2001). A wide breadth of knowledge, experience, willingness to take professional risks, and enough self-confidence to deal with complexities one has not considered are important characteristics of the instructor in a seminar. Without these characteristics, the instructor may become defensive when things do not move in expected directions. Such defensiveness is not productive and will quash student discussion, exploration, and risk-taking.

The seminar is our favorite teaching model by far, EXCEPT when we hate it. There is so much excitement, growth, and new thinking for students and instructors when the process is working at its best and everyone is involved. But during difficult times in the group process, we wonder if maybe we should just lecture and not deal with the frustrations. If we did not have the confidence and energy to hang in there knowing that we can work the process over time, we would do what we have done at some times in the past: take one or two student comments and then talk for the remainder of the time. In such instances, a class of 10 may be seminar size, but becomes just a small lecture class that might as well have 50 students.

For example, there have been times in one of my (JoLynn) seminar classes where we have had less than productive involvement from the students and both they and I felt disappointed. Self-preservation tells me to develop a lecture for the next class so I can have better control and students will gain information. I have done that in the past and it produces less anxiety and yet, I believe less learning. My self-efficacy needs to be strong enough to fight through the urge to reduce discussion and increase lecture based on confidence in myself and the ability to utilize the seminar process. It is not more content that is needed from me, but more confidence that I can make the seminar process work successfully.

EVALUATING SEMINAR EFFECTIVENESS

Effective assessment of students and instructors in a seminar begins long before any assessment is designed and utilized. Comprehensive evaluation begins with the instructor establishing expectations of students at various points during the course or class lesson. Student learning objectives in a true seminar course must begin with higher levels of Bloom's Taxonomy (Bloom et al., 1956) and not the lower knowledge level of the model. The information in Figure 4.1 demonstrates how objectives, selected for a given class session or course, guide instructor roles to encourage the desired responses from students. This, in turn, is expected to promote outcomes that can demonstrate achievement of those objectives.

The model outlined in Figure 4.1 can be used to develop procedures to evaluate student outcomes, faculty performance, and overall course quality. Instructors can develop specific teaching roles that can then be evaluated based on student reactions to them and student outcomes. Instruments to assess student learning can be developed based on specific tasks they should be expected to accomplish that match the objectives. Student course evaluations can focus on their skill development and growth rather than general questions about course satisfaction.

Examples of Evaluating Learning

As an assessment example for Bloom's analysis-level, we use theoretical conceptualization of a client's profile as a topic in an advanced theory course in which doctoral students explore and evaluate traditional and contemporary counseling theories. Students, for example, need to recognize what factors grounded within various theoretical orientations might be causing and/or maintaining a client's diminished functioning in order to propose viable interventions. The task is to break down the general problem (e.g., understanding the impact of the client's psychosocial and cultural identities on functioning) into causative factors and assess potential resources before looking for a solution. A sample analysis question

Objectives for Students	Instructor Roles	Effective Student Responses	Student Assessment Tasks	
Knowledge (Remember or recognize specific information)	directs tells shows examines	responds absorbs remembers recognizes	define repeat list name match identify	memorize record relate label locate select
Comprehension (Understand the information given)	demonstrates listens questions compares contrasts examines	explains translates demonstrates interprets	restate describe explain identify estimate group	summarize recognize express locate review rearrange
Application (Use techniques, concepts, principles, & theories in new situations)	shows facilitates observes criticizes	solves problem demonstrates use of knowledge constructs	translate apply employ practice illustrate demonstrate	solve dramatize use schedule compute modify
Analysis (Break complex ideas, concepts or behaviors into their constituent elements or parts)	probes guides observes acts as a resource	discusses uncovers lists dissects	calculate test contrast criticize differentiate questions solve experiment	appraise diagram compare separate inventory infer analyze outline
Synthesis (Original, creative thinking that forms a whole by putting constituent elements or parts together)	reflects extends analyzes evaluates	discusses generalizes relates compares contrasts abstracts	compose propose formulate assemble construct hypothesize manage summarize	plan design modify collect create organize invent generate
Evaluation (Developing & applying standards & criteria to judge the value of ideas, actions & methods)	clarifies accepts harmonizes guides	judges disputes develops criteria	judge discriminate compare score choose estimate measure support	appraise predict rate value select assess justify criticize

FIGURE 4.1. Instruction and Assessment Actions Via Bloom's Taxonomy. Adapted by permission of the publisher; Adapted from Bloom, Benjamin S. *Taxonomy of Educational Objectives Book 1/ Cognitive Domain*, 1st Ed. @1984. Reprinted by permission of Pearson Education, Inc., Upper Saddle River, NJ. Adapted by permission of the publisher. From Richard J. Hazler, *Helping in the hallways*, 2nd ed., Corwin Press, Thousand Oaks, CA. Copyright @2008.

for discussion or written examination might then be, "From the feminist theory literature, identify and prioritize based on their impact, factors influencing the client's daily level of functioning. Provide a rationale for each factor selected."

Synthesis is another advanced thinking level emphasized in seminars that can be evaluated through discussion or written assignments. Using the example above, students could be asked to literally diagram from their theoretical orientation major obstacles and supports that impact client functioning. Completing this level of synthesis allows students to differentiate the complex issues of diverse clients and analyze various trajectories as outlined by their orientation. A final evaluation question could ask about judgments and reasoning pertaining to theories that fit the synthesized problem.

An Example of Evaluating the Instructor

Evaluating whether the faculty member performed his or her roles can be done by identifying, for example, the number of faculty statements or amount of talk that matches the analysis instructor roles versus how many times other instructor roles from Bloom's Taxonomy were exemplified in statements (see Figure 4.1). Student assessments of faculty could use Bloom's language (e.g., guided the discussion, probed for our ideas, provided necessary expertise to help our thinking) in assessment instruments.

Instructors can also assess the implementation of their roles by observing student responses. Are they discussing, listing ideas, dissecting generalities, and uncovering new ideas? These would be important aspects of an analysis-focused discussion. A faculty member could even develop a check sheet to code/categorize student comments as well as their own comments to see how effectively student analytic responses are being drawn out by the faculty member.

SUMMARY

The complexities of using a seminar as the primary teaching format require appropriate course goals/objectives, students at suitable developmental levels, and faculty with instructional self-efficacy. We strongly believe that critical higher order thinking skills are developed and enhanced through purposeful application of instructor/facilitator and student roles. Learning through these proactive, engaged, often student-led experiences yields significant personal and professional growth for students and instructors. We acknowledge the demands that the seminar format can place on all participants, but wholeheartedly support its continued use as an instructional method in counselor education.

REFERENCES

Benner, P. (1984). *From novice to expert: Excellence and power in clinical nursing practice.* Menlo Park, CA: Addison-Wesley.

Bernard, J. M. (1979). Supervisor training: A discrimination model. *Counselor Education and Supervision, 19,* 60–68.

Bloom, B. S., Engelhart, M. D., Furst, F. J., Hill, W. H., & Krathwohl, D. R. (1956). *Taxonomy of educational objectives: Cognitive domain.* New York, NY: McKay.

Corey, M. S., Corey, G., & Corey, C. (2010) *Groups process and practice* (8th ed.). Belmont, CA: Brooks/Cole CENGAGE Learning.

Council for Accreditation of Counseling and Related Educational Programs [CACREP]. (2009). *2009 standards for accreditation.* Alexandria, VA: Author.

Creswell, J. W. (2009). *Research design: Quantitative, qualitative, and mixed methods approaches.* Thousand Oaks, CA: Sage.

Granello, D. H. (2000). Encouraging the cognitive development of supervisees: Using Bloom's Taxonomy in Supervision. *Counselor Education and Supervision, 40,* 31–46.

Granello, D. H. (2001). Promoting cognitive complexity in graduate written work: Using Bloom's Taxonomy as a pedagogical tool to improve literature reviews. *Counselor Education and Supervision, 40,* 292–307.

Granello, D. H., & Hazler, R. J. (1998). A developmental rationale for curriculum order and teaching styles in counselor education. *Counselor Education and Supervision, 38,* 89–105.

Hazler, R. J. (2008). *Helping in the hallways* (2nd ed.). Thousand Oaks, CA: Corwin Press.

Liese, B. S., & Beck, J. S. (1997). Cognitive therapy supervision. In C. E. Watkins, Jr. (Ed.), *Handbook of psychotherapy supervision* (pp. 114–133). New York, NY: John Wiley & Sons.

Merriam-Webster online. (2012). *Seminar.* Retrieved from http://www.merriam-webster. com/dictionary/seminar

Moore, W. S. (1994). Student and faculty epistemology in the college classroom: The Perry schema of intellectual and ethical development. In K. W. Prichard & R. M. Sawyer (Eds.), *Handbook of college teaching: Theory and applications* (pp. 45–67). Westport, CT: Greenwood Press/Greenwood.

Pascarella, E., & Terenzini, P. (2005). *How college affects students.* San Francisco, CA: Jossey-Bass.

Smith, K. E., & McCormick, D. M. (1992). Translating experience into learning: Facilitating the process for adult students. *Adult Learning, 3,* 22–25.

Stoltenberg, C. D., McNeill, B., & Delworth, U. (1998). *Integrated developmental model of supervision.* San Francisco, CA: Jossey-Bass.

Tsui, L. (2001). Faculty attitudes and the development of students' critical thinking. *The Journal of General Education, 50,* 1–28.

Tsui, L. (2002). Fostering critical thinking through effective pedagogy. *The Journal of Higher Education, 73,* 740–763. doi: 10.1353/jhe.2002.0056

Tsui, L. (2006). Cultivating critical thinking: Insights from an elite liberal arts college. *The Journal of General Education, 55,* 200–227.

Tsui, L., & Gao, E. (2006). The efficacy of seminar courses. *The Journal of College Student Retention, 8,* 149–170. doi: 10.2190/DJ96-47XT-N103-K451

Connecting Experiential Education and Reflection in the Counselor Education Classroom

MARK E. YOUNG

GULNORA HUNDLEY

The experiential approach to family therapy is based on the simple premise that clients should have a real experience during the counseling session that changes how they think and feel. Similarly, experiential teaching and learning rest on the assumption that the most powerful learning experiences are the result of important experiences in the classroom. The major element of experiential learning is "doing," which includes engaging in activities that make sense to students and which have an authentic impact. Experiential theory asserts that a student acquires knowledge from his or her own actions, perceptions, and personal involvement (Osborn, Daninhirsch, & Page, 2003).

Personal involvement means that students' prior knowledge and feelings are activated, a process that Rogers (1994) called "significant learning." Arthur and Achenbach (2002) further defined experiential learning as, not only learning by doing, but also learning while being *emotionally* engaged. The emotions most often associated with experiential learning are interest/excitement, surprise, disgust, sadness, and anger. It is relatively easy to provide exciting, shocking, and provocative experiences for students, but experiential learning can only be effective when students are directly in touch with something that is also meaningful to them, and when they experience guided reflection on and analysis of that experience (Magnuson & Norem, 2002).

KOLB'S STAGES

Kolb (1984) is the name most often associated with experiential learning theory. He took earlier ideas about experiential learning and systematized them (Kolb, Boyatzis, & Mainemelis, 2001). Kolb used the term "experiential" to differentiate the approach from cognitive and behavioral learning theories. Experiential learning theory is in line with the ideas of educational theorists such as Dewey (1960) and Piaget (1967) and has been popular in counselor education since its inception (see Atkinson & Murrell, 1988). The model itself proposes that there are four kinds of experiences that a learner can have: Mode 1, concrete experience; Mode 2, reflective observation; Mode 3, abstract conceptualization; and Mode 4, active experimentation (Kolb et al., 2001).

Thus, the process of experiential education and learning begins with a concrete experience and ends with application. For example, in counselor education students might participate as members of a triadic group activity during a "Techniques of Counseling" course (Mode 1; Young, 2013). After learning a particular skill such as confrontation, small group activity continues with intentional and guided reflection on that experience (Mode 2). This reflective debriefing allows students to process the experience and asks them to react verbally in class or to write a reflection paper or journal as a homework assignment. The next stage, abstract conceptualization (Mode 3), represents both the integration of learning experiences and generation of new ideas. In our example of the triadic group activity, a student may recognize that he or she used closed questions frequently during a mock counseling session and decides to practice more open-ended questions in the future. In the final stage of experiential education and learning, active experimentation (Mode 4), new ideas learned by the student in the previous stage are tested by putting them into practice. In this case, the student attempts to use more open-ended questions compared to closed questions. Kolb stressed that the learning process can begin at any point of this cycle, but it should ideally include all four phases (Kolb et al., 2001).

EXPERIENTIAL LEARNING IN COUNSELOR EDUCATION

Experiential learning has played an important role in counselor education (Cummings, 2001), which often includes these experiential activities: role playing, demonstrating therapeutic techniques, presenting and discussing cases and critical incidents, and utilizing in-class simulations. Counselor education involves the acquisition of skills and that makes experiential learning appropriate. In addition, counselor education is aimed at older more mature learners who are less open to sitting in lectures and answering multiple choice exams. Thus, the counselor educator recognizes that experiential learning is a match developmentally.

Andragogy, the approach that explains how adults learn, is different from pedagogy, the approach that defines how children learn (Pollio & Macgowan, 2010). A major difference is that pedagogy rarely takes into consideration previous life experiences, which are crucial when teaching adults. The counselor educator must find a way to link past experiences with new learning. Another difference is that the emphasis in andragogy is on the instructor as a facilitator rather than teacher. Adults prefer an active role as a user of education rather than being a passive recipient (Knox, 1986). Because adults learn through doing, instruction should emphasize tasks that mature students can perform, rather than information that they must memorize.

When Experiential Learning Goes Bad

Experiential education can be criticized when experiences are not somehow connected with application (Kayes, 2002). For example, in a recent qualitative study of experiential learning in multicultural counseling, students consistently objected to multicultural learning experiences when they could not see how the classroom experiences were related to counseling practice (Young, Butler, Hutchinson & Gutierrez, 2011). When students watched examples of prejudicial treatment of minorities, they experienced a number of conflicting emotions from guilt to anger but they expressed frustration when there was no way to reconcile these feelings with appropriate action.

At other times, experiential classroom activities may portray a client problem or dilemma in an over-simplified manner. For example, role-play or simulation involving a person suffering from a debilitating physical illness may lead to a simplistic view of all individuals with that disease (Grayson & Marini, 1996). The problem then, is how to find exciting classroom experiences that students can readily apply and, at the same time, supply them with sufficient knowledge so that their learning is not superficial and that their enthusiasm sparks further study.

The Importance of Reflection

Reflection is the process of mentally reviewing our actions, assumptions, thoughts, feelings, and guiding theories in a particular situation (cf., Griffith & Frieden, 2000). Whereas Kolb's model in Mode 2 specifically identifies reflection as an integral part of the paradigm, in practice, experiential exercises are frequently presented without clear guidance and then poorly processed (Brackenreg, 2004).

One of the ways that educational theorists and counselor educators have recommended dealing with this gap between experiences, content knowledge, and application is to incorporate more reflection into classroom learning (Granello & Young, 2012; Larrivee, 2000, 2008). Thus, this chapter highlights the importance of reflection, not because it is theoretically distinct from experiential education but out of concern that it is underutilized and because it helps students finish the "experiential loop" by helping them see how they can apply what they have learned (Takeda, Marchel, & Gaddis, 2002).

The following quote by Donald Schön, in *The Reflective Practitioner* (1983), while using sexist language, shows the connection between: (a) having an experience that suggests a new way of thinking; (b) reflecting on the experience and (c) trying out a new behavior to match the new perspective:

> The practitioner allows himself to experience surprise, puzzlement, or confusion in a situation which he finds uncertain or unique. He reflects on the phenomenon before him, and on the prior understandings which have been implicit in his behaviour. He carries out an experiment which serves to generate both a new understanding of the phenomenon and a change in the situation. (p. 68)

Based on Schön's ideas, how can the counselor educator capitalize on classroom experiences through reflection? One example involves a student who had viewed a film about older adults in a class and had an emotional reaction. The student became aware of avoiding older people and feeling anxious in their presence. The student commented on having little contact with older individuals since entering college. The student discussed concerns of getting older and having to take care of aging parents in the future. In this case the instructor suggested carrying out an experiment that would allow for positive contact with an older person. One of other classmates further suggested that they visit an older person and that was the beginning of a change for the student. The point of this discussion is that without including reflection, the student might not have processed concerns and instead may have tried to forget the movie as quickly as possible. Thus, reflection becomes a vehicle for extending learning experiences beyond the classroom and challenging students to deal constructively with the emotions aroused by experiential education (Wong-Wylie, 2007).

Content Learning

So far, we have said that experiential education sometimes ends too quickly without sufficient reflection. Another criticism of experiential learning is that "fun learning" is not always "good learning." Some of us may be familiar with engaging instructors who receive high student evaluations but do not cover much material.

The *Dr. Fox effect* (see Williams & Ware, 1977) was discovered in an experiment where an actor was coached to give a lively lecture full of doubletalk and contradictions. Three separate audiences of psychiatrists, psychologists, and graduate students gave glowing evaluations of his teaching. The Dr. Fox effect states that if the enthusiasm of the lecturer is high, then students will evaluate low content lecturers the same as high content lecturers even though they learn more in the high content condition (Naftulin, Ware, & Donnelly, 1973). In other words, exciting instructors do not necessarily inform their audiences. One of the conundrums this helps to explain is the excellent ratings for teachers who fail to teach important content and also the popularity of motivational speakers. On the other hand, when the amount of content is held constant in these experiments, the exciting, seductive lecturer is more highly rated by students and the students do better on achievement tests (Williams & Ware, 1977). Counselor educators must, it seems, be able to create a high interest/high content classroom situation if they want to improve achievement and make students happy. One of the common methods for increasing interest is through experiential exercises that enliven content in the classroom.

EXPERIENTIAL EDUCATION IN COUNSELOR EDUCATION WITH AN EMPHASIS ON REFLECTION

We have said that both reflection and content learning should be integral parts of an experiential learning approach to counselor education. The paradigm we suggest is not revolutionary or entirely new, but it is one way of thinking about how to provide an experience, supply important content and, at the same time, consider how the learning is to be applied. Consider the following steps:

Preparation. Students are prepared for the experience by giving them some initial theoretical or content material to orient them to the context. For example, let us say that in the Theories of Counseling class, the topic is behavior therapy. The instructor refers to the readings for the week and gives a brief (15–20 minute) lecture on the theory of behaviorism while differentiating between positive reinforcement, punishment, and negative reinforcement. It is emphasized that reinforcement is the central motivator in the theory because all behavior can be explained in terms of its consequences. This is done so that students grasp the importance of the lesson.

Experience. In the second phase, students are engaged in an experience with clear instructions. In this case, three students are asked to step outside the room while the rest of the class arranges the desks and chairs into a maze. Each of these three experimental subjects navigates the maze blindfolded under separate conditions and their attempts to solve the same maze are timed. The first subject receives positive reinforcement in the form of clapping for a correct turn in the maze, the second subject receives "boos" for incorrect turns (punishment), and in the third condition (negative reinforcement), the students boo constantly until the subject makes a correct turn, in which case the students cease booing.

Processing the exercise (verbal reflection). In this third phase, students share with the class their emotional and other reactions to the exercise. They are challenged by the instructor to consider how they would apply these types of reinforcement in the treatment of maladaptive behaviors such as misbehavior in children and cigarette smoking in adults. In this phase, the instructor again brings up the weekly readings and helps them place their learning in the context of counseling theories. There are a number of avenues for this kind of reflection aimed at integrating previous knowledge and theories. This might be a small group discussion or an assignment to journal on the topic, "How behavior therapy fits with my ideas about change." In addition, students may be encouraged to go deeper and consider the ethical, social, and multicultural implications of the experience. Finally, students can be asked to apply their knowledge to an in-class case study in which they are to develop a behavior management program for a particular client or they might be asked to conduct a homework experiment in a structured way. In the case of the homework experiments, students might be instructed to conduct a functional analysis of a personal bad habit such as nail biting and develop a treatment plan using behavior therapy principles.

TYPES OF EXPERIENTIAL ACTIVITIES IN THE CLASSROOM

In this section, we list and describe four types of experiential exercises: experiments, simulations, case studies/critical incidents, and problem-based learning. Later, we discuss some other methods including role-playing and reflecting teams as we look at how they can be incorporated in particular courses.

▶ *Experiments.* Previously we gave the example of how being anxious with some older people could be addressed through experimenting with new behavior. In addiction classes, students are sometimes required to become abstinent from something they do with frequency. For example, students may give up chocolate or caffeine or some activity such as bike riding. To help students remember and analyze this experience, they are asked to journal about their desires, environmental cues, and the effect of their "sobriety" on other aspects of their lives.

An associated method is called "discovery learning" (Alfieri, Brooks, Aldrich, & Tenenbaum, 2011; Bruner, 1961). In discovery learning, instead of the student being told the basic principles they are to learn, they engage in experiences where they uncover these principles themselves. In our Techniques of Counseling class, for example, we conduct an experiment in which one member of the class describes a minor problem they are having. Then every member in the classroom writes down his or her best advice for the student. As a group we identify the 10 best pieces of advice while the student with the problem waits outside. When the student returns to the classroom, the instructor reads the advice to the student. The following week, that student is asked to tell us what advice he or she remembered and what advice was taken. Almost universally, the student/client remembers only a small proportion of the advice and has put none of it into practice. They usually report that they had already tried most of the ideas that were suggested and other pieces of advice were not appropriate to their situation. When the student has followed the advice, it generally tends to be those suggestions that were very general such as, "Think about what you really want to do in this situation." The students are then asked to reflect on (discover) principles for giving advice and how they should approach it in practice (Young, 2013). This kind of experience has a much greater impact than the instructor warning students about the dangers of premature advice giving.

▶ *Simulations.* A simulation is a "controlled representation of a real situation" (Miller, 1971, p. 2). Simulations, here, are differentiated from role-plays by the fact that they involve an entire class and they are extended over a whole class period or more than one class. For example, there are simulations for experiencing differences in socioeconomic status (SES), which may last for an entire day. In those simulations, the high status groups are even served filet mignon and the low SES group gets peanut butter and jelly. An important characteristic of a simulation is that, as time goes on, the roles become more and more real. One is reminded of the Stanford Prison Experiments in which Zimbardo (1971) simulated a prison environment with college students who played "guards" and "prisoners." The experiment showed that even in simulated circumstances, people respond to authority and control in similar ways. Although in-class simulations do not usually reach the same level of intensity as Zimbardo's prison, they can engender strong emotions. Simulations suitable for counselor education range from job search simulations (Aiken, Lutrick, Kirk, Nickerson, & Wilder, 2001), to research simulations (Hummel, 1993), to assessment and treatment planning for substance abuse clients (Fussell, Lewy, & McFarland, 2009), and marriage and family therapy situations (Hodgson, Lamson, & Feldhousen, 2007).

▶ *Case study and critical incident analysis.* Depending on the course in which it is used, the case study can be a clinical vignette (see Grant, 2006) that presents a therapeutic dilemma or diagnostic puzzle. For a case study to be experiential, the focus must be on the impact the case has for learners. Therefore, participants must be asked to gauge its emotional effect and then to reflect and respond by noting how they would apply what they have learned from the case rather than merely identifying the factual content or analyzing the dilemmas that it poses. This method is frequently used in teaching ethics (Heaton &

Black, 2009), but case studies also have advantages in advanced classes such as Diagnosis and Treatment where students begin to recognize that not all decision making is black and white, and that labels and treatment plans have important consequences for clients. The important point is that, in order for a case study to be experiential, it must bring an emotional or intellectual challenge to students and it is not presented merely as an illustration.

Critical incident analysis is slightly different than a case study. It is a brief case study or vignette, which includes a "reflective examination of the incident" (Collins & Pieterse, 2007, p. 17) from both a theoretical and a practical perspective. For example, a common incident in practicum is when a client makes veiled threats about suicide. The class can be divided into groups who look at the incident from the point of view of all the participants including the counselor, supervisor, client, and police when involuntary hospitalization is required.

▶ *Problem-based learning in counselor education.* Problem-based learning or "project-based learning" is similar to case study and critical incident analysis in that students are presented with a simulated case commonly encountered in practice (Albanese & Mitchell, 1993). We, however, view problem-based learning as centered more on systemic components of problem resolution (e.g., making use of human service resources), whereas a case study concentrates on diagnostic and counseling treatment strategies, and critical incident analysis focuses on an incident within a case, for example, responding to a client's suicidal ideation. Consider the example of a mother who has a 14-year-old daughter with autism. She has been denied public assistance, and because she is Spanish speaking, she is having difficulty dealing with the bureaucracy. In addition, she does not have the money for an attorney to assist her. Here, the students may be asked to collaboratively solve the problem in a group setting based on their assigned readings and on research that they acquire outside of class. For example, students might research community-based resources such as an autism support group and opportunities for bilingual assistance. The focus is on recommending a plan that has a systemic component and showing that the literature (e.g., literature on autism) has been consulted in order to bring evidence into the mix. The case above may be a group project lasting only a couple of weeks. On the other hand, problem-based learning may take an entire semester when it is focused on a major project with a systemic scope such as dealing with funding for a community agency or developing a suicide prevention program for a middle school (Peterson & Myer, 1995).

Problem-based learning can increase student motivation to learn concepts being taught in-class because students can see a connection to actual practice. In addition, students can realize that there are previously neglected sources of information pertinent to the problem. Students, for example, may locate relevant information through professional readings as well as through discussions with social service agencies, consultations with medical or educational facilities, or consultations with legal services. Finally, problem-based learning simulates a realistic situation, that is, a case conference where students work together to help resolve a difficulty. Problem-based learning can also demonstrate the advantages of consulting research when faced with typical problems encountered in a counselor's office (Blumenfeld et al., 1991).

Problem-based learning may occasionally become bogged down by group (student) conflict. Using advanced graduate students as facilitators may help ease this difficulty (Stewart, 1998) and could benefit these advanced students who are learning facilitation skills. It should also be noted that problem-based learning focuses not on the student's personal experiences, but on problem-solving, knowledge acquisition, and applying that knowledge to real world situations. Reflection can be encouraged if facilitators take time to allow group discussions in which students think about the processes of information gathering and problem-solving.

EXPERIENTIAL LEARNING IN VARIOUS COURSES

▶ *Couple and family systems.* Carl Whitaker (1976), one of the originators of experiential family therapy, emphasized the therapeutic impact of in-session experiences for families. Similarly, experiential teaching methodologies in couples and family counseling including the use of role-plays, sculpturing à la psychodrama, reflecting teams, and simulated families can be powerful teaching tools. Role-play is a standard component of couple and family programs and an effective tool that helps students to increase their counseling self-efficacy. Video recording of a role-play activity, which the student watches later, seems to increase learning (Bandura, 1977; Gabriel, 1982; Robinson & Cabianca, 1985).

The reflecting team, introduced by Tom Andersen (1991), has become an important method for teaching counselors and for counselors in practice (Long & Young, 1995). Reflecting teams are groups of counselors (or students and faculty) who watch a real or mock counseling session and then reflect on their thoughts and feelings in full view of the clients. Reflecting teams have been utilized in marriage and family therapy since the late 1980s and provide opportunities for the family to learn more about itself from a team of professionals (Cole, Demeritt, Shatz, & Sapoznik, 2001). The one-way mirror approach is the most common way of working with reflecting teams. It begins with the reflecting team situating itself behind the one-way mirror and observing the live session between the counselor and family. The reflecting team and the family then switch places 15 or 20 minutes into the session and the counselor and the family listen to the team's discussion and observations. When the reflecting team concludes the discussion, they return to the one-way mirror and the counselor and the family go back to the counseling room and discuss the comments made by the team. This switching may occur several times during the session. The reflecting team teaches students how to develop the ability to see the client's situation from multiple perspectives and creates an opportunity for the family to reconsider their views (West, Watts, Trepal, Wester, & Lewis, 2001). Long and Young (1995) and Harrawood, Parmanand, and Wilde (2011) have used the reflecting team in the classroom setting and have found it to be effective in teaching family therapy skills even when students role-play the parts of counselor, client, and observation team member.

▶ **The multicultural counseling class.** Traditionally, the multicultural class in counselor education includes the following competencies: (a) knowledge, (b) personal attitudes and self-awareness, and (c) skills (e.g., Arredondo et al., 1996; Sue, Arredondo, & McDavis, 1992). The knowledge component can be achieved by presenting information about values, beliefs, customs, and other factual data regarding the history and customs of specific cultural, ethnic, and racial groups to students in a didactic manner. The skills component is often neglected but can be addressed through watching video of skillful counselors and through skill practice. On the other hand, the awareness or attitude dimension is most often presented through experiential activities (Kim & Lyons, 2003). Experiential activities in a multicultural course may include simulations, role-playing with clients from different cultures, conducting focus groups, performing cross-cultural interviews, and writing cultural autobiographies (see Pope, Pangelinan, & Coker, 2011).

"Bafa Bafa" (Shirts, 1977) is a simulation game that may be used in multicultural courses. The purpose of this game is to introduce students to the concept of culture and help students understand ways to facilitate cross-cultural communication. Participants are instructed to create a simulated culture with specific rules, customs, and traditions. Students are divided into Alpha and Beta cultures and are required to not only develop their own rules, but also exchange visitors with the other group and learn about their culture. After completion of these activities, students process their experiences in a large group facilitated by the instructor. Bafa also helps students to become aware of inaccurate assumptions we make about people from different cultures or ethnic groups due to lack of knowledge or understanding of norms and customs.

"Step forward, step back" (Singh, 2004) is another experiential game that simulates the ways in which culturally afforded privileges can determine who gets ahead in real-life situations. In this game, students are instructed to move forward or backward based on their past experiences of advantage or disadvantage. Students are read a set of sentences such as, "Take two steps forward if you were never a victim of a crime." By the end of this game students can see who is ahead and by how far. This game can be utilized to enhance awareness of privilege that exists based solely on demographic characteristics (e.g., race, gender, and ethnicity). This game also helps students to reflect on advances they have (or have not) made in life compared to other people from different socioeconomic, ethnic, or cultural backgrounds.

▶ *The group counseling class and the written journal.* The group counseling class in some counselor education settings is an exemplar of the combination of experiential education and reflection (Anderson & Price, 2001; Osborn et al., 2003). Routinely, students have a period of classroom instruction and are participants in a personal growth group. Reflective practice can be built into this course by including a journal (see Hubbs & Brand, 2005); however, to truly be called reflective, the journal cannot be merely a catalog of one's personal feelings. It must incorporate a look at one's assumptions, theories, and thoughts.

Ieva, Ohrt, Swank, and Young (2009) studied the influence of experiential groups on counseling students who attended a group class and journaled about their personal growth group experiences on a weekly basis. Students were asked to reflect upon what happened in each group session on the following topics (Carlock, 1976):

Participation—Who are the high and low participators?
Influence—Who influenced the group today?
Group Atmosphere—What is the "voice" of the group?
Feelings—What are the primary feelings expressed or unexpressed today?
Curative Factors—What curative factors did you see at work?
Cohesiveness—How cohesive is the group at this point in time?
Norms—What norms are becoming accepted in the group?
Relationships—Are there personal relationships developing? Are any alienations or conflicts brewing?
Group Development—What stage is the group in or cycling through?
Leadership—What leader or member interventions did you think were helpful today?

The authors concluded that students became aware of the importance of experiential groups. Students reported that experiential groups helped them learn group leadership skills. They also supported requiring students to participate in these groups and indicated that the journal was a useful tool for identifying issues to bring up in the group and for understanding group dynamics.

EVALUATION AND ASSESSMENT OF EXPERIMENTAL LEARNING IN THE COUNSELOR EDUCATION

One reason for the lack of research support, relative to experiential learning, is that identifying and specifying outcomes of experiential learning can be problematic, and creating instruments to measure the unique outcomes of experiential learning remains elusive. Often what the student learns is not what the teacher anticipated. Authentic assessment of experiential learning needs to recognize the fact that experiential methods may not emphasize content as much as other methods of teaching. Thus asking, "Did it stick?" must be answered by looking at emotional impact, the student's thinking process around the issue, and the ability to apply the information and not just the ability to recite facts. Therefore, assessment and tests should attempt to get at outcomes beyond content and also determine whether students can apply what they have learned. Barkley, Cross, and Major (2005) noted that performance-based assessment methods are more authentic ways of assessing the impact of experiential learning in the counselor education classroom. For example, in the beginning family systems class, one common experiential exercise is to ask the class to divide into simulated families that stay together for part of the term. Through playing a family member and observing other families, students gain an understanding of family dynamics. For example, what are the rules and roles of their mock family? While ordinary assessment might require students to define these terms on an examination, a performance based assessment method might also be used in this situation. Students in this class have an opportunity to observe other "families" in their classroom and conduct counseling sessions with them. Evaluation by the teacher can be based on goals, treatment plans, or counseling interventions that students devise for the other families. Teachers may use rubrics to grade the student's ability to work with simulated families.

One challenge in conducting an in-class evaluation is that it is difficult to provide a safe, low stress environment when students recognize that they are being evaluated (Shurts et al., 2006). Students are less likely to feel anxious and be more fully engaged in the learning activity when the grading does not occur right after the activity, but this presents the instructor with the dilemma of how to provide meaningful feedback and grading during the class (Arnold, 1993; Helmeke & Prouty, 2001). One option is to utilize self-evaluation by the students who grade themselves with the same rubric the instructor uses. While it does not replace feedback from the instructor, self-evaluation is integral to counselor education because counselors need to be constantly reflecting on their own performance when they go into practice (Bennetts, 2003).

Another method for self-evaluation and reflection is the portfolio, a summative evaluation of everything the student has learned. The portfolio can also be utilized in each course as a capstone project for students (Curry & Lambie, 2007). A key aspect of the portfolio is to include artifacts that show student development with the requirement that the student reflect on his or her development and change over time based on these work samples (Engels et al., 2009).

CONCLUSION

Experiential education encourages learning through participation, using role-playing, games, experiments, simulations, and case studies. Whereas experiential education is widely used in counselor education, too often it amounts to a disorganized set of classroom activities, which are inconsistent with Kolb's (1984) theory or good educational principles. The three greatest sins in experiential learning are: (a) classroom activities are not carefully planned to provide students with practice-oriented insights, that is, after the exercise, students cannot identify specific learning associated with that week's content; (b) exercises are not fully processed in the classroom and students are left emotionally aroused with no avenue for closure; and (c) students are not asked to reflect on what they have learned during or between classes or how they might apply it. Thus, learning is superficial and not integrated with previous experiences or current material. Considering these three concerns, it is clear that experiential learning in the counselor education classroom is not a teaching shortcut. It requires thoughtful preparation and clear goals. Moreover, assessing experiential learning remains a problem for instructors who are not familiar with authentic assessment strategies and, at first, students may find it difficult to self-evaluate and they may struggle to identify what the instructor wants. Despite the difficulties in creating and evaluating experiential learning, no other teaching method has the potential to bring close-to-real-life experiences into the classroom while energizing students and instructors.

REFERENCES

Aiken, R., Lutrick, A., Kirk, J. J., Nickerson, L., & Wilder, G. (2001). *Pounding the pavement*. Retrieved from ERIC database. (ED362474)

Albanese, M., & Mitchell, S. (1993). Problem-based learning: A review of literature on its outcomes and implementation issues. *Academic Medicine, 68*, 52–81.

Alfieri, L., Brooks, P. J., Aldrich, N. J., & Tenenbaum, H. R. (2011). Does discovery-based instruction enhance learning? *Journal of Educational Psychology, 103*(1), 1–18.

Andersen, T. (Ed.). (1991). *The reflecting team: Dialogues and dialogues about the dialogues*. New York, NY: W.W. Norton.

Anderson, R. D., & Price, G. E. (2001). Experiential groups in counselor education: Student attitudes and instructor participation. *Counselor Education & Supervision, 41*, 111–119.

Arnold, M. (1993). Ethnicity and training marital and family therapists. *Counselor Education & Supervision, 33*, 139.

Arredondo, P., Toporek, R., Brown, S., Jones, J., Locke, D.C., Sanchez, J., & Stadler, H. (1996). *Operationalization of the multicultural counseling competencies*. Alexandria, VA: Association for Multicultural Counseling and Development.

Arthur, N., & Achenbach, K. (2002). Developing multicultural counseling competencies through experiential learning. *Counselor Education & Supervision, 42*, 2–14.

Atkinson, G., & Murrell, P. (1988). Kolb's experiential learning theory: A meta-model for career exploration. *Journal of Counseling and Development, 66*, 374–377.

Bandura, A. (1977). *Social learning theory.* Upper Saddle River, NJ: Prentice Hall.

Barkley, E. F., Cross, K. P., & Major, C. H. (2005). *Collaborative learning techniques; Handbook for college faculty.* San Francisco, CA: Jossey-Bass.

Bennetts, C. (2003). Self-evaluation and self-perception of student learning in person-centered counselling training within a higher education setting. *British Journal of Guidance & Counselling, 31*(3), 305–323.

Blumenfeld, P. C., Soloway, E., Marx, R. W., Krajcik, J. S., Guzdial, M., & Palincsar, A. (1991). Motivating project-based learning: Sustaining the doing, supporting the learning. *Educational Psychologist, 26*, 369–398.

Brackenreg, J. (2004). Issues in reflection and debriefing: How nurse educators structure experiential activities. *Nurse Education in Practice, 4*, 264–270.

Bruner, J. S. (1961). The act of discovery. *Harvard Educational Review, 31*, 21–32.

Carlock, C. J. (1976). The group journal. Unpublished manuscript.

Cole, P. M., Demeritt, L. A., Shatz, K., & Sapoznik, M. (2001). Getting personal on reflecting teams. *Journal of Systemic Therapies, 20*, 74–87.

Collins, N. M., & Pieterse, A.L. (2007). Critical incident analysis based training: An approach for developing active racial/cultural awareness. *Journal of Counseling & Development, 85*, 14–23.

Cummings, A. L. (2001). A model for teaching experiential counseling interventions to novice counselors. *Counselor Education and Supervision, 32*, 23–30.

Curry, J., & Lambie, G. W. (2007). Enhancing school counselor accountability: The large group guidance portfolio. *Professional School Counseling, 11*(2), 145–148.

Dewey, J. (1960). *On experience, nature, and freedom.* New York, NY: Liberal Art Press.

Engels, D. W., Barrio Minton, C. A., Ray, D. C., Bratton, S. C., Chandler, C. K., Edwards, N. A., . . . Smith, M. R. (2009). *The professional counselor: Portfolio, competencies, performance guidelines, and assessment* (4th ed.). Alexandria, VA: American Counseling Association.

Fussell, H. E., Lewy, C. S., & McFarland, B. H. (2009). Evaluating and training substance abuse counselors: A pilot study assessing standardized patients as authentic clients. *Substance Abuse, 30*, 47–60.

Gabriel, J. A. (1982). Using role play as a training and supervisory tool. *Child Welfare, 61*, 383–387.

Granello, D. H., & Young, M. E. (2012). *Counseling today: Foundations of professional identity.* Upper Saddle River, NJ: Pearson.

Grant, J. (2006). Training counselors to work with complex clients: Enhancing emotional responsiveness through experiential methods. *Counselor Education & Supervision, 45*, 218–230.

Grayson, E., & Marini, I. (1996). Simulated disability exercises and their impact on attitudes towards persons with disabilities. *International Journal of Rehabilitation Research, 19*, 123–131.

Griffith, B. A., & Frieden, G. (2000). Facilitating reflective thinking in counselor education. *Counselor Education & Supervision, 40*, 82–93.

Harrawood, L. K., Parmanand, S., & Wilde, B. J. (2011). Experiencing emotion across semester-long family role-play and reflecting team: Implication for counselor development. *The Family Journal, 19*, 198–203.

Heaton, K. J., & Black, L. L. (2009). I knew you when: A case study of managing preexisting nonamorous relationships in counseling. *The Family Journal, 17*, 134–138.

Helmeke, K. B., & Prouty, A. M. (2001). Do we really understand? An experiential exercise for training family therapists. *Journal of Marital and Family Therapy, 27*, 535–544.

Hodgson, J. L., Lamson, A. L., & Feldhousen, E. B. (2007). Use of simulated clients in marriage and family therapy. *Journal of Marital and Family Therapy, 33*, 35–50.

Hubbs, D., & Brand, C. F. (2005). The paper mirror: Understanding reflective journaling. *Journal of Experiential Education, 28*, 60–71.

Hummel, T. J. (1993). A research simulation for counselor trainees. Paper presented at the annual meeting of the American Educational Research Association, Atlanta, GA. Retrieved from ERIC database. (ED362474)

Ieva, K. P., Ohrt, J. H., Swank, J. M., & Young, T. (2009). The impact of experiential groups on master students' counselor and personal development: A qualitative investigation. *Journal for Specialists in Group Work, 34*, 351–368.

Kayes, D. C. (2002). Experiential learning and its critics: Preserving the role of experience in management learning and education. *Academy of Management Learning & Education, 1*, 137–149.

Kim, B. S., & Lyons, H. Z. (2003). Experiential activities and multicultural competence training. *Journal of Counseling and Development, 81*, 400–408.

Knox, A. B. (1986). *Helping adults learn.* San Francisco, CA: Jossey-Bass.

Kolb, D. A. (1984). *Experiential learning.* Englewood Cliffs, NJ: Prentice Hall.

Kolb, D. A., Boyatzis, R. E., & Mainemelis, C. (2001). Experiential learning theory: Previous research and new directions. In R. J. Sternberg & L. Zhang (Eds.), *Perspectives on cognitive, learning, and thinking styles* (pp. 227–249). Mahwah, NJ: Lawrence Erlbaum.

Larrivee, B. (2000). Transforming teaching practice: Becoming the critically reflective teacher. *Reflective Practice, 1*(3), 293.

Larrivee, B. (2008). Development of a tool to assess teachers' level of reflective practice. *Reflective Practice, 9*(3), 341–360.

Long, L. L., & Young, M. E. (1995). The reflecting team in counselor education. *Counselor Education and Supervision, 23*, 112–118.

Magnuson, S., & Norem, K. (2002). Reflective counsellor education and supervision: An epistemological declaration. *Reflective Practice, 3*(2), 167–173.

Miller, T. V. (April, 1971). Simulation in counselor education. Paper presented at the American Personnel and Guidance Association Annual Convention, Atlantic City, NJ.

Naftulin, D. H., Ware, J. E., Jr., & Donnelly, F. A. (1973). The Doctor Fox lecture: A paradigm of educational seduction. *Journal of Medical Education, 48*, 630–635.

Osborn C., Daninhirsch, C., & Page, B. (2003). Experiential training in group counseling: Humanistic processes in practice. *Journal of Humanistic Counseling, Education and Development, 42*, 14–28.

Peterson, S. E., & Myer, R. A. (1995). The use of collaborative project-based learning in counselor education. *Counselor Education And Supervision, 35*, 150–158.

Piaget, J. (1967). Cognition and conversations: Review of J. S. Bruner and others, studies in cognitive growth. *Contemporary Psychology, 12*, 530–533.

Pollio, D. E., & Macgowan, M. J. (2010). The andragogy of evidence-based group work: An integrated educational model. *Social Work with Groups: A Journal of Community and Clinical Practice, 33*(2–3), 195–209.

Pope, M., Pangelinan, J. S., & Coker, A. D. (2011). *Experiential activities for teaching multicultural competence in counseling.* Alexandria, VA: American Counseling Association.

Robinson, S. E., & Cabianca, W. A. (1985). Effects of counselor's ordinal position when involved in role play practice triads. *Counselor Education and Supervision, 24,* 365–371.

Rogers, C. (1994). *Freedom to learn.* New York, NY: Macmillan.

Schön, D. A. (1983). *The reflective practitioner: How professionals think in action.* New York, NY: Basic Books.

Shirts, R. G. (1977). *Bafa bafa: A cross culture simulation.* Del Mar, CA: Simulation Training Systems.

Shurts, W., Cashwell, C. S., Spurgeon, S. L., Degges-White, S., Barrio, C. A., & Kardatzke, K. N. (2006). Preparing counselors-in-training to work with couples: Using role-plays and reflecting teams. *The Family Journal, 14,* 151–157.

Singh, R. (2004). Exploring culture in practice: A few facets of a training course. *Journal of Family Psychotherapy, 15,* 87–104.

Stewart, J. B. (1998). Problem-based learning in counselor education. *Canadian Journal of Counselling, 32,* 37–49.

Sue, D.W., Arredondo, P., & McDavis, R.J. (1992). Multicultural counseling competencies and standards: A call to the profession. *Journal of Counseling and Development, 70,* 477–486.

Takeda, A., Marchel, C. A., & Gaddis, R. (2002). Performing reflective practice in college education and counselor training. *Japanese Journal of Counseling Science, 35*(2), 145–154.

West, J. D., Watts, R. E., Trepal, H. C., Wester, K. L, & Lewis, T. F. (2001). Opening space for client reflection: A postmodern consideration. *The Family Journal, 9,* 431–437.

Whitaker, C. A. (1976). The technique of family therapy. In G. P. Sholevar (Ed.), *Changing sexual values and the family (pp. 144-157).* Springfield, IL: Charles Thomas.

Williams, R. G., & Ware, J. E. (1977). An extended visit with Dr. Fox: Validity of student satisfaction with instruction ratings after repeated exposures to a lecturer. *American Educational Research Journal, 14,* 449–457.

Wong-Wylie, G. (2007). Barriers and facilitators of reflective practice in counsellor education: Critical incidents from doctoral graduates. *Canadian Journal of Counselling, 41*(2), 59–76.

Young, M. E. (2013). *Learning the art of helping* (5th ed.). Upper Saddle River, NJ: Pearson.

Young, M. E., Butler, S. K., Hutchinson, T. S., & Gutierrez, D. (2011). A qualitative study of experiential learning in the multicultural class. Unpublished manuscript.

Zimbardo, P. G. (1971). The power and pathology of imprisonment. *Congressional Record.* (Serial No. 15, 1971-10-25). Hearings before Subcommittee No. 3, of the Committee on the Judiciary, House of Representatives, Ninety-Second Congress, *First Session on Corrections, Part II, Prisons, Prison Reform and Prisoner's Rights: California.* Washington, DC: U.S. Government Printing Office.

CHAPTER 6

Using Out-of-Class
Learning Activities

JASON McGLOTHLIN

DIANA L. VANWINKLE

KELSEY GEORGE

T he concept of out-of-class learning activities, or what traditionally has been called "homework," has remained a part of the educational process since the inception of formal education (Gill & Schlossman, 2000). Today, homework has become an integral part of K–12, undergraduate, and graduate education. So to write a chapter on such a topic could be epic. Instead we have focused on the practicalities of out-of-class learning activities in counselor education from the instructor's and the student's perspective because we believe that in order for learning to occur, a reciprocal appreciation of homework is required. Jason will share thoughts on homework from the perspective of a faculty member, and Kelsey and Diana will reflect on homework from the students' perspective.

RATIONALE FOR USING HOMEWORK
FROM AN INSTRUCTOR'S PERSPECTIVE

The notion of homework should be familiar to counselors as it is an integral part of clinical care (Hay & Kinnier, 1998; L'Abate, L'Abate, & Maino, 2005). In many clinical settings, homework helps to enhance the therapeutic process (Engle, Beutler, & Dunlap, 1991), helps clients' progress after counseling has terminated

(Shelton & Ackerman, 1974), helps develop new ideas to be discussed in session (Woods, 1991), gives responsibility and ownership to clients for their own progress (Cummings, 1991), and enhances the outcomes of counseling (Startup & Edmonds, 1994). Homework in an educational setting has the same basic purpose as in a clinical setting: to help build upon or enhance in-class (or in-session) learning.

Depending on the type of homework assigned, instructors hope that students can accrue a wide variety of skills, knowledge, and personal achievements. I have required a number of different homework assignments, but none has been more important than reading. In some of my classes, I talk about reading on a 5 point Likert-type scale where 1 = not read or opened the book; 2 = glanced through the reading and read the main headings; 3 = skimmed through the reading; 4 = read; and 5 = read and studied like a professional. "Read and studied like a professional" means that one thoroughly reads the material, reads the footnotes, marks or highlights the readings appropriately, generates questions from the readings, and considers how to follow up on the readings. In a perfect world, and if I could guarantee that all students were reading at a "5," I would consider no other form of homework for some classes.

I have seen graduate students (both master's and doctoral level students) who read materials at a 3 or below level. I can recall times in class where I have said "would you prefer to go to a surgeon who reads like a professional or one who skims through the various readings? Is our role as counselors any less important to clients?" The benefit of reading is monumental. Overall, it has been found that those who read more thoroughly write better, remember more, understand complex concepts better (Adams, Simmons, Willis, & Pawling, 2010), do better on examinations, have a deeper understanding of classroom discussions, and participate more in class (Lei, Bartlett, Gorney, & Herschbach, 2010; Sappington, Kinsey, & Munsayac, 2002). Although there is no specific literature on the benefits of reading for counselors-in-training, one could hypothesize that the more thoroughly students read the better they will (a) write case notes, treatment plans, and reports; (b) conceptualize client care; (c) discuss client cases; and (d) work with complex clientele.

In the above list of benefits of reading for counselors-in-training, you will notice "the better they will do on exams" was not mentioned. Whereas this is probably true, this statement was intentionally left out because I do not support students reading for exams. Students need to read to be better professionals and to work with clients at a higher level of competency and professionalism. Weimer (2002) said it best in that students who only read and study for exams have short-term gains and long-term losses.

In addition to reading assignments, having students write papers to reflect their learning is commonplace. Assigned papers come in various formats that provide different benefits to students. First, reflection papers (or journals) allow students to express their feelings and opinions about specific topics or experiences. This allows instructors to gain insight into the unique understandings and experiences of students. Second, comprehensive papers are lengthy assignments that allow students to provide a synthesis of various issues and elaborate on relationships. This allows instructors to see if students are conceptualizing issues in a multifaceted yet useful manner. Third, scholarly papers are typically technical papers or manuscripts for potential publication, and from these manuscripts, instructors can evaluate a student's writing abilities and research and theoretical skills. Fourth, assessment reports and treatment plans are typically beneficial because they allow students to conceptualize clients from multiple standpoints, from diagnostic and conceptual perspectives to positions that consider therapeutic interventions. Overall, assigned papers help improve writing skills, increase knowledge, and allow students to convey their own unique understandings of an issue.

Applied to counselor education, skill development homework may occur when students role-playing different skills with other students outside of the classroom setting. The role-plays can be audio or video taped and then critiqued by instructors. Next, skill development homework is typically done by seeing clients in practicum and internship. Such homework is supervised and provides students with a wealth of knowledge and skill for clinical practice. While the benefits of supervised skill development are beyond the scope of this chapter, such homework has been considered one of the hallmarks of counselor education (Bernard & Goodyear, 2009). While reading and writing certainly contribute to one's overall learning and knowledge base, skill development homework also contributes to learning through applying one's knowledge.

In a similar fashion, service learning furthers the learning process through the blending and application of knowledge and skill. Service learning and experiential homework such as immersion experiences provide students with opportunities to explore new contexts. Overall, students can benefit from such homework by learning about new cultures or environments, by being exposed to unfamiliar and sometimes uncomfortable surroundings, and by shadowing professionals in real-life situations. In addition, service learning activities can have a positive impact on the community because students are typically providing a service for the overall good of the community (Conway, Amel, & Gerwien, 2009).

Most importantly in my mind, service learning activities can help students gain a closer and more meaningful connection with classroom content because they can see how the content applies to and directly impacts real-life situations (Barry, 2011). Service learning activities have particular relevance in counselor education. For example, service learning activities might include volunteering at a crisis "hotline," at a residential treatment facility, or in a school counseling department within a local school system. Service learning activities have been shown to improve multicultural awareness and cultural sensitivity (Amaro-Jimenez, 2012); help students learn assessment, statistical, and research concepts (Hewett & Porpora, 1999); assist in a deeper understanding of values and ethical decision making (Billings & Halstead, 2012); and improve leadership and advocacy skills (Longo & Gibson, 2011). Overall, service learning activities have multiple uses in helping counselor trainees understand and conceptualize course content.

Finally, technology has provided various opportunities for homework assignments. Blogging on a specific topic, doing real-time role-plays in Second Life˚, creating digital stories, and developing websites, are only a few examples how such homework assignments can help develop a student's technology capabilities. Developing the technology competencies of students has become a typical expectation within counselor education (CACREP, 2009).

Lang (2008) commented that instructors need to provide a wide variety of homework assignments to give students multiple opportunities to grow and challenge themselves. At the same time, instructors need to be creative and aware of how students are responding to homework; remaining open to altering one's course and homework assignments to best meet the needs of students continues to be critical.

REFLECTING ON THE RATIONALE FOR HOMEWORK FROM A STUDENT'S PERSPECTIVE

In general, and from a popular perspective, the notion of homework has often been fitted with negative connotations (Gill & Schlossman, 2000). Students can also share such negative perceptions of homework, "Which professor should I take for this course? Certainly the one who requires the least amount of homework." I (Kelsey) am as guilty as the next person of looking for the path with the least "head wind." It has also been those courses with the least amount of meaningful work in which I experienced the smallest amount of learning. Instead, it is often the work done outside of class that I have retained and used in a professional manner. Generally speaking, I read, think, and challenge myself the most when I take ownership of a piece of work. It allows me the opportunity to research something that is personally and professionally meaningful.

Assignments that become particularly compelling to me are those that allow for creativity. In one of my graduate courses, students were asked to give a short presentation about applying counseling skills to an oppressed clientele. The only requirement for this project was to provide an annotated bibliography. In other words, the demonstration could take any form (e.g., PowerPoint, skit, discussion) and we were encouraged to be creative. With such little direction for this assignment, I first felt overwhelmed. Over the course of a few weeks, I became less overwhelmed and genuinely surprised myself. With the professor encouraging creativity and me giving myself permission to step outside of my comfort zone, I worked harder to develop a project that was different from anything I had previously done. I became inspired by the opportunity to teach about clients with disabilities, because I was passionate about this group. I was moved to take risks by putting so much of myself into the project and I was challenged to try different technologies (i.e., iMovie) that I had never used before. In the end, my decision was to share information with the class about counseling individuals with physical disabilities. Each student was given a piece of yarn and told to tie themselves to their chair to represent being bound by a wheelchair. The class was shown a digital story (i.e., the practice of telling a story using computer tools, such as digital photos, music, recorded audio voice-overs, and video clips) exemplifying how their life would change if they lost their mobility. Images and narrations of sports they could no longer play, inaccessible houses and buildings, and obstacles in travelling and transportation elicited an emotional response, and stimulated the students acoustically and visually. I then sounded a mock fire alarm to highlight the challenges of escaping from a high-rise building without the use of an elevator. A short presentation and discussion about the unique issues faced by this population followed.

Although not all courses bestow a forum for ingenuity, homework assignments (from content heavy to experientially-based courses) can give students an opportunity to personalize information. For some, retaining facts from a PowerPoint lecture is difficult and it is not until they work with the material in a deeper sense that it becomes meaningful, thus memorable. Homework becomes something of a "tiramisu"—layering course content with the instructor's voice, research articles, and previous experiences. This integration of information and experiences is how I remember complex issues.

IMPLEMENTING HOMEWORK FROM AN INSTRUCTOR'S PERSPECTIVE

In counselor education there are, obviously, a variety of courses that each requires homework opportunities and challenges. Whereas each class develops differently, the overall goal is similar to that posed by Vatterott (2010), that is, "The best kind [of homework] deepens student understanding and builds essential skills" (p. 10). Furthermore, Vatterott (2009, 2010) suggested that homework should be multifaceted and contain several key characteristics. The following bullets describe Vatterott's key characteristics and, here, they have been contextualized for counselor education.

▶ *Homework should be purposeful.* Instructors should clearly develop purposeful assignments and convey the purpose to students. Developing purposeful homework rests in an understanding of what needs to be evaluated in the course (e.g., knowledge, skill development, case conceptualization and treatment planning abilities, etc.). Assignments can then be tied to evaluative measures and, consequently, show the purpose of the assignments.

▶ *Homework should be efficient.* Students don't want to do things that waste their time, and more homework does not necessarily equate to more learning. More learning comes from the greater amounts of meaning students derive from an assignment. Therefore, instructors should be efficient in what they assign and focus on meaningful homework assignments. At the same time, homework can be lengthy, time consuming, difficult, and at times overwhelming, as long as it is meaningful.

▶ *Homework should be owned.* I have said to students, "Don't tell me what you think I want to hear. If you don't agree with something, please let me know. I want you to take what I say and make it your own." I believe that students should have a voice and not regurgitate what instructors want to hear. Therefore, homework needs to allow students to be creative, have a voice, and grow according to their individual learning styles.

▶ *Homework needs to provide opportunities for students to feel competent.* Students really do earn grades rather than receive them from faculty members. I use this language on syllabi, in talking with students, and in evaluating homework. As I reflect on my own education, the courses from which I learned the most and in which I felt the most sense of accomplishment were courses where I struggled and at times earned lower grades. Much like in counseling, growth comes from struggle.

In addition to the characteristics posed by Vatterott (2010), there are several other aspects of homework that instructors might be mindful of in order to help enhance the student's learning.

▶ *Instructors need to empower students' sense of responsibility.* Similar to Vatterott's (2010) notion that homework should be owned, students need to be responsible for their learning and the best way to achieve this is by including students in the development of assignments (Weimer, 2002). For example, I have taught a basic appraisal course that covers the CACREP core curriculum standards in the assessment area. In the syllabus I state that 50% of their overall grade will be derived from a "festival of knowledge" (my term for an examination). The first assignment I have in this course requires them to write a brief 2–3 page paper indicating how they would like to be assessed; since this is an appraisal course, it is a natural fit that students must determine how they will be assessed. In this assignment, they must answer the following questions: "How many festivals of knowledge would you like? What do you want them to cover? What type of questions would you prefer (e.g., essay, multiple choice, matching, etc.)? Do you want a take home or in class examination?" I provide the class with some parameters to their choices (e.g., a take-home "festival" will require more specificity than an in-class "festival," an in-class "festival" will not be in an open-book format, etc.). In-class discussion of this assignment helps me develop the remainder of the course. Involving students while ensuring academic rigor is a hallmark of helping students feel responsible for their learning.

▶ *Empower critical thinking about homework assignments.* Most academics believe that critical thinking is a necessity in higher education (Macalister, 1999). Keeley, Shemberg, Cowell, and Zinnbauer (1995) suggested that helping students develop critical thinking skills not only assists them in developing a sense of responsibility around their learning but also helps them develop as better professionals. They recommended explaining the rationale behind each homework assignment (e.g., why you require it and why it is important and beneficial to professional practice), having students paraphrase the assignment to ensure understanding, and providing students with opportunities to discuss homework activities at points prior to completion and after homework has been submitted.

▶ *Meeting accreditation and licensure requirements.* When implementing homework, instructors must be mindful that students are not the only entity to be considered. Courses typically include specific curricular experiences required by accreditation and licensure boards. In many circumstances, these curricular experiences are evaluated through homework activities. For example, CACREP (2009) required the "assessment of student learning and performance" (p. 8). In many circumstances, this would include homework activities (e.g., papers, demonstration of clinical skills, etc.). Overall, the "CACREP Standards are written to ensure that students develop a professional counselor identity and master the knowledge and skills to practice effectively" (CACREP, 2009, p. 2).

▶ *Feedback equals growth.* The feedback instructors provide on homework is almost as valuable as the homework itself. Instructors want to provide feedback that is timely and that can help students build upon future content. Also, providing feedback with suggested detail and that can be acted upon is critical. I occasionally find myself writing "let's chat" on papers so I can meet individually with students to help build on their learning. Now, I have learned that when students see "let's chat" it may instill fear. However, when introducing the syllabus, I inform the class that meetings may occur to better provide them with useful feedback so, consequently, meetings are to be expected.

▶ *Provide feedback that is legible.* I have horrible handwriting, so I have created typed comment keys that are a list of my most frequently used notions on homework (e.g., 1 = well written; 2 = APA style problem, 3 = grammar problem, etc.). I basically write numbers on students' homework and on occasion I will write something that is not on my typed comment key. This practice has not only saved me time grading homework but also reduces the trouble that students have reading my handwriting. It also provides students up front with a list of things I may say about their homework; essentially, if they read my comment key, they could almost grade the homework themselves.

In addition to individual instructor benefits, discussing homework assignments at a programmatic level could assist faculty in seeing whether a diverse range of homework (e.g., exams, papers, demonstration of skill) could produce positive program modifications. For example, such discussions can produce homework assignments that build upon prior homework. In courses where there is prerequisite coursework, developmental homework assignments can be used (Ruggiero, 1988). If a counseling theories course and a counseling techniques course are prerequisites to practicum, and practicum is a prerequisite to internship, then there could be four assignments that ultimately fuse into one comprehensive assignment. In counseling theories and counseling techniques, students could write a paper that compares and contrasts different theories and techniques. In the practicum, students could use this information to write a reflection paper on how they conceptualize their clients. Finally, in internship, they could prepare a paper and presentation that shows their development and deeper understanding of the three previous homework assignments. This model of homework across the curriculum reflects the recent occurrence of portfolios, which have been shown to help build a student's academic and professional identities, facilitate learning across courses and time, and assist students as they reflect on their academic achievements and limitations (Miller & Morgaine, 2009).

REFLECTING ON IMPLEMENTATION OF HOMEWORK FROM A STUDENT'S PERSPECTIVE

From a student's perspective, homework should be an expectation of graduate studies. Out-of-class learning is a norm in educational settings (Hong, Wan, & Peng, 2011). Each semester contains coursework outlined in syllabi, explaining assignments for in class and out-of-class learning. Homework has been an integral part of the learning experience, so much so that the thought of no homework leaves me (Diana) feeling a bit lost. Homework provides structure and guidance as students are immersed in a new area of study. For students, this structure provides an informed path towards engaging with the course content throughout the term.

Yet at times, I have been guilty of skimming syllabi to find the "assignments" heading and asking myself "How am I ever going to get all of this done?" If, however, homework cannot be managed and completed as thoroughly as the instructor intended, students miss a learning opportunity. In my mind, the first step in implementing homework, so that students are fully engaged in the learning process, begins with the student-instructor relationship. Instructors help students engage in the homework process. Crawley, Curry, Dumois-Sands, Tanner, and Wyker (2008) discussed a student-instructor relationship as "full-contact pedagogy" calling educators to fully engage students in the learning process by drawing them into a shared enthusiasm and providing a "guided inquiry" in which the instructor creates space for students to explore the subject and join the instructor on a journey of exploration, reflection, and learning (p. 14). In the student-instructor relationship, there are two primary responsibilities; instructors need to create classroom dialogue to engage students in homework, while also indicating that much of the out-of-class learning is the student's responsibility. Ongoing interaction with the course instructor can be a motivating force helping the student begin and follow through with homework. Hong, Milgram, and Rowell (2004) commented that instructors are vital to the implementation of homework and as such set the bar for the student's commitment to out-of-class learning, though the ultimate responsibility for engagement rests with the students.

A common belief regarding homework is the equation homework + completion = learning (Hong et al., 2011). It may be, however, that some readers can remember completing homework and earning a high grade even though little learning actually occurred. For homework to promote and cultivate learning, a student must be engaged in the assignment.

A course assignment titled, "Reflection on Complexity," created an opportunity for me as a learner to grow in new ways. While reviewing the syllabus, the instructor explained the intent of the homework and how it provided an opportunity for learning. The assignment required me to choose a novel that reflected a culture different from my own and to view a character's "life complexity" while incorporating theories of counselor supervision. Here, the chosen character became the client while I was in the role of the supervisor. As the supervisor, I applied supervision theory to a multicultural counseling context. The instructor dedicated portions of class time throughout the term to allow students to engage in dialogue about the assignment and their readings. Students worked together to locate books and share, outside of the formal class setting, their individual experiences with various novels. The assignment provided an environment where there was initial engagement of course concepts in a setting that also allowed for discussion and continued application of supervision theory. The overall intentionality of "Reflections on Complexity" created a purposeful experience, owned by students using critical thinking to engage in the essential goal of learning about supervision.

The "Reflection on Complexity" during out-of-class learning provided a clear intent, and empowered students with practical supervision theory, while also removing anxiety that may occur in actual supervisory experiences. The opportunity to engage in critical reflective thinking supported ownership of my emerging professional identity as a counselor and supervisor.

EVALUATING THE EFFECTIVENESS OF HOMEWORK

The typical means for soliciting feedback on the usefulness of out-of-class learning activities is from the institution's formal and standardized course evaluations completed by students at the end of the term. This is a means for students to give anonymous feedback to instructors. Typically, institutions will include a comments section on teaching evaluations that reference the appropriateness, rigor of homework, and so forth. These evaluations can provide instructors with insight on the appropriateness of their homework assignments and may help in making modifications to improve the homework assignments in the future.

In some cases, teaching evaluations may include items pertaining to the amount of homework in the class. For example, if students say that the amount of work was appropriate for the class, some could consider this as a signal that the instructor did not challenge students or provide enough homework. On the other hand, if students say that there was too much homework, some may consider this positively (i.e., rigorous), or negatively (i.e., too demanding). Student evaluations have been scrutinized over the years due to concerns with reliability, validity, and their utility (Nilson, 2003). We, however, believe that student evaluations can provide opportunities for reflection and possible course modification. In addition, there can be other procedures for soliciting feedback on the usefulness of out-of-class learning activities:

▶ *Informal student evaluations.* Similar to the standardized student evaluations mentioned above, instructors could develop their own anonymous evaluations and distribute them after each homework assignment is due or at least at mid-term. This could provide feedback for homework or course modifications during a successive term.

▶ *Class discussions.* Open class discussion regarding the usefulness of homework could generate themes of how homework is perceived and processed. If using this form of evaluation, the instructor needs to be intentional about focusing the discussion on providing constructive feedback with the aim of bettering education rather than lessening the workload.

▶ *Peer Reviews.* Having another instructor (from within your discipline or from outside the discipline) review teaching methods, homework, and syllabi can be beneficial. Compared to students, other instructors may have a more experienced perception of teaching practices. In this form of evaluation, instructors might solicit peer reviews from senior faculty and faculty that would provide critical feedback rather than a placating "good job."

▶ *Consultation.* Whether from a new instructor or a seasoned professor, soliciting feedback from trusted colleagues is a valuable endeavor. Similar to a clinical setting where consultation is a standard of practice (Brown, Pryzwansky, & Schulte, 2006), faculty should consult as well. Being open to and continually soliciting feedback from colleagues on the implementation of homework, clarity of homework assignments, grading practices, and alternative homework assignments could be beneficial.

▶ *Earned grades.* Grades may be an evaluative measure of homework usefulness. If everyone is failing, then the homework may be too difficult or not clearly conceived. At the same time, if everyone is getting 100%, then it may be too easy or not graded with appropriate rigor. Alteration of grading scale, grading practices, or the homework assignment itself could be a result of such evaluations.

▶ *Instructor's investment.* It may be important to do a cost/benefit analysis on the instructor's investment in grading homework, for example, given the amount of homework, how long each assignment takes to grade versus what is needed to thoroughly evaluate the students' learning. More is not always better, and at the same time, less is not always better.

▶ *Student's investment.* Similar to instructors, it is important to look at the student's investment in homework. As stated earlier, the amount of homework is to be considered. However, the evaluation of homework can also be measured by the depth and thoroughness with which the assignment is completed. At the graduate level, we believe that students should convey a rich understanding of materials from a multitude of standpoints. Evaluating homework according to the thoroughness and depth of the completed work can inform instructors about how assignments might be introduced, graded, and modified.

The notion of student investment is a primary perspective to consider in order to know whether out-of-class learning activities are having a desired impact on the classroom environment. If most students are demonstrating well-developed views from assigned readings and thoughtful writing, homework assignments are probably having a desired effect on the classroom.

CONCLUSION

The fundamental underpinning of homework is to help students conceptualize and further develop information and experiences gained from time spent in class. For this to happen, both the instructor and the students must play a role in the development, implementation, and continual assessment of the effectiveness of homework.

REFERENCES

Adams, A., Simmons, F., Willis, C., & Pawling, R. (2010). Undergraduate students' ability to revise text effectively: Relationships with topic knowledge and working memory. *Journal of Research in Reading, 33*(1), 54–76.

Amaro-Jimenez, C. (2012). Service learning: Preparing teachers to understand better culturally and linguistically diverse learners. *Journal of Education and Teaching, 38* (2), 211–213.

Barry, M. (2011). Research for the greater good. *College and Research Libraries News, 72*(6), 345–348.

Bernard, J. M., & Goodyear, R. K. (2009). *Fundamentals of clinical supervision* (4th ed.). Columbus: OH, Pearson.

Billings, D. M., & Halstead, J. A. (2012). *Teaching in nursing: A guide for faculty* (4th ed.). St. Louis, MO: Elsevier/Sanders.

Brown, D., Pryzwansky, W. B., & Schulte, A. C. (2006). *Psychological consultation and collaboration: Introduction to theory and practice* (6th ed.). Boston, MA: Pearson.

Conway, J. M., Amel, E. L., & Gerwien, D. L. (2009). Teaching and learning in the social context: A meta-analysis of service learning's effects on academic, personal, social, and citizenship outcomes. *Teaching of Psychology, 36,* 233–245.

Council for Accreditation of Counseling and Related Educational Programs [CACREP]. (2009). *The 2009 Standards.* Alexandria, VA: Author. Retrieved from http://www.cacrep.org/doc/2009%20Standards%20with%20cover.pdf

Crawley, S. L., Curry, H., Dumois-Sands, J., Tanner, C., & Wyker, C. (2008). Full-contact pedagogy: Lecturing with questions and student-centered assignments as methods for inciting self-reflexivity for faculty and students. *Feminist Teacher, 19*(1), 13–30.

Cummings, N. A. (1991). Assigning homework. In C. S. Austad & W. H. Berman (Eds.), *Psychotherapy in managed health care: The optimal use of time and resources* (pp. 40–62). Washington, DC: American Psychological Association.

Engle, D., Beutler, L. E., & Dunlap, R. J. (1991). Focused expressive psychotherapy: Treating blocked emotions. In J. D. Safran & L. S. Greenberg (Eds.), *Emotion, psychotherapy and change* (pp. 169-196). New York, NY: Guilford Press.

Gill, B., & Schlossman, S. (2000). The lost cause of homework reform. *American Journal of Education, 109*(1), 27–62.

Hay, C. E., & Kinnier, R. T. (1998). Homework in counseling. *Journal of Mental Health Counseling, 98*(2), 122–132.

Hewett, T. T., & Porpora, D. V. (1999). A study report on integrating statistics, problem-based learning, and computerized data. *Behavior Research Methods, Instruments, and Computers, 31*(2), 244–251.

Hong, E., Milgram, R. M., & Rowell, L. L. (2004). Homework motivation and preference: A learner-centered homework approach. *Theory Into Practice, 43*(3), 197–204.

Hong, E., Wan, M., & Peng, Y. (2011). Discrepancies between students and teachers perceptions of homework. *Journal of Advanced Academics, 22*(2), 280–308.

Keeley, S. M., Shemberg, K. M., Cowell, B. S., & Zinnbauer, B. J. (1995) Coping with student resistance to critical thinking: What the psychotherapy literature can tell us. *College Teaching, 43*(4), 140–145.

L'Abate, L., L'Abate, B. L., & Maino, E. (2005). Reviewing 25 years of professional practice: Homework assignments and length of therapy. *The American Journal of Family Therapy, 33,* 19–31.

Lang, J. M. (2008). *On course: A week-by-week guide to your 1st semester of college teaching.* Cambridge, MA: Harvard University Press.

Lei, S. A., Bartlett, K. A., Gorney, S. E., & Herschbach, T. R. (2010). Resistance to reading compliance among college students: Instructors' perspectives. *College Student Journal, 44*(2), 219–229.

Longo, N. V., & Gibson, C. M. (2011). *From command to community: A new approach to leadership education in colleges and universities.* Medford, MS: Tufts University Press.

Macalister, H. E. (1999). Women's studies classes and their influences on student development. *Adolescence, 34,* 283–292.

Miller, R., & Morgaine, W. (2009). The benefits of e-portfolios for students and faculty in their own words. *Peer Review, 11*(1), 8–12.

Nilson, L. B. (2003). *Teaching at its best: A research-based resource for college instructors* (2nd ed.). San Francisco, CA: Jossey-Bass.

Ruggiero, V. R. (1988). *Teaching thinking across the curriculum.* New York, NY: Harper & Row.

Sappington, J., Kinsey, K., & Munsayac, K. (2002). Two studies of reading compliance among college students. *Teaching of Psychology, 29*(4), 212–221.

Shelton, J. L., & Ackerman, I. M. (1974). *Homework in counseling and psychotherapy: Examples of systematic assignments for therapeutic use by mental health professionals.* Springfield, IL: Thomas.

Startup, M., & Edmonds, I (1994). Compliance with homework assignments in cognitive-behavioral psychotherapy for depression: Relation to outcome and methods of enhancement. *Cognitive Therapy and Research, 18,* 567–579.

Vatterott, C. (2009). *Rethinking homework: Best practices that support diverse needs.* Alexandria, VA: ASCD.

Vatterott, C. (2010). 5 hallmarks of good homework. *Educational Leadership, 68*(1), 10–15.

Weimer, M. (2002). *Learner-centered teaching: Five key changes to practice.* San Francisco, CA: Jossey-Bass.

Woods, P. J. (1991). Orthodox RET taught effectively. In M. E. Bernard (Ed.), *Using rational-emotive therapy effectively: A practitioner's guide* (pp. 85–96). New York, NY: Plenum Press.

CHAPTER 7

Using Technology in Teaching

MARTY JENCIUS

esktop computers may seem to have always been part of the workplace for counselor educators, but it has only been about 25 years since they became commercially available. In those 25 years there have been many changes that we currently take for granted. This chapter focuses on the technology tools that counselor educators can use to enhance their teaching. Fouts (2000) provided rationale for using technology in teaching. Much of the research he summarized concluded that the inclusion of technology in teaching can increase student learning in basic skill areas, provide higher academic achievement in certain areas, allow students to learn more quickly and have greater retention, and improve students' attitudes about learning. Including technology in counselor training creates an environment where students assume responsibility for learning through student-centered strategies. Technology used in conjunction with face-to-face instruction allows the instructor to make the best use of in-class time with activities that require interpersonal interaction (Noeth & Volkov, 2004).

The chapter in this text by Albrecht and Jones focused on distance education platforms using technology, where all or most of the coursework is delivered through a software package that instructors use to engage their students' learning. Albrecht and Jones' focus was on deployment of counselor training using a technology delivery system. This chapter focuses on the development of training using various tools that could be part of a distance education course or could be used to supplement traditional face-to-face classroom education. The chapter also provides examples of how these technology tools have been used in counselor preparation and provides a pathway for counselor educators to adopt new technologies as part of their teaching portfolio.

Previous work by the author can provide the reader with tools for utilizing technology in a variety of counseling and counselor education environments. Wilson, Jencius, and Duncan (1997) provided one of the first manuscripts that discussed the potential use of the Internet and computers for teaching and practice in counselor education. The article described the development of the Internet and World Wide Web, the new potential that Internet technologies provided practicing counselors and counselor educators, and the ethics of using this new platform. Jencius (2003) focused on using the Internet and computers to facilitate the development of cultural competence using technology platforms that typify human interactions. Jencius, Baltimore, and Getz (2010) reviewed the use of technology in supervision including typology (hardware and software platforms), digital video production, teaching clinical supervision via videoconferencing, and adoption of technology in supervision. Jencius (2010) provided guidelines for using technology in counselor training clinics addressing technology-based records management; computer assessments; technology used to assist in the supervision process; and preparing, acquiring, implementing, and maintaining new technology. The above sources cover a range of information about the use of technology in counseling. To understand the tools and their impact on teaching, one has to follow the development of the Internet as a teaching platform.

WEB DEVELOPMENT

The teaching tools described in this chapter parallel the natural evolution of the Internet. The development of the Internet can be described using version terms based on shifts in what the capabilities of the Web were and how it was used. If you follow the emergence of each version you will see a timeline for technology teaching tools.

Web 1.0 (1990–2000) is also known as "the static web" and involved the dissemination of information from an expert user (Web author) to a consumer of information (Farber, 2007). Web 1.0 consisted of websites that provided content but did not allow for interaction with the consumer of the content. Web 2.0 (2000–2010) is known as "the social web." The purpose of Web 2.0 was to include opportunities for the users and producers of content to interact. Content provision to the Web was no longer the purview of specialists who wrote the code but was now readily available to anyone given a simple set of tools. Tools for teaching emerged in the Web 2.0 era, including micro blogs, blogs, wikis, social networks, RSS feeds, photo and video-sharing sites, and virtual world. Web 3.0 (2010–2020) is not a dramatic shift from Web 2.0, but in Web 3.0 these separate services are connected, communicate with each other, remember user preferences, and become smarter as they are used more often. Because 3.0 uses the text input of the user to develop a database about the user that can predict the user's interests, it is referred to as "the semantic web." Web 3.0 also includes many devices not originally thought of as being "computers": smartphones, home appliances and security systems, tablets, and so forth. The computers are all interconnected without it being obvious to the user and at the same time ubiquitous. Spivak (2007) prognosticated Web 4.0 (2020–2030) will be the first development of ambient and artificial intelligence, where computers can independently create models of thinking beyond the content that is programmed into them. The teaching tools focused on in this chapter are those related to Web 2.0 as they have developed a sound platform of use but are still newly adopted by counselor educators.

DECIDING ON USING THE APPROPRIATE TECHNOLOGY TOOL

There is a plethora of tools that instructors can use to augment their teaching. If you follow new technology tools, you will notice that one has to resist the temptation to grab the shiniest new toy for the classroom. How do counselor educators evaluate potential tools and make technology choices that will enhance their teaching and student learning? In selecting tools to use for instruction, one should question pedagogical purpose, affordability, user support, and permanence.

Pedagogical purpose should be the foundational question that counselor educators ask when thinking of adopting a technology. How does using this tool replace traditional instruction or augment the instructional objectives that I have for the course? The tool may allow for some direct instructional objectives to be obtained as part of the learning students do outside of the classroom, leaving more time in classroom meetings for learning objectives that require the gathering of students in one location. Affordability should be considered given the potential additional cost to a faculty member or student budget. The trend in technology is to offer some tools free with limited scope of use and then add a surcharge should the user wish to have expanded resources from the tool. User support and the availability of online help should be considered when choosing a tool. Students may time shift their work to all parts of the day and having a resource to help them use the tool prevents you from providing 24-hour tech support. Permanence is a question about the tool's sustainability. Will this tool be available for use years from now and how likely will it be that people continue to use this tool? Permanence is hard to predict with technology tools but looking at relative numbers of users of a particular tool will give you guidance about whether to venture toward adoption. The tools presented for your consideration here will demonstrate pedagogical purpose, affordability (free in many cases), user support, and permanence in the market.

In choosing tools for this chapter, the author focused on tools beyond what has been described in the counseling literature (previously described tools such as email, listservs, websites, PowerPoint; Buono, Uellendahl, Guth, & Dandeneau, 2010; Wilson et al., 1997). Instead the focus is on tools that provide a greater user presence and immediacy in the teacher-student interaction. As technology teaching tools for counseling develop they do so with the opportunity to create greater *virtual presence* (Jencius, 2009; Patrick, 2002). Virtual presence can be defined as the visceral sense a person has when they are engaged in a relationship with another person that transcends the technology they are using. We experience virtual presence when we sit in a movie theater and watch a film; engrossed in the story and the multimedia experience, we lose the context of the theater environment, and become involved in the characters and the story. Web 2.0 and 3.0 tools can engage virtual presence to such a degree that the glass, wires, keyboard, and mouse disappear for users in the experience. Emerging tools presented here have begun to demonstrate the potential for engaging students in virtual relationships that they report are just as real and satisfying as traditional relationships (Jencius, 2009).

As a matter of fact, the reader may want to engage in developing a protocol for learning new technology. Readers of this chapter may come from various levels of technology ability, each with a different set of skills and a different set of professional development needs. To get a good overview of what skills you will need, look at the Technical Competencies for Counselor Education (ACES Technology Interest Network, 2007). The competencies present a list of technology skills that a counselor educator should acquire, and they have a skill set for master's degree level graduates and an additional skill set for doctoral degree level graduates.

Furthermore, Jencius (2003) provided suggestions for counselors who might want to engage in web-based resources and the suggestions hold relevance for any counselor educators attempting to further develop their technology skills. First, realize that the Internet and tools that we may use for teaching are constantly expanding, and as such, it will be impossible for one to learn all the available teaching tools. Instead of learning how to use all the tools, it is recommended that you learn how to search and find the tool that meets your pedagogical need. Learn from those around you who are using technology tools. Attend workshops, speak with technology support personnel, look to colleagues who have demonstrated skill in teaching with technology. A final suggestion for learning new technology is to expand your skills by following the natural development of technology tools. In light of what has been said in this chapter, consider becoming familiar with Web

1.0 resources (email, listservs, search engines, websites, presentation software) and then move on to learning Web 2.0 resources (text and video chat, micro blogging, blogs, wikis, social networking, and virtual worlds). Counselor educators will then be more prepared to implement emerging technology in teaching.

IMPLEMENTING EMERGING TOOLS FOR TEACHING WITH TECHNOLOGY

▶ *Micro blogging.* Micro blogging involves the publication of small messages of 140 characters or less. These small messages can be used as a method of communication with students around interesting content related to a course. The messages can include hyperlinks that direct readers to larger content on websites, documents, pictures, sound files, and movies. Twitter.com is the most well known of the micro blogging platforms and has over 400 million subscribers (TechCrunch.com).

One of the useful functions that can be included in a micro blog post is a "hash tag." Hash tags are a way that you can make your posts searchable so you can find your and other classmates' posts. A hash tag is a piece of text included in the user's post with the format "#_____." Hash tags have become the shorthand for large groups of users in order to easily cluster posts on a collective topic of interest. An example of professional use of hash tags is at events or conferences. Users at the event can include an agreed upon hash tag in their posts and then everyone can follow comments on the event by searching the feed for the hash tag. The American Counseling Association (ACA) and the Association for Counselor Education and Supervision (ACES) have used hash tags for posts at their recent conferences so those attending the conference (and those not attending) could receive and post information on conference updates and activities.

Similarly micro blogging using hash tags can be incorporated into the learning activities of a counseling course. The author teaches an online psychopathology course and has desired to increase students' exploration of the clinical literature. Students for the course created Twitter accounts and were expected to find current research and stories about disorders and post them to their Twitter account with a hyperlink to the original source and a hash tag, #CHDSPsycho. Students were asked to follow the stream of posts by searching for the #CHDSPsycho hash tag and then read and respond to another student's post. This process broadened the students' understanding of the disorder, pointed to contemporary treatments, and enriched the level of discourse in the class.

▶ *Real Simple Syndication (RSS).* Real Simple Syndication or RSS is a web format used to create websites that regularly have new material added to them. RSS works well for news pages, blogs, audio and video feeds, or any content that has regularly updated additions to the website. With Web 1.0, as web content was updated the user could only know this by regularly going to the website. With the RSS format, the updates are automatically delivered to you in one location on your computing device.

Using RSS readers as a technology and information tool is becoming more common in counselor education. Many counseling related journals have RSS feeds that update with each new addition. In the past, if we did not subscribe to a particular journal, we would need to go to the library and browse through the shelves of new issues, select, and then photocopy articles of interest. RSS feeds bring that information directly to your desktop or portable device. In many cases, the feed will have hyperlinks to retrieve the complete document, web page, or multimedia. The American Counseling Association has nine of its journals with RSS feed updates (see http://tinyurl.com/6qjkx5x). As of February 2012, ACES Spectrum shifted its publication to include an RSS feed (see http://feeds.feedburner.com/ACESOnline) so one can read news as it develops instead of waiting for the Spectrum quarterly publication. Using RSS feeds provides students with a time saving method to keep up on current news and scholarly publications. Students can scan through the table of contents of many journals easily with any computing device during a short break in their schedule.

The author teaches the use of RSS feed readers in his online psychopathology class as part of the assignment to update the Twitter feed with current literature. Students seek out articles using a feed reader, review the articles, and then post comments and links to the Twitter feed. Doctoral students engaged in research have also found the RSS feed aggregators to be a valuable tool in following the literature. Instead of having to visit a variety of sites to review content, they can skim the feeds from multiple locations, all of which are easily viewed and stored in their aggregator. Content can be bookmarked and full versions can be retrieved then or at a later time.

▶ *Blogs.* Web page publication used to be under the purview of programmers who would take an author's text and convert it into Hyper Text Markup Language (.html) and design the web page for publication. Getting a web page from publication to the Internet required a separate set of skills in setting up the structure of the website and loading the files. Web 2.0 automated all those tools so there is no need for programming knowledge to create content for the Web. Blogs are one of the best examples of content production by authors, moving from author to direct web publication.

Blogs are personal web pages, generally text content heavy, that give the opportunity for any one author or set of authors to add content to the website in serial fashion. Content can be added through the hosting blog website interface or through apps used with portable devices. Colleges and universities using learning management systems (Blackboard, Moodle, Desire2Learn) have blogging tools built into their system. The difficulty with learning management systems is that they lack mobile applications that allow students to use their handheld devices for blogging. With the increasing use of smartphones and tablets, counselor educators may be wise to use third party blogging services like Blogger.com or Wordpress.com that have apps for portable devices. These third party blogging services are free services that students and instructors can use to establish their own blog and limit access should they choose.

The author created a private Wordpress blog, collegeteaching.wordpress.com, for use in his doctoral course on college teaching in counselor education. Each of the students in the class was added as an author for the blog. The blog was used for posting a variety of assignments in the course so the class could react and respond to each other's work. Teaching philosophies developed by each student were posted, read, and commented on by other students in the class. Students were responsible for doing chapter summaries and posting questions to the group to which other students had to respond. As the semester continued, the blog included posts from the instructor with links to recent articles in the *Chronicle of Higher Education*, requests from students looking for help conceptualizing research on teaching, and posts from students seeking help for common classroom management issues. The blog posts of assignments and classmates' reactions/responses paralleled the kind of evaluative activities that the doctoral students will be doing with their own classrooms one day.

▶ *Wiki.* Wikis, like blogs, can be single-user or multiple-user websites where the user can have editing rights to add or modify content on a page using a web browser interface. Whereas blogs have posts that are added sequentially by the author and in a linear fashion, wikis are structured around content areas in the form of separate pages. Multiple authors can contribute and edit pages in wikis, whereas with blogs the content, once posted, usually is not altered. Most wikis are produced so they do not allow for responses or comments. Wikis are generally static in their content compared to blogs where readers can have fluid conversations with authors.

Wikis are best suited for collaborative projects where groups of students can contribute to the development of content around a particular project. For my online psychopathology class, it was my intent to get students to learn more about psychotropic medications and to be more actively engaged in that learning. Groups of students were given a framework of content that they were expected to cover pertaining to various classes of psychotropic medications. Each group was assigned a particular medication class and as a team developed a page in the wiki. Teams had to cover the requested content for each of the classes of medications and build the content into a wiki page. The wiki format can record changes to the wiki and who performs them, so an instructor can get a record of each student's involvement in the creation of the wiki page.

▶ *Social networks.* Social networks have become a popular means of connecting with friends, relatives, and consumers, around common areas of interest or relationship. Facebook, one of the largest social networks had 845 million users as of December 31, 2011(Protalinski, 2012). Because social networks are so widely used by students, counselor educators consider it a potential tool for teaching. Social networks are typically a web-based format from which each member has the ability to create their own web page and link friends with various levels of permission to one's content. Examples of web-based social networks include Facebook, Google+, and MySpace. The definition of social networks is now extending to technology platforms not typically accessed through web pages (e.g., Twitter, Linkedin, Foursquare), but instead accessed by applications on handheld devices. Content that users place on social networking sites can include a list of friends and a profile about the user that includes demographic information, education, employment, location, and interests. Content that can be regularly updated by the member includes their "status" (a text message declaring their current experience), and hyperlinks, pictures, or embedded multimedia. Some social networking sites have user-selected applications that members can interact with such as games, surveys, and questionnaires.

For counselors and counselor educators the growing concern with social media sites is the question of professional boundary (Centore, 2011). A user account, if not set for privacy, can be open for anyone in the social network to find, including clients and students. Boundary issues and the lack of privacy with social networks abound in the media (CBS News, 2011) and have resulted in firings and sanctions by professional associations. Professional associations are now warning teachers (Zagier, 2011), judges (Schwartz, 2009), and doctors (Conaboy, 2011) about boundary concerns with social networks. As of this writing, no directives regarding the use of social networks have emerged from professional counseling associations to direct their members.

Given the privacy and boundary concerns, the best use of social networks in counselor education is limited to disseminating information for programs or associations. Counseling organizations and university programs have created Facebook pages for the purpose of sharing information with their members or students. The American Counseling Association has a Facebook page (http://tinyurl.com/7t2nc8r) and a LinkedIn page (http://tinyurl.com/7w7p95n). Similarly the Association for Counselor Education and Supervision has a Facebook page (www.facebook.com/acesonline) and a LinkedIn page (http://tinyurl.com/8a7qlzz). Should a counselor educator consider using a Facebook page for instructional support purposes, it is recommended that they make a separate personal Facebook account and make sure that their personal account has privacy security settings (Centore, 2011).

▶ **Virtual Worlds.** Virtual worlds are defined as "a synchronous, persistent network of people, represented by avatars, facilitated by network computers" (Bell, 2008). In virtual worlds users are represented as 3-dimensional avatars. The users control their avatar and through that avatar interact and manipulate the virtual world. Virtual worlds are *synchronous* in that when users enter the world using their computers, the action is happening in real time, at the moment they are "in-world." If they are interacting with another user/avatar, that user is simultaneously sitting at his or her computer manipulating an avatar and the environment. Virtual worlds are *persistent* in that once the user logs off the computer, the virtual world remains intact on the server for a later time when he or she will return. The look and feel of a virtual world appears to be much the same as a modern video game. The difference between video games and true virtual environments are their customizability. Virtual worlds are customizable by the developer/user. Everything within a virtual world has been created and placed in the virtual world by the user/developer whereas the videogame environment is generally a closed, unchanging environment predetermined by the videogame programmer. Also, video games have predefined goals by the programmer, whereas virtual worlds do not require goals as a purpose for interaction. Virtual world interactions have more open-ended objectives, like developing social interactions, than do the goals of programmed video games.

The most common virtual world platform is Second Life® with 27 million registered members and an average of 50,000 online at any time. Second Life® has a thriving business economy with 1.4 million dollars in daily transactions (Shepherd, 2012). Second Life® is not just made up of individual members but is also a venue for corporate marketing with many corporation sims, from companies such as IBM, Cisco, Reebok, Starwood Hotels, the American Cancer Society, and Wells Fargo, all of which have a virtual world presence.

Universities have created a presence in virtual worlds for marketing purposes and for online education. Counselor education programs have also adopted virtual world experiences as a platform for training. Edina Renfro-Michel from Montclair State University has created "The Theorists Project," a portion of an island sim that has houses dedicated to various counseling theorists. Students are assigned houses and are responsible for furnishing the houses with objects and information about the counseling theorist. Victoria Walker, working with Regent University, developed a virtual world counseling training facility for students to practice basic counseling skills with each other. Deb Pender at Northern Illinois University has used the virtual world environment in a sim clinic to enact clients with various diagnoses and has also developed an emergency response site simulation to teach first responders crisis response techniques. Tarrell Portman at the University of Iowa used a virtual world conference center for meeting her doctoral internship class. She had a private conference room inworld where her students would gather weekly for engagement and supervision.

The Counselor Education in Second Life (CESL) center was created by the author with doctoral student Debra London in November of 2008. The CESL provides training space and consultation for counselor educators who wish to utilize virtual worlds for training projects, classroom meetings, and professional conferences. Services have been provided free of charge to interested educators. Counselor educators are using the space for weekly classroom meetings, opportunities for group supervision, and virtual office hours for students. The CESL center has offered 4-day annual conferences since 2009. The 3rd Virtual Conference on Counseling had over 200 attendees, 40 program presentations, and representation from over 13 different countries, completely offered through this computer virtual environment.

▶ *Digital textbooks.* The rising cost of college textbooks has impacted student budgets. Textbook publishers have attempted to provide added value to material through digital videos available for classes, test banks for the course, PowerPoint slides, and online classrooms for discussion. The additional teaching elements may increase the product value but does little to reduce the cost. Even when traditional publishers provide e-book versions of their textbooks as a purchase option, the overall cost and return value of the e-book does not save the student money in the bottom line (DeSantis, 2012).

The digital media movement brings the producer of content closer to the consumer of content. Getting the content producers (counselor educators) closer to the content consumers (counseling students) meets the needs of the counseling students better through knowing what they need to learn and reducing the cost of the production. New digital textbook software puts publishing tools directly in the hands of counselor educators allowing them to produce materials for their students that can be closely related to their students' needs.

E-books, or e-pubs, differentiate themselves from traditional textbook media in that they are *revisable, responsive,* and *portable.* Content is revisable immediately. If I want to alter or change content in the e-book, I can do so and upload the new version for consumers in a matter of minutes. The consumer can re-access the revised edition of the book for download. E-books are responsive in that the e-book has the ability to alter its layout based on the device used for reading. E-books are user responsive as the reader can adjust properties of the book such as font size and style, background image, and brightness. The responsive e-book can be read on desktops, tablets, or smartphones. They also have the ability to have hyperlinks to Internet resources and multimedia embedded in the book itself which makes the e-book format a much richer learning device pedagogically. They are portable and meant to be used on portable devices like laptops, tablets, e-readers, and smartphones.

The author with collaboration of doctoral students in his college teaching course created an e-book containing information on developing a teaching philosophy, college teaching methods, addressing classroom behavior, experiential learning, designing a syllabus, creating an evaluation rubric, and other practical skills for teaching. The e-book contains dynamic content links and will be used to supplement other texts used in the course. It will be available for download through online bookstores (e.g., counselingpress.com). This initiative has sparked the development of a second similarly formatted e-book on supervision.

IMPLEMENTING A NEW TECHNOLOGY FOR TEACHING

As teaching professionals we have to learn to make continuous adjustments to our pedagogy. New courses, a new group of students, a new textbook, are all common situations to which new counselor educators must adjust. Starting a new technology in the classroom requires a process of similar adjustment. Jencius (2010) has developed a strategy for adapting new technology in counseling training clinics that includes steps for preparing, acquiring, implementing, and maintaining new technologies. Many of the ideas in that article should be considered in teaching with technology. Framing your implementation around teaching, the steps to consider when starting a new technology in the classroom include:

▶ *Think pedagogically.* Reflection on the learning outcomes for your class should be the driving force behind choosing or not choosing to use a particular technology. What knowledge and skills would your students need to acquire in the class and how might this technology be of assistance? Can this part of your curriculum be addressed through independent work? Another way to look at pedagogical application of technology is, "Will the use of this technology away from the classroom open space in the classroom schedule for me to work with students on topics that are best considered as a group?"

▶ *Think purposefully.* Once you have made a decision based on your pedagogical intent to use a new technology for a learning experience, ask yourself the question, "How does this tool help with the learning process in this class?" There are lots of flashy new technologies that you can add to a counselor training experience, but if they do not serve a pedagogical purpose, it is probably better to rethink the use of the tool.

▶ *Think portability.* Can the tool be used on a variety of devices and multiple operating systems? Look to see if the tool you are using can be used on common operating systems (Windows, Mac OS, Android, Linux). Explore to see if there are app versions of the tool that will allow for the tool to be run on laptops, tablets, portable readers, and smartphones.

▶ *Think about your learning curve.* You need to spend time learning about the tool before you can frame the tool within the context of your course. How do you learn best? Reading about the tool? Practice lessons with the tool? Do you intuitively play without a set plan? If you want to micro blog with your class you need to spend time using and exploring micro blogging tools. Look for online guides and start to keep a pool of resources on a tool you plan to use. This will come in handy as students have questions.

▶ *Think collaboratively.* Look for colleagues within the counselor education field who are using the tool and also look for those outside our field for inspiration on how to implement technology tools in the classroom. Since many of the Web 2.0 tools are text-based interactive writing platforms, the author finds lots of ideas by watching how academics in the humanities are using these tools. If you find a colleague using the tool, ask them if they would be willing to share their ideas. Often they are proud of being innovative and will be able to tell you what to look out for when using the technology.

▶ *Think support for students.* What kinds of training are you willing to provide for students prior to using the tool? As an instructor, do you do an in-class demonstration or have a tech support person take time to provide training during your class? If you have resources from your own learning, you can post or send these to students to help them learn and adapt to using the new tool.

▶ *Think practically.* If the tool becomes obsolete or is not useful, drop it, and move onto something else to achieve your pedagogical purpose. The author used to check out CD-ROMs of video segments to students that they would watch and evaluate outside of class. When the ability for placing this video into a course management system became available, distributing CD-ROMs became an obsolete tool.

▶ *Think potentiality.* If the tool is useful in one class, what is the potential value of the tool in other classes that you teach? Look at its pedagogical function in the current class and think about how it might or might not be useful in similar assignments in other courses that you teach. Students having already used the tool in one class will more readily adopt it in another class setting.

TRANSFORMING YOUR TEACHING

The author has found his use of technology in teaching has transformed students' learning as well as his teaching. Technology in teaching can provide students with diverse learning styles opportunities to learn in ways best suited for them (Grasha, 2000). Technology tools also allow learning to be time-shifted to a better place and time for the student. Technology has transformed my teaching by freeing up face-to-face classroom time and requiring me to be more intentional with things I do in the classroom. I now have time in the classroom to work on activities that require student face-to-face interaction, transforming my classroom from a more passive learning environment to a more active learning environment that requires the presence of others.

Transforming one's teaching can, in part, be connected with evaluating the worth of the technology used in the course. Tools used can be evaluated formatively (during the semester) and summatively (at the end of the semester). For example, students may be asked, "What challenges have you had in using this tool?" "To what degree have you developed a sense of competence with this tool and how is this different from when you started using the tool?" "How has the technology facilitated your understanding of the course content?" and "What suggestions would you have for new students using the tool?" Every technology plan should include a multimodal evaluation. Noeth and Volkov (2004) suggested that assessment of technology-based learning in education should consider the stakeholders' impressions (students and teachers). Specific to counselor education, the reader might consider the following:

- What were the students' impressions of the technology used in the course?
- How did the students and/or teacher view the technology impacting the students' level of involvement with others in the course and with the course content?
- What did the teacher see as fostering or impeding his or her use of technology?
- According to the teacher and/or students, what about the classroom environment was supportive or challenging to the use of technology, for example, the students' prior exposure to the tool, actual cost to students purchasing the technology, the presence of functional/operational technology in the classroom, and so forth?
- In what ways did the teacher's level of comfort, understanding, and competency with the technology impact student learning?

Noeth and Volkov (2004) have also supported the teacher's assessment of the types of technology used and their fit with the method of instruction. Such assessment in counselor education might consider the following:

- How does the teacher view the choice of technology fitting with learning styles of students?
- Was the chosen mode of technology beneficial in delivering specific course content, for example, using role plays in Second Life˚, following a blog as a means of developing class discussion, using RSS feed for providing content on current research, and so forth?
- In what ways does the teacher see the use of technology being aligned with the pedagogical purpose of the course, for example, introductory exposure to new content, skill acquisition, advanced understanding of professional information, and so forth?
- What additional technology options does the teacher see as helping to accomplish identified learning outcomes?

Evaluation should look at the process of implementing the technology as well as expected and unexpected outcomes. Reflecting on the expected and unexpected outcomes might lead to other pedagogical uses of the technology in other classes. Whether done formally through student evaluation questionnaires or through informal discussion throughout the course, counselor educators should explore with students how technology has impacted their involvement in the course and their ability to achieve learning outcomes.

REFERENCES

ACES Technology Interest Network (2007). Technical competencies for counselor education: Recommended Guidelines for program development. Retrieved from http://files.acesonline.net/doc/2007_aces_technology_competencies.pdf

Bell, M. (2008). Toward a definition of "virtual worlds." *Journal of Virtual Worlds Research, 1*(1). Retrieved from https://journals.tdl.org/jvwr/article/view/283/237

Buono, L. L., Uellendahl, G. E., Guth, L. J., & Dandeneau, C. J. (2010). The use of technology in counselor education and supervision. In G. McAuliffe & K. Eriksen (Eds.), *Handbook of counselor preparation* (pp.377-392). Los Angeles, CA: Sage.

CBS News. (2011). *Did the Internet kill privacy?* Retrieved from http://www.cbsnews.com/stories/2011/02/06/sunday/main7323148.shtml?tag=stack

Centore, A. (2011). *Online social networking with counseling clients: Six "Facebook" rules.* Retrieved from http://my.counseling.org/2011/04/20/online-social-networking-with-counseling-clients-six-"facebooking"-rules/

Conaboy (2011). *For doctors, social media a tricky case.* Retrieved from http://www.boston.com/lifestyle/health/articles/2011/04/20/for_doctors_social_media_a_tricky_case/?page=full

DeSantis, N. (2012). *E-textbooks saved many students only $1.* Retrieved from http://chronicle.com/blogs/wiredcampus/new-study-shows-e-textbooks-saved-many-students-only-1/34793

Farber, D. (2007). *From semantic Web (3.0) to the WebOS (4.0).* Retrieved from http://www.zdnet.com/blog/btl/from-semantic-web-30-to-the-webos-40/4499

Fouts, J. T. (2000). *Research on computers and education: Past, present, and future.* A report to the Bill and Melinda Gates Foundation. Seattle, WA: Seattle Pacific University.

Grasha, A. (2000). Integrating teaching styles and learning styles with instructional technology, *College Teaching, 48*(1), 2–10.

Jencius, M. (2003). Applications of technological advances for multicultural counseling professionals. In F. D. Harper & J. McFadden (Eds.), *Culture and counseling: New approaches* (pp. 350–362). Boston, MA: Allyn and Bacon

Jencius, M. (May, 2009). Training and counseling in a virtual world. *Counseling Today,* pp. 28–29.

Jencius, M. (2010). Technology Enhanced Counselor Training Clinics. In K. Mobley & J. Myers (Eds.), *Developing and maintaining counselor education laboratories.* Alexandria, VA: American Counseling Association. Retrieved from http://www.acesonline.net/wp-content/uploads/2011/08/mobley_myers.pdf

Jencius, M., Baltimore, M. L., & Getz, H. (2010). Innovative uses of technology in supervision. In J. R. Culbreth & L. L. Brown (Eds.), *State of the art in clinical supervision* (pp. 63-86). New York, NY: Taylor Francis/Routledge

Noeth, R. J., & Volkov, B. B. (2004). *Evaluating the effectivness of technology in our schools: ACT policy report.* Retrieved from http://www.act.org/research/policymakers/pdf/school_tech.pdf

Patrick, A. (2002). *The psychology of virtual presence: Research ideas.* Retrieved from http://www.andrewpatrick.ca/virtual-presence/presence-ideas.html

Protalinski, E. (2012). *Facebook has over 845 million users.* Retrieved from http://www.zdnet.com/blog/facebook/facebook-has-over-845-million-users/8332

Schwartz, J. (2009). *For judges on Facebook, friendship has limits.* Retrieved from http://www.nytimes.com/2009/12/11/us/11judges.html

Shepherd, T. (2012). *Second Life Grid Survey.* Retrieved from http://gridsurvey.com/index.php

Spivak, N. (2007). *How the webOS evolves?* Retrieved from http://www.novaspivack.com/technology/how-the-webos-evolves

Wilson, F. R., Jencius, M., & Duncan, D. M. (1997). Introduction to the Internet: Opportunities and dilemmas. *Counseling and Human Development, 29,* 1–16.

Zagier, A. S. (2011). *Mo. teachers protest Facebook crackdown.* Retrieved from http://www.msnbc.msn.com/id/44034102/ns/technology_and_science-tech_and_gadgets/#.T05qC1H1bjp

CHAPTER 8

Using Distance Learning in Teaching

ANNETTE C. ALBRECHT

DENNIS G. JONES

According to Staklis (2010), during the 2007–2008 academic year, more than 20% of post-secondary students in the United States were involved in some type of distance learning program. This demand for distance learning coupled with greater availability of high-speed Internet access has created a "perfect e-storm" (Kim & Bonk, 2006, p. 22) for meeting the needs of adult learners with high quality distance courses. This is not to suggest that every student wants to be enrolled in distance learning courses, nor that the technology and network access are perfect. However, the growth of distance learning programs suggests an upward trend in this phenomenon. For example, "during the 2006–07 academic year, two-thirds (66 percent) of 2-year and 4-year Title IV degree-granting postsecondary institutions reported offering online, hybrid/blended online, or other distance education courses" (Parsad & Lewis, 2008, p. 2).

DEFINITIONS OF DISTANCE LEARNING

Distance learning has many definitions. For the purposes of this discussion, distance learning is defined as academic-related coursework in which students and instructors are separated by space or time, and technology is used as the medium to bridge this space/time gap. Course delivery occurs along a continuum from 100% face-to-face (i.e., no separation by space or time) with no distance learning component, to 100% distance learning with no face-to-face component. Course formats between these two extremes are described as "hybrid" or "blended."

BENEFITS OF DISTANCE LEARNING

Benefits of a high quality distance learning program can be viewed from multiple perspectives (e.g., institutions, faculty members, students).

Institutions

Most institutions of higher education are being expected to do more with less. According to the American Association of State Colleges and Universities (2010), public universities are continuing to mandate hiring freezes. Similar funding issues are present at many private institutions. However, the number of students entering into higher education continues to grow (Snyder & Dillow, 2011). Therefore, one approach to bridge the gap between the availability of faculty and the growing number of students is to implement distance learning.

Faculty Members

Some faculty members find that distance learning provides them with more flexibility in meeting the other demands of their profession (Lei & Gupta, 2010). For those who have previously traveled to off-campus sites on a weekly basis to teach class, distance learning may provide an opportunity to gain back several commuting hours each week. Additionally, many faculty members who are engaged in distance learning find the reflective opportunities incorporated into many courses to be a value added experience for students (Rizopoulos & McCarthy, 2009). For example, when utilizing a discussion board, students may be asked to post comments and react to the comments of other students throughout the semester on a specific topic.

Students

In discussing the role of distance learning in the counselor preparation process, Chandras, DeLambo, and Eddy (2005) suggested that one of the benefits of distance learning programs is that they will provide opportunities "for those students with disabilities or those working full time. One's place of residence does not pose a barrier for educational access" (p. 253). Opening doors of opportunity for students who are place bound and/or time bound is not only something that counselor education programs should do, but many would argue that they must do.

DISTANCE EDUCATION LEARNING ENVIRONMENTS

Distance education learning environments are interactive technology-based systems that use a combination of media to bridge the space/time gap between instructors and students. Typically, these media include: (a) text, (b) audio, (c) video, (d) graphics, and (e) motion graphics (i.e., 2D & 3D animations). The various distance education learning environments are delineated by the mix of these media, and the nature of the interactivity between instructors and students, as well as the space/time relationship.

A primary criterion for differentiating distance education learning environments is related to the space/time gap. Synchronous distance learning is when students are separated from the instructor by space. Asynchronous distance learning is when students are separated from the instructor and other students by time. Some distance learning courses include both synchronous and asynchronous components.

Synchronous Distance Education Learning Environments

The following approaches are considered primarily synchronous; however, they may be complemented with one or more asynchronous components.

Two-Way Interactive Television (ITV). The ITV systems allow faculty members to interact in real-time (synchronous) with students in remote classrooms. These systems reduce the need for faculty members to travel to remote campuses to teach courses. In many ways, this environment most closely resembles a face-to-face classroom as it allows the faculty member and remote students to see and hear each other.

One of the authors teaches a research methods course between ITV classrooms on the main campus and classrooms at two remote campuses (each campus is approximately 90 miles from the main campus). The classrooms are close enough that the instructor travels to each of the remote sites once a month to develop personal relationships with the students.

Desktop Videoconferencing (DVC). This technology provides faculty members the ability to interact with students at individual computers while in their homes or offices. If the instructor's and students' computers have audio (e.g., headphones with microphones) and video (e.g., webcams), this technology is somewhat similar to ITV. The fundamental difference between these environments is that DVC students are not required to be in the same classroom.

A variation in desktop videoconferencing is a webinar format where the instructor has the capability to send audio and video to students. During the webinar, students have the opportunity to interact with the instructor and other students through a telephone-based audio conference. According to Mann Layne and Hohenshil (2005):

> In counselor education, using interactive television and high-bandwidth videoconferencing to provide training opportunities for students in remote areas, satellite campuses, and foreign countries is becoming relatively routine and will continue to expand because it not only provides education for underserved groups of students, but it also makes effective use of faculty and facilities and can be a tool for increasing diversity. (p. 225)

Text chat. Another tool for real-time communication among faculty members and students is text chat (e.g., text-based messages are typed on a keyboard). In almost all situations, this type of tool is used in conjunction with other synchronous and asynchronous components. A variation of text chat is instant messaging. The authors will often have students contact them using text chat to ask a question during online office hours.

Virtual whiteboards. Web-based collaboration tools that allow multiple students to diagram in a common shared virtual space are referred to as whiteboards. This type of tool is often used in lieu of chat when working with statistical formulas or figures because these symbols are easier to draw free hand than type. Like text chat, virtual whiteboards are often used to complement other synchronous and asynchronous components. One of the authors requires virtual teams in an online course to complete a group identity exercise. This project entails the team developing a group logo. It is not uncommon to find teams using this shared diagramming space to complete the task.

3D virtual environments/virtual worlds. In virtual environments, faculty members and students utilize avatars to interact with each other. Most virtual worlds allow users to use audio and/or text chat to interact. Like a traditional classroom, faculty members can lead discussions and conduct presentations using an avatar. One of the most popular virtual worlds (Wiecha, Heyden, Sternthal, & Merialdi, 2010) for educators (Girvan & Savage, 2010) is Second Life®. The authors recently conducted a presentation using Second Life® at the 2nd Virtual Conference on Counseling (2VCC). One of the best resources for learning about virtual worlds in counselor education is Counselor Education in Second Life (http://sl.counseloreducation.org).

Asynchronous Distance Education Learning Environments

Collectively, online courses serve as the primary tool for asynchronous distance education. "Online education provides opportunities to learn or complete training programs for those individuals with the type of constraints that prevents attendance within the traditional classroom (e.g., disability, full-time job, geographical region, family, etc.)" (Chandras & Chandras, 2010, p. 2). Most online courses are composed of multiple asynchronous tools that may be combined with synchronous tools. Additionally, the majority of online courses are delivered through some type of learning content management system (LCMS). A LCMS is a set of software tools that combines the features of a learning management system (LMS) and content management system (CMS). A LMS encompasses the components of an online course that perform administrative functions. Such tasks include enrolling students, documenting online activities, tracking users, utilizing grade books, and generating reports. A CMS provides the means for instructors and students in an online course to share information (e.g., text, audio/video files) as well as tools to collaborate (e.g., text chat, bulletin boards). Most institutions involved in online course delivery have adopted some type of LCMS (e.g., Blackboard, Desire2Learn) in order to facilitate online course delivery.

Content delivery. An essential element of online courses is some type of instructor provided content that ranges from text-based lecture notes, to presentations (with or without "voice over"), to audio/video demonstrations. Developing content is the most time consuming component of online courses for most faculty members. Specifically, it is the place where the faculty member can best customize the course based on personal experiences. Many textbook publishers provide some prepared online content (e.g., PowerPoint slides, video clips) that can be imported into the LCMS. It is the experience of the authors that publisher provided content is a great place to start; however, the personalization of this content to meet the faculty member's course objectives is essential.

Threaded discussion/bulletin board. Tools that allow instructors and students to post and respond to threaded discussions related to a topic or issue are common in most online courses. Some courses include instructor-initiated postings that require student responses, which may be evaluated as part of the course grade. One of the authors regularly incorporates bulletin board activities into courses. For example, in a psychopathology course, she has students work in virtual teams to develop appropriate diagnoses based on written case studies.

Wiki/blog. Although similar to threaded discussions, wikis tend to evolve in a less formal manner. As explained by Mirk, Burkiewicz, and Komperda (2010):

> A wiki functions like a collaborative word processing document but is viewed like a web page. Multiple users are able to contribute to the formation of one dynamic document, at different times and in different geographic locations. One of the benefits of a wiki is that the educator is able to monitor group progress and track who has contributed to a group collaborative effort. (p. 73)

Electronic journals. To encourage students to post comments and observations throughout a course on various topics, faculty members incorporate electronic journals. Unlike threaded discussions and wikis, these journals are usually accessible to only the student and the instructor.

E-mail. In addition to traditional e-mail that is used by faculty members and students to communicate, most LCMS platforms include some type of internal e-mail for instructors and students to correspond with each other. From a course management perspective, internal e-mail assists an instructor in keeping all the correspondence related to the course in one location.

Assessments. Most LCMS platforms allow faculty members to create and deliver online quizzes, and enable students to upload and submit assignments (e.g., papers, reports). However, due to system limitations, most of these platforms will not allow students to upload large video files (e.g., mock counseling sessions).

Mobile LCMS. Most online courses are accessed through a web browser on a desktop or notebook computer with an Internet connection. The ability to access these courses through mobile devices such as smartphones (e.g., iPhone, Blackberry) is slowly becoming more prevalent and will soon become a standard.

BEST PRACTICES IN DISTANCE LEARNING FOR COUNSELOR EDUCATORS

Over the years, several authors (e.g., Lou, Bernard, & Abrami, 2006; McGinnis, 2010; Reynolds, 2006; Summers, Waigandt, & Whittaker, 2005; Wang, Solan, & Ghods, 2010) have published lists of strategies for effectively teaching at a distance. Most, but not all, of these recommendations have been generated in the context of non-counseling related courses. Although the delivery of high quality counselor preparation programs shares many elements with other disciplines, the following suggestions incorporate principles of best practice related to distance learning with the nuances of helping students develop counseling skills in a distance learning environment.

▶ *Learning to become a distance teacher.* In addition to knowing the course content and the students in the program, distance learning faculty members need to understand both the distance learning technologies and the experiences of a distance learning student. In other words, becoming a distance teacher is a process that evolves through experiences (i.e., both good and bad).

Institutions committed to providing high quality distance education experiences for their students will have some type of distance learning instructional support office that will assist faculty and students in learning to use the distance education technologies. These offices can help answer the "how to" questions. In discussing the development and delivery of counseling courses in an online environment, Patrick (2005) emphasized that "it is essential that instructors receive training and preparation prior to embarking on online course instruction" (p. 241). However, becoming an effective distance learning instructor goes beyond understanding the technologies. It requires that counselor educators understand the overall distance learning experience.

A method to gain a deeper understanding of distance learning is to "observe" the distance course of a colleague at one's home institution, or at another institution. For example, a colleague of the authors recently taught an online counseling course that included the ability to access the course through Blackboard Mobile (http://www.blackboard.com/Platforms/Mobile/overview.aspx). Being provided the experience of seeing Blackboard Mobile in use will make us better prepared to work with students using this technology when it becomes available on our campus.

In an online course, faculty members need to learn how to interact with students. Counselor educators could apply some of the same techniques that are used in online counseling sessions. In discussing training students to provide online counseling, Trepal, Haberstroh, Duffey, and Evans (2007) concluded that "counselor educators can and should encourage students to become aware of the differences in communicating in cyberspace (e.g., language issues, condensed messages)" (p. 275). Gaining an understanding of these differences in an online course compared to a face-to-face course can assist faculty members in becoming more effective communicators.

▶ *Planning.* Forsyth, Pizzica, Laxton, and Mahony (2010) documented the importance of planning in the distance learning process. Ideally, the planning process to convert an existing course for delivery via distance learning should begin approximately one year prior to the course being taught in this new environment. In a previous publication (i.e., Albrecht & Jones, 2001), the authors outlined a month-by-month timeline for preparing a distance learning course.

However, at many institutions, this timeline is not feasible due to a variety of unforeseen circumstances (e.g., a faculty member unexpectedly leaving the department). Recently, one of the co-authors was asked to convert one of her face-to-face courses to a totally online class with less than one month's notice. The following is a brief summary of steps that she went through to plan this conversion for a career counseling course:

1. Review the concepts from previous offerings of the course in a face-to-face environment that were most difficult for students to master. Then, begin thinking about how to articulate these concepts in a completely online environment. For example, in this course, the most challenging issues are explaining the details of each theory and the explicit expectations for the final case study project.
2. Identify existing learning resources (e.g., textbook, websites) to be incorporated into the course.
3. Prepare a list of additional learning resources that need to be developed (e.g., lecture notes and presentation materials that need to be converted into an electronic format).

4. Determine course evaluation methodology (e.g., how exams will be administered).
5. Develop a detailed week-by-week schedule of activities and assignments that assist the students in meeting the course objectives.
6. Begin developing additional resources by converting existing materials and identifying new resources (e.g., videos from TeacherTube and YouTube, podcasts from CounselorAudioSource.Net). For the mentioned example of a career counseling course, this included posting detailed lecture notes concerning each theory.
7. Begin developing detailed instructions for each activity/assignment to provide students with the instructor's expectations. For the example of a career counseling course, this included posting a very detailed description of the case study project.
8. Prepare the course website by uploading learning resources and activity/assignment instructions.

Given the importance of interactivity in a distance learning environment, it is imperative that faculty members design purposeful interactions among students, instructors, and the content into these courses (Bernard et al., 2009). In a face-to-face course, it is possible for a faculty member to "wing it." However, when students are separated by space or time, the opportunities for meaningful impromptu interactions are limited. Whereas most interactions will need to be planned, many faculty members provide students opportunities for spontaneous interactions through chat rooms or discussion boards that are not monitored by the instructor (i.e., much like the discussions that occur among students before or after a face-to-face class).

▶ *Provide various levels of user support.* Gu, Zhang, Lin, and Song (2009) defined learner support as "all resources that a learner can access in the learning process, including materials, learning communities, teachers/facilitators, and media/technology, to achieve experiential learning objectives as ingredients of a major effort to facilitate experiential distance learning by teachers" (p. 115). Based on a number of factors (e.g., previous experiences in the distance learning environment, prior knowledge related to course content), some students will need limited support and others will need extensive support. The concept of providing varying levels of support for learners is often referred to as scaffolding. For example, one of the authors has taught a data analysis course online and expected all students to work through at least one example for each statistical technique. By providing the opportunity for students to work through multiple examples, those students who wanted more learner support were able to utilize the additional problems while students familiar with the concept could move on to the next topic.

▶ *Student–instructor interaction.* In distance learning courses, faculty members need to establish understandable parameters related to the methods of interaction between students and instructors. Without clear expectations in an online course, it is not uncommon for a faculty member to feel like he or she is teaching individual correspondence courses. A technique used by one of the authors to proactively address this issue is referred to as "three then me." Using this model, when a student contacts the instructor with a question, the student provides the three resources to which he or she first looked for the answer. The first part of this interaction whether via telephone, text, or e-mail is about the quality of the three sources. This model assists students in becoming independent learners. Additionally, the number of unnecessary contacts (e.g., When is the final exam?) for faculty is reduced to allow more time for value-added interactions.

Some authors have found chat rooms (i.e., web-based environment for text-based chat) and e-mail to be particularly helpful in student–instructor interactions. For example, Finlay, Desmet, and Evans (2004) reported that "the chat room—is particularly conducive to interactivity between teacher and students" (p. 175).

Many faculty members who teach distance learning courses establish regular virtual office hours using the tools included in the LCMS (e.g., chat, audio conferencing, video conferencing) for "meeting" with students. This provides a great opportunity for the instructor and the students to discuss class assignments and review drafts of papers. If the instructor has the students working in some type of team, the faculty member can meet with the entire group at one time.

The LCMS often includes tools (e.g., electronic journals, private discussion boards, personal WIKIs) for students to post reflections that can be viewed only by the student and the instructor. These tools allow the faculty member to engage in a personal dialog with each student related to course topics.

Some faculty members prefer to conduct telephone conferences with students. For example, one of the authors teaches a research methods course using ITV and schedules regular telephone conferences with students to review their research proposals. During these conversations, they are able to discuss the students' questions. Additionally, these conversations allow the instructor to expand on his written feedback from earlier drafts of the proposal.

▶ *Student–content interaction.* In addition to interacting with the instructor, students need to interact with the course content. This interactivity is especially important in online courses because most of the content will be provided to the student through some type of LCMS. To the greatest degree possible, the content should actively engage the student, rather than passively require a student to read a series of lecture notes or review a presentation with the instructor's "voice over." A typical way to build meaningful interactivity into the content is to build "check for understanding" quizzes into the materials. For example, after reviewing a set of course content materials, the student completes a quiz. The quiz is not part of the course grade; however, the student may not proceed to the next part of the content until successfully completing the quiz.

The incorporation of student–content interaction has been documented. In discussing skill development for pharmacy students, Flowers, Vanderbush, Hastings, and West (2010) concluded that "interactive Web-based multimedia training vignettes presented by experts have the potential to improve student training and subsequent patient care" (p. 1). Additionally, Hawthorne, Prout, Kinnersley, and Houston (2009) described an interactive distance learning module related to diversity skills training for medical students. These same types of student-content interactions have application to counselor preparation.

▶ *Student–student interaction.* Adams (2008) reported that "peer interaction distinguishes an online course from a correspondence or independent study course. A successful online experience creates a sense of community among learners allowing them to interact and contribute reciprocally to the learning process" (Quality of Instruction section, para. 1).

This same type of interaction is important in ITV courses. One of the authors utilizes numerous small group activities during class and has students report back to the larger group. Clear guidelines and timelines are crucial for successful activities in an ITV environment because instructors will want to mute the microphones during the activities to reduce background noise that will be sent to all sites.

As suggested by Curtis (2004), chat room discussions have the potential to replace small group activities in face-to-face courses. This type of interaction can also occur through bulletin boards and virtual whiteboards. A feature of many online courses is some type of asynchronous discussion among students through bulletin boards where the instructor will post discussion questions and have students respond.

In order to encourage student-to-student interaction, one of the authors creates virtual teams in his online data analysis course. The purpose of these teams is twofold: (a) to help students "connect" with other students, and (b) to provide opportunities for peer-to-peer learning. In face-to-face courses, it is important for students to understand group dynamics within their teams; however, in an online course communication can be more difficult because of the space/time gap. Therefore, the first activity of these virtual teams is to complete an online assignment that requires the team members to address group dynamics. Specifically, the students develop a team name and motto, and then they work through a series of group process questions (e.g., how they plan to handle disagreements). The team submits a written report that summarizes the team members' responses to these questions and outlines the team's expectations of each member (e.g., providing timely feedback to each other, having final team projects ready for submission at least one day prior to the deadline). Students report that this type of activity is very beneficial in allowing the team members to get to know each other.

▶ *Provide clear expectations.* Whether in an ITV course or online course, it is especially important to provide students with clear directions because the instructor does not have the ability to read non-verbal feedback cues that are present in face-to-face courses. For example, when providing students with directions for conducting role plays in a psychopathology course delivered by ITV, one of the authors supplements verbal directions with a written handout at both the local and remote classrooms.

In online courses, one of the authors describes himself as being redundant through the extensive use of hyperlinking within the LCMS platform. For example, an assignment is posted in the assignment folder on the course home page. The author also provides hyperlinks to this assignment from the course calendar, a weekly reminder update, and the assignment submission tool.

▶ *Engaging students in active learning.* In discussing the development of online counseling courses, Osborn (2009) cautioned faculty members to remember that "each online activity should be tied in with one of the course's objectives, and not just be technology for technology's sake" (p. 335). In a face-to-face course, engaging students may be easier because the instructor is standing in the front of the room. However, in distance environments, the technology tools replace the instructor's physical presence and need to help serve as a catalyst to engage students in the learning process.

For example, one of the authors makes extensive use of threaded discussions to support the peer review process of student projects in both ITV and online courses. Specifically, each research team (three to four students) is assigned a bulletin board within the LCMS where team members are required to post their projects and teammates are expected to provide feedback based on the course content. This process provides students the opportunity to apply course content through the peer review process.

▶ *Evaluating student learning.* As noted by Wall (2000), with proper planning, technology-mediated assessments can be very effective in the evaluation of student learning. Most LCMS platforms provide tools for delivering quizzes and receiving assignments. However, especially in online courses, many instructors express concern about whether a student is actually completing his or her own work. To address this issue, one of the authors requires one proctored essay exam in each online course. The student is required to find his or her own proctor and have this person approved by the university. One of the authors explains to the students at the beginning of the semester, he will be reading the proctored essay not only for content, but will be looking at writing style to verify that it is consistent with the student's discussion postings throughout the semester. In over a decade of teaching online courses, the author has never had a reason to suspect that the student completing the proctored exam was not the same person who completed the discussion postings.

▶ *Overcoming technology challenges.* Technological competence of faculty members and students in a distance learning environment (especially an online environment) is essential. In discussing the results of a survey of students enrolled in online counseling courses, Chandras et al. (2005) remarked that students with stronger technology skills believed they performed better in online courses. Some faculty members teaching online courses require students to attend a face-to-face course orientation meeting at the beginning of the semester (Ali & Leeds, 2009), or a program in an on campus computer lab. During this orientation, the faculty member will review with students how to use the tools within the LCMS platform. Additionally, this time can be used to allow students to meet the other members of their virtual team, and discuss the process for submitting assignments.

However, despite the best efforts, both online and ITV courses will experience technical issues from time to time. It is important for the faculty member to remain relaxed and convey this feeling to his or her students. Also, most institutions with high quality distance learning programs provide some type of Help Desk to assist faculty and students with issues. Therefore, it is essential that faculty and students know how to contact this resource.

EVALUATING THE EFFECTIVENESS OF DISTANCE LEARNING

Like other teaching methodologies, distance learning at both the individual course, and program level, can be evaluated using internal as well as external benchmarks. After completing these evaluations, the outcomes will most likely mirror the results reported by Vismara, Young, Stahmer, Griffith, and Rogers (2009) who concluded, "our findings clearly demonstrate that teaching via distance learning technology was as effective as teaching using live interaction" (p. 1646). Additionally, the instructor can utilize a number of techniques for evaluating the student's involvement in the learning process.

Internal Benchmarks

Internal benchmarks considered by counselor preparation programs could include the following.

Student performance compared to face-to-face courses. For counselor education programs offering two sections of the same courses using different delivery methods (e.g., face-to-face & ITV), it is appropriate to compare student performance between sections. Of course, this assumes pre-course similarities between students. Ideally, regardless of format, the course includes some consistent learning outcomes that can be measured (e.g., written assignments evaluated with a standard rubric).

Student performance in future courses. In most counselor preparation programs, courses are sequenced to allow development to occur based on experiences in prerequisite courses. Conducting some type of assessment at the beginning of a subsequent course based on an established benchmark allows the faculty to assess the knowledge and skill retention of students from a prior distance learning course.

Student performance on comprehensive examinations. Many programs include some type of comprehensive examination that occurs near the end of the program. Performance on this examination provides an excellent measure for comparison against both current and former students in face-to-face tracks of the program. This becomes more difficult when students are mixing and matching face-to-face and distance courses throughout the program.

Student feedback. Although not as methodically robust as other evaluation techniques, soliciting thoughtful feedback from students can provide individual faculty members and program coordinators with valuable information. For example, the following elements are reported by Conn, Roberts, and Powell (2009) as important to student satisfaction in distance learning classes: "clear course expectations, prompt response to student questions, encouragement of student participation, use of varied instructional techniques, access to the instructor, and timely feedback to students about their work" (p. 298).

External Benchmarks

External benchmarks considered by counselor preparation programs could include the following.

Student performance in field experiences. Regular feedback from clinical (on-site) supervisors provides important information to faculty members concerning all students. However, for students in distance learning programs this type of information is especially valuable because the faculty members could be less familiar with the students.

Student performance on state or national-level licensure or certification exams. Whether completing an exam to become a Licensed Professional Counselor or school counselor, student performance on these exams can provide a good point of reference when compared to both current and former students in face-to-face tracks of the program. However, like comprehensive exams, this becomes more difficult when students completed courses in a variety of learning environments.

Evaluating Student Involvement in the Learning Process

The overall purpose of student evaluation activities is to encourage students to reflect on their learning experiences. One of the authors has been teaching a research methods course via ITV for three years and has received positive feedback from students related to "forcing me to think about what I am learning." This student evaluation is accomplished through use of a two-prong approach. The first approach is student self-report and the second is peer feedback.

Three types of self-report are utilized. First, each written assignment includes a self-evaluation component that focuses on both the assignment's content and what the student learned from completing the assignment. Throughout the semester, the student will submit approximately 10 written assignments with the final assignment being a completed research proposal. Second, the final exam includes an essay item where a student reflects on (a) what he or she knew about the research process prior to the course, (b) what new knowledge and skills the student gained as a result of the course, and (c) what additional skills the student will need to be a successful researcher. Finally, the student completes an evaluation of the members of his or her learning team (this group works together all semester completing an ongoing team case study as well as providing peer feedback on all written assignments). The team evaluation provides the student an opportunity to reflect on his or her contribution to the team as well as the contributions of other team members.

Additionally, each written assignment includes a peer feedback component that focuses on the assignment's content. The student is expected to summarize the feedback that he or she received from team members on the assignment, and to submit this summary with the assignment.

FUTURE DIRECTIONS IN USING DISTANCE LEARNING IN TEACHING

Counselor education programs help develop students who can meet the needs of an ever changing society by advocating for those who do not have a voice. Through technology (e.g., Facebook, Twitter) our worldview continues to become more universal, and we now are in the process of seeing and realizing the evolving needs of a truly global society. Clearly, technology will allow institutions to provide counselor education programs to students throughout the world.

In 2000, Granello surmised that the "possibility of using artificial intelligence programs to provide case simulations . . . may seem like it is science fiction, but if history informs us we know that the counseling and computer relationship will continue to evolve and grow" (p. 2). This same type of relationship will continue to progress between distance learning and counselor preparation.

REFERENCES

Adams, A. J. (2008). Choosing an online doctorate: Five things that all counselors should know. In *VISTAS 2008*. Retrieved from http://counselingoutfitters.com/vistas/vistas 08/Adams.htm

Albrecht, A. C., & Jones, D. G. (2001). *High tech/high touch: Distance learning in counselor preparation.* Alexandria, VA: Association for Counselor Education and Supervision (ACES).

Ali, R., & Leeds, E. M. (2009). The impact of face-to-face orientation on online retention: A pilot study. *Online Journal of Distance Learning Administration, 12*(4). Retrieved from http://www.westga.edu/~distance/ojdla/winter124/ali124.html

American Association of State Colleges and Universities. (2010, November). *State outlook: Fiscal and state policy issues affecting postsecondary education.* Retrieved from http://www.congressweb.com/aascu/docfiles/StateOutlook-Nov2010.pdf

Bernard, R. M., Abrami, P. C., Borokhovski, E., Wade, C. A., Tamim, R. M., Surkes, M. A., & Bethel, E. C. (2009). A meta-analysis of three types of interaction treatments in distance education. *Review of Educational Research, 79,* 1243–1289. doi: 10.3102/0034654309333844

Chandras, K. V., & Chandras, S. V. (2010). A survey of online doctoral degrees in counseling as perceived by doctoral graduates by race and gender and recommendations for online development. In *VISTAS 2010* (Article 64). Retrieved from http://counseling outfitters.com/vistas/vistas10/Article_64.pdf

Chandras, K. V., DeLambo, D. A., & Eddy, J. P. (2005). A survey of online counseling course satisfaction/dissatisfaction of graduates by race and gender and recommendations for online course development. In *VISTAS 2005* (pp. 253–256). Retrieved from http://www.counseling.org/Resources/Library/VISTAS/vistas05/Vistas05.art 55.pdf

Conn, S. R., Roberts, R. L., & Powell, B. M. (2009). Attitudes and satisfaction with a hybrid model of counseling supervision. *Journal of Educational Technology & Society, 12*(2), 298–306.

Curtis, R. (2004). Analyzing students' conversations in chat room discussion groups. *College Teaching, 52*(4), 143–149. doi: 10.3200/CTCH.52.4.143-149

Finlay, W., Desmet, C., & Evans, L. (2004). Is it the technology or the teacher? A comparison of online and traditional English composition classes. *Journal of Educational Computing Research, 31*(2), 163-180. doi:10.2190/URJJ-HXHA-JA08-5LVL

Flowers, S. K., Vanderbush, R. E., Hastings, J. K., & West, D. (2010). Web-based multimedia vignettes in advanced community pharmacy practice experiences. *American Journal of Pharmaceutical Education, 74*(3), Article 39.

Forsyth, H., Pizzica, J., Laxton, R., & Mahony, M. J. (2010). Distance education in an era of eLearning: Challenges and opportunities for a campus-focused institution. *Higher Education Research & Development, 29*(1), 15–29. doi: 10.1080/07294360903421350

Girvan, C., & Savage, T. (2010). Identifying an appropriate pedagogy for virtual worlds: A communal constructivism case study. *Computers & Education, 55*(1), 342–349. doi: 10.1016/j.compedu.2010.01.020

Granello, P. F. (2000). *Historical context: The relationship of computer technologies and counseling* (ED446333). Greensboro, NC: ERIC Clearinghouse on Counseling and Student Services.

Gu, X., Zhang, B., Lin, X., & Song, X. (2009). Evaluating online solutions for experiential support of distance learning by teachers in China. *Journal of Computer Assisted Learning, 25*(2), 114–125. doi: 10.1111/j.1365-2729.2008.00291.x

Hawthorne, K., Prout, H., Kinnersley, P., & Houston, H. (2009). Evaluation of different delivery modes of an interactive e-learning programme for teaching cultural diversity. *Patient Education and Counseling, 74*(1), 5–11. doi: 10.1016/j.pec.2008.07.056

Kim, K., & Bonk, C. J. (2006). The future of online teaching and learning in higher education: The survey says... *EDUCAUSE Quarterly, 29*(4), 22–30.

Lei, S. A., & Gupta, R. K. (2010). College distance education courses: Evaluating benefits and costs from institutional, faculty and students' perspectives. *Education, 130*(4), 616–631.

Lou, Y., Bernard, R. M., & Abrami, P. C. (2006). Media and pedagogy in undergraduate distance education: A theory-based meta-analysis of empirical literature. *Educational Technology Research and Development, 54*(2), 141–176. doi: 10.1007/s11423-006-8252-x

Mann Layne, C., & Hohenshil, T. H. (2005). High tech counseling: Revisited. *Journal of Counseling & Development, 83*(2), 222–226.

McGinnis, M. (2010). Program profiles John Tracy Clinic/University of San Diego graduate program: A distance learning model. *Volta Review, 110*(2), 261–270.

Mirk, S. M., Burkiewicz, J. S., & Komperda, K. E. (2010). Student perception of a wiki in a pharmacy elective course, *Currents in Pharmacy Teaching and Learning, 2*(2), 72–78. doi: 10.1016/j.cptl.2010.01.002

Osborn, D. S. (2009). Wikis, podcasts and more . . . Program policy considerations with online teaching. In *VISTAS 2009* (pp. 329–336). Retrieved from http://counselingout fitters.com/vistas/vistas09/Article_29_Osborn.pdf

Parsad, B., & Lewis, L. (2008). *Distance education at degree-granting postsecondary institutions: 2006–07* (NCES 2009–044). Washington, DC: National Center for Education Statistics, Institute of Education Sciences, U.S. Department of Education.

Patrick, P. K. S. (2005). Online counseling education: Pedagogy controversies and delivery issues. 239-242. In *VISTAS 2005* (Article 52). Retrieved from http://www.counseling .org/Resources/Library/VISTAS/vistas05/Vistas05.art52.pdf

Reynolds, G. P. (2006). Techniques and tips for using computers in teaching counseling courses. In *VISTAS 2006*. Retrieved from http://counselingoutfitters.com/Reynolds. htm

Rizopoulos, L., & McCarthy, P. (2009). Using online threaded discussions: Best practices for the digital learner. *Journal of Educational Technology Systems, 37*(4), 373–383. doi:10.2190/ET.39.4.c

Snyder, T. D., & Dillow, S. A. (2011). *Digest of Education Statistics 2010* (NCES 2011-015). Washington, DC: National Center for Education Statistics, Institute of Education Sciences, U.S. Department of Education.

Staklis, S. (2010). *Web tables—Profile of undergraduate students: 2007–08* (NCES 2010-205). Washington, DC: National Center for Education Statistics, Institute of Education Sciences, U.S. Department of Education.

Summers, J. J., Waigandt, A., & Whittaker, T. A. (2005). A comparison of student achievement and satisfaction in an online versus a traditional face-to-face statistics class. *Innovative Higher Education, 29*(3), 233–250. doi: 10.1007/s10755-005-1938-x

Trepal, H., Haberstroh, S., Duffey, T., & Evans, M. (2007). Considerations and strategies for teaching online counseling skills: Establishing relationships in cyberspace. *Counselor Education & Supervision, 46*(4), 266–279.

Vismara, L. A., Young, G. S., Stahmer, A. C., Griffith, E. M., & Rogers, S. J. (2009). Dissemination of evidence-based practice: Can we train therapists from a distance? *Journal of Autism and Developmental Disorders, 39*(12), 1636–1651. doi: 10.1007/s10803-009-0796-2

Wall, J. E. (2000). *Technology-delivered assessment: Diamonds or rocks* (ED446325). Greensboro NC: ERIC Clearinghouse on Counseling and Student Services.

Wang, J., Solan, D., & Ghods, A. (2010). Distance learning success – A perspective from socio-technical systems theory. *Behaviour & Information Technology, 29*(3), 321–329. doi: 10.1080/01449290903544645

Wiecha, J., Heyden, R., Sternthal, E., & Merialdi, M. (2010). Learning in a virtual world: Experience with using Second Life for medical education. *Journal of Medical Internet Research, 12*(1), e1. doi: 10.2196/jmir.1337

CHAPTER 9

Teaching to Encourage Professional Involvement

COURTLAND C. LEE

GOEUN NA

ROXANNA N. PEBDANI

The essence of counselor education is to help students develop the competencies to be effective helping professionals. Counselor education generally consists of a series of both theoretical/conceptual and experiential learning components. Significantly, a great deal of counselor training consists of learning by doing. The literature suggests that experience based learning techniques are often used in counselor education (Froehle & Robinson, 1983; Rabinowitz, 1997). While gaining counseling skills through experiential learning is generally attended to in counselor education, employing experiential learning to teach active professional involvement has not been widely considered in the counselor education literature. The purpose of this chapter is to present pedagogical strategies for promoting the importance of active professional involvement among students. These strategies are based on a belief that active professional involvement throughout one's career is the hallmark of counseling professionalism. The chapter explores curriculum experiences and teaching practices that foster such learning among counselors in training.

The notion of learning by doing in counselor training is underscored by the Council for Accreditation of Counseling and Related Educational Programs (CACREP) Standards (2009). Whereas the Standards call for students to engage in active learning in practicum and internships, they also mandate that students have experiences in which they learn the importance and value of active involvement in the counseling profession (CACREP). Professional involvement has been an important aspect in the growth and credibility of counseling as a helping profession. Some of the best examples of this involvement are the advocacy efforts counselors engaged in throughout the country that eventually led to the enactment of counselor licensure laws in all 50 states and the District of Columbia (Shallcross, 2009). Such involvement underscores the importance of counselors moving beyond their individual offices to become actively involved in the profession. Licensure offered counselors the opportunity to provide quality human services to a broad array of citizens. Given this, it is important that students have the opportunity to learn about and engage in professional involvement activities as part of their professional training.

The rationale for including the importance of professional involvement in counselor training is that it will help students to better understand what it means to be a professional counselor. Much has been written about the professional identity of the counselor and the importance of advocating for the integrity of the profession (Collison, 2000; Smith, 2001). Understanding the nature of professional involvement, therefore, will underscore the importance of working to advance counseling as a profession (Engels & Bradley, 2001; Myers, Sweeney, & White, 2002). In addition, as students begin to comprehend the importance of advancing the profession through their own involvement, they will also come to better appreciate how their involvement in a profession helps to move it in more effective ways to help clients and promote societal well-being (Lee, 2007).

This chapter discusses the importance of promoting active professional involvement among students. It will present examples of how a counselor education program promotes learning with the assistance of professional involvement. Experiences, like those discussed in this chapter, should be considered an integral part of counselor preparation and infused throughout the counselor education curriculum.

PROMOTING THE IMPORTANCE OF ACTIVE PROFESSIONAL INVOLVEMENT

Promoting the importance of active professional involvement among students in a counselor education program should be approached in a systematic fashion. The nature of learning experiences related to active professional involvement should be seen as integral to the training curriculum. The following are guidelines for infusing these experiences throughout a counselor education program.

▶ *Include active professional involvement as a part of the program mission statement and objectives.* CACREP Standards require that counselor education programs have a comprehensive mission statement that describes the program's intent and purposes. Likewise, objectives should be developed that are directly related to program activities. Therefore, active professional involvement should be clearly delineated as a part of a program's intent and purposes as well as specified in behavioral objectives. For example, a mission statement might include wording such as *"The Counselor Education Program prepares professionals who seek leadership positions to advocate for clients and the profession of counseling."* A statement such as this makes explicit the program's intent that active professional involvement will not only advance counseling, but also promote client well-being.

Additionally, behavioral objectives such as *"develop leadership skills in counseling, supervision, consultation, and collaboration for promoting human growth and development,"* and *"develop depth and breadth in professional growth and continued lifelong learning"* provide a framework for developing the types of learning experiences related to active professional involvement that follow.

▶ *Model membership and active involvement in professional associations.* Teaching the importance of involvement in the profession must begin by counselor education faculty not only promoting such involvement, but modeling it as well. Counselor educators who demonstrate competency as active members of the profession, actively advocating for counselors and their clients, move students' understanding of professional involvement from the theoretical to the applied setting. It is difficult to promote professional involvement among students when they do not see members of their faculty displaying such a commitment to the profession. Therefore, it is mandatory that counselor educators are active members of professional associations such as the American Counseling Association (ACA), at the national and/or branch level, or one of its divisions like the Association for Counselor Education and Supervision (ACES). Significantly, CACREP requires that counselor education units have faculty who engage in activities of the counseling profession and professional organizations. This includes engagement in professional development activities, research and scholarly activities, and service and advocacy initiatives (see 2009 CACREP Standard I.W.5.a-c).

▶ *Infuse professional involvement throughout curricular experiences.* It is crucial for counselor educators to infuse the importance of professional involvement throughout the curriculum. Professional involvement issues such as leadership, service, counselor advocacy, scholarship, and public policy should be included in both didactic and practical coursework. Counselor educators are encouraged to think of creative ways to incorporate professional development activities into the curriculum. For example, in a career development class the instructor might have students conduct an interview with an ACA leader about his or her path to professional involvement. Asking questions such as: (a) What is your philosophy of leadership? (b) How do you view your leadership style? (c) What skills do you possess that have helped you as a leader? (d) Who and what influenced the development of your leadership skills and style? (e) What has been your greatest leadership challenge? (f) What has been your greatest leadership success? (g) How do you reconcile being a leader with being a professional counselor? and (h) What advice would you give emerging leaders? can give students an idea of how a career path that includes active professional involvement and leadership might unfold.

Likewise in a professional orientation class, the faculty member might create a Leader Scavenger Hunt in which, as a class assignment, students must attend a professional meeting and collect the signatures of as many leaders as possible who are in attendance. Similarly in this class, students might be required to complete an assignment in which they are required to do volunteer work in a community setting as a way to better understand the role of a counselor as an advocate and leader.

In any number of courses, students might be required to engage issues of public policy. As an example, students might be required to conduct an analysis of an educational, rehabilitation, mental health, or career development policy to better understand how this impacts upon client or student well-being. Such an analysis is important because it provides students with insight into the significance of policies to the delivery of quality counseling services. It also enables students to develop an understanding of policy at a level that allows them to become more successful advocates for their clients and for the profession.

Finally, as students are introduced to research methodology, counselor educators should attempt to emphasize the meaningfulness of research. In particular, students should be encouraged to formulate research questions within the context of broad social issues. They should also be encouraged to think about the implications of research findings for developing or modifying policies.

▶ *Promote active professional involvement.* From the initial orientation to the program to its conclusion, faculty should promote active professional involvement among students. Whereas students must join ACA or the American School Counselor Association (ASCA) in order to obtain liability insurance, it is incumbent upon faculty to ensure that student involvement does not end there. Students should be strongly encouraged to attend conferences, workshops, and other professional activities throughout the duration of their studies. Faculty members can consider ways to make active professional involvement a part of coursework and, more specifically, as assignments during the semester. For example, students might be encouraged to become student volunteers at state, regional, or national conferences. Similarly, students can be encouraged to apply to serve on ACA branch or division committees. It is anticipated that an ongoing emphasis on active participation throughout their program will result in a commitment to continue such active involvement as professionals.

In addition to promoting external professional involvement, students should understand the importance of being good department, college and university citizens. Students should therefore be encouraged to get involved in a variety of campus service activities that contribute to their counselor training. This might include serving as a student representative at counseling department meetings, serving on a graduate student committee where decisions are made about supporting student scholarship, or serving on a faculty search committee. It might also involve serving on the college or university senate or other bodies where decisions are made and policies created concerning curriculum, financial or other student-related issues. For doctoral students in particular, developing such a commitment to being a good university citizen through service activities will be an important aspect of their future advancement in academia.

▶ *Promote scholarly activity in the profession.* Professional involvement also includes making scholarly contributions to the theory and practice of counseling. In addition to advancing knowledge, students should come to understand that the generation of new knowledge should also help to promote societal well-being. It is therefore incumbent that counselor educators find ways to promote scholarly activity among students. This is especially crucial for those students involved in doctoral studies, whose career success will often be predicated on the ability to present and publish for career advancement. This should begin with the modeling of such activities on the part of faculty members, by being actively involved in scholarly writing, and by being engaged in professional presentations. Again, CACREP Standards require counselor educators to engage in research and scholarly activity (see CACREP Standards I.W.5.b). Importantly, those faculty members who are active professional presenters and authors are encouraged to invite students to collaborate with them on scholarly projects. Similarly, students should be encouraged to submit presentation proposals to professional conferences. In addition, faculty members can set an expectation that selected written coursework should be prepared in such a way that it could be submitted for publication in state or national journals as well as professional newsletters. Likewise, faculty members can help students in preparing proposals for presentations at conferences. For example, it may be a course requirement that prior to doing a class presentation, students submit a proposal for the presentation that is modeled after a conference proposal submission process.

It is important that a culture be established in the program in which faculty actively involve students in scholarly activities. This includes having students present with faculty members at conferences. It also involves faculty and students collaborating on research and writing projects. In addition, faculty can encourage scholarship in their teaching by commenting on and discussing professional literature in classes. Students can be further encouraged to thoughtfully critique professional literature as part of class assignments. Such an activity provides students with the skills to carefully analyze professional writing.

PROMOTING ACTIVE PROFESSIONAL INVOLVEMENT: A PROGRAM

Program Background

As a way to underscore the ideas that have been discussed in this chapter, aspects of a counselor education program that actively promotes professional involvement among its students is now presented. The program is CACREP-accredited and is located at a major research university in the Middle Atlantic part of the United States, training both master's and doctoral students. The program is coordinated by an internationally known leader in the field of counseling. In addition to the co-ordinator, other program faculty members have extensive records of professional involvement.

The program clearly states in its mission that it prepares counselors, at both the master's and doctoral level for leadership positions in the counseling profession. One of the program objectives is to develop leadership skills among students. This development is a part of the assessment process in many courses in the program. The faculty members use as outcome measures of leadership, active student involvement with professional organizations, student presentations at conferences, and student publications. These outcomes are discussed in more detail at the end of this chapter.

Program Curricular Experiences

The nature of leadership and the importance of professional involvement are in-fused throughout the program curriculum. With respect to professional involve-ment, membership in professional associations is required of all students. Whereas the importance of this membership for liability insurance purposes is stressed, students also learn about the importance of active involvement in professional organizations, not only for advancement of their career, but as a way to actively serve their clients and in order to advance society as well. For example, through coursework, students are introduced to professional associations, an experience which often includes attendance at professional meetings as a class requirement. Because of the program's location, students often have the opportunity to visit the national headquarters of professional counseling associations in conjunction with class assignments. For example, in learning about counselor advocacy as a way to improve the profession and to better serve clients, students may be required to visit the office of Public Policy and Legislation at the ACA headquarters to interview staff members about this topic. Students must then develop an action plan, which spells out how they will become effective advocates for the profession and for the population with which they plan to work.

The development of leadership skills is essential to coursework in the program. The nature of leadership is a critical concept that is covered in a number of class assignments. For example, through readings and reflective assignments, students are required to assess their own leadership style and ability. At the doctoral level, students are required to conduct an interview (via email, telephone, or in person) with a past President of ACA about his or her perceptions of leadership. After the interview, students must write a paper in which they reflect upon knowledge gained from the presidential interview and how that relates to their own leadership style.

These educational experiences related to leadership have influenced how students perceive the nature of professional involvement. Students are constantly encouraged by program faculty to become actively involved in the profession. As a result of this, students in the program routinely volunteer at national and state ACA conferences. They are also encouraged by the faculty to seek out other leadership positions at the state and/or national level. This has resulted in program students holding a number of important leadership positions, including serving as the Graduate Student Representative on the ACA Governing Council and being a reviewer on the national panel that selects programs for the annual ACA conference. Program students have also held important leadership positions within the state counseling association. In addition, the program has had several students selected as Leadership Fellows with Chi Sigma Iota, the international counseling honor society. As stated previously, such experiences help to instill in students the importance of active professional involvement to the promotion of their careers, counseling, and ultimately, the betterment of society as well.

Likewise, scholarly activity is actively promoted in the program curriculum. In their coursework, doctoral students learn how to prepare conference proposals and are often required to submit papers for professional presentations. A unique aspect of this is when doctoral students must do a presentation in class, they are required to submit the equivalent of a conference presentation proposal to the professor in order to have their topic approved. The professor then acts as a mock conference review panel and either "accepts" or "rejects" the students' proposals. The proposals are reviewed based on the rationale, learning objectives, educational content, target audience, area of application, presentation structure, materials, expertise, and so forth. This provides students with feedback from the professor on the strengths and weaknesses of their "proposals." The procedure allows students to develop skills that will help them prepare proposals with a high likelihood of being accepted for professional conferences. As a result of this process, program students are comfortable submitting conference proposals regularly and therefore present at the ACA conference on an annual basis.

Another example of promoting scholarly activity involves students being encouraged to publish papers that are written for class. An important extension of this is that often faculty and students collaborate on writing projects that evolve out of class discussions and activities. One such example is a collaboration that took place several years ago when doctoral students in an advanced multicultural counseling class complained about the textbook they were using. The students urged the professor to write a better book. The professor, in turn, challenged the students to write such a book. The students took up the challenge and the professor then helped the students develop a proposal for the book and then found a book publisher who accepted the proposal. The professor also helped the students secure contributors for the book. As the students developed their chapters, he provided editorial feedback on their work. The result of this collaborative project was a multicultural counseling textbook published jointly by the students and the professor.

Significantly, in recent years the program has begun to promote professional involvement on an international level. Students have been encouraged to submit proposals to present at international conferences. As a result of this, several students have had the opportunity to present scholarly work overseas. In addition, several students are involved in a leadership development program conducted by the International Association for Counselling (IAC). This program pairs students with IAC leaders in a mentor-mentee relationship in an effort to nurture future professionals for counseling leadership on a global scale. This international activity has allowed students to develop new perspectives on professional involvement in an increasingly interconnected counseling world.

EVALUATING THE USE OF PROFESSIONAL INVOLVEMENT IN TEACHING

It is anticipated that a significant portion of the learning that takes place in counselor training will be experiential in nature. The richest teaching experiences in training counselors occur when students have the opportunity to apply theory to practice. It is impossible to teach about leadership and professional involvement in counseling without having students experience these concepts firsthand. Given this, it is important that they have learning experiences that serve to introduce them to service to the profession, to clients, and to society.

In an era when performance-based outcomes form the basis of counselor training, it is important that counselor educators explore meaningful methods of assessing student learning. Within this context, the following are possible behavioral outcomes that can be used in evaluating teaching that encourages professional involvement:

- Student submits at least one manuscript for publication.
- Student is an active member of a faculty/student research team during the course of his or her graduate studies.

- Student develops and submits at least one program proposal for presentation at state, regional, national, or international counseling conferences during the course of his or her graduate studies.
- Student interviews a past President of the American Counseling Association about his or her perceptions on the concept of leadership and writes an analysis of the interview with his or her perceptions on the nature of leadership.
- Student completes a Community Leadership Assignment in which he or she is to become active in the leadership and helps to shape policy of a community advocacy agency/organization.
- Student conducts a detailed analysis of a problematic counseling or related policy of an institution and provides alternative policies for promoting client welfare.
- Student presents evidence of active involvement in ACA and its divisions as well as CSI at the national and state level by applying for and obtaining leadership and advocacy positions.
- Student presents evidence of active involvement in service at the program, department, college, or university level that advances the quality of counselor education.

In addition, as students complete ongoing assignments on the way to achieving these learning outcomes, faculty can obtain formative data about how students comprehend the importance of active professional involvement related to counseling professionalism and client and societal well-being.

CONCLUSION

Whereas it is realized that unique institutional realities may preclude many training programs from adopting all aspects of such a model for helping students learn about the nature of professional involvement, experiences of this nature should be an essential part of counselor development. Therefore, training programs must make a commitment to ensure that students have the competencies to become actively involved in the counseling profession. Every student should be seen as a potential leader and active contributor to the profession above and beyond the expected crucial role of being an excellent service provider to clients.

REFERENCES

Collison, B. (2000). The counselor's professional identity. In H. Hackney (Ed.), *Practice issues for the beginning counselor* (pp. 9–22). Boston, MA: Allyn & Bacon.

Council for Accreditation of Counseling and Related Educational Programs [CACREP]. (2009). *2009 Standards*. Alexandria, VA: Author.

Engels, D. W., & Bradley, L. J. (2001). Advocacy for the counseling profession. In D. C. Locke, J. E. Myers, & E. L. Herr (Eds.), *The handbook of counseling* (pp. 569–579). Thousand Oaks, CA: Sage.

Froehle, T. C., & Robinson, S. E. (1983). Enhancing the effects of modeling through role-play practice. *Counselor Education and Supervision, 22,* 197–206.

Lee, C. C. (Ed.). (2007). *Counseling for social justice.* Alexandria, VA: American Counseling Association.

Myers, J. E., Sweeney, T. J., & White, V. E. (2002). Advocacy for counseling and counselors: A professional imperative. *Journal of Counseling and Development, 80,* 394–402.

Rabinowitz, F. E. (1997). Teaching counseling through a semester-long role play. *Counselor Education and Supervision, 36,* 216–224.

Shallcross, L. (2009). Counseling profession reaches the big 5-0. *Counseling Today.* Retrieved from http://ct.counseling.org/?s=big+5-0

Smith, H. (2001). Professional identity for counselors. In D. C. Locke, J. E. Myers, & E. L. Herr (Eds.), *The handbook of counseling* (pp. 569–579). Thousand Oaks, CA: Sage.

Reflecting on Student-Teacher Relationships Within Counselor Education

JANINE M. BERNARD

MELISSA LUKE

There may be instructors who diminish the importance of relationship with students, but we doubt that many of them are counselor educators. As members of the counseling profession, relationship is endemic to what we do. Furthermore, the courses we teach often revolve around, or are related to, topics that are interpersonal in nature. This symbiosis between course content, profession, and student-teacher relationships makes the latter somewhat of an "of course." Yet, although relationship is highly valued, and even *because* it is highly valued, it is incumbent upon counselor education faculty to manage relationships appropriately within the classroom.

To date, the emphasis on student-faculty relationships within the counselor education literature has been on the dangers of multiple relationships, including sexual liaisons (e.g., Kolbert, Morgan, & Brendel, 2002; Kress & Dixon, 2007). Certainly, our profession is not alone in its concerns about boundary violations. In addition to exploitative boundary crossings, there is concern about nonsexual, yet inappropriate, student-faculty relationships as well. For example, with the explosion of social networking, the issue of having faculty as "friends" on *Facebook* has emerged (Browder & Burke, 2009). Some faculty may view this as a modern day strategy for getting to know their students. But Browder and Burke identified the problem when they reported one graduate student saying, "With the power of instructors, how can I just say no when they request me to be their 'friend'?" (p. 5).

Beyond boundary issues, the clinical supervision literature within the mental health professions has been replete with contributions that address a variety of relationship issues and dimensions (Bernard, 2005); however, counselor education pedagogical literature has been mostly silent on the issue. Fortunately, other disciplines, including teacher education and social psychology, provide research and insight about the centrality of the student-faculty relationship for student learning.

"The nature of teacher-student relationships is consequential to a successful outcome" (Henderson & Nash, 2007, p. 17). This is a consensus of teacher education in general, both when students are children and when they are adults. Research supports that faculty relationships and mutual respect are important to students (e.g., Magolda, 1987) and that a faculty member's ability to communicate empathy and concern for students in the classroom is positively correlated with students' perception of teaching effectiveness (Keiter, 2000). Perhaps more importantly, teacher-student relationships have also been found to correlate with student motivation toward learning (Christensen & Menzel, 1998; Wilson & Taylor, 2001).

The manner in which relationship issues are discussed by education scholars is familiar territory for counselors. McKeachie and Svinicki (2006) included among their "teaching tips" a number of suggestions that would be reframed in counselor education as "handling transference and countertransference" in the classroom. For example, McKeachie and Svinicki raised the issue of having students in classes who exhibit problem behaviors. They suggested: "Remember that your problem students are human beings who have problems and need your empathy and help . . . no matter how much you would like to strangle them" (p. 189).

Hammer (2005) applied social psychology research to teaching and identified three categories relevant to student-faculty relationships. The first of these is *attributional style*, that is, the patterns faculty display in explaining student behavior. Broadly, these styles are either student-promoting and relationship-enhancing (e.g., "Something must have happened to make Joan late for class."), or student-distancing and distress-maintaining (e.g., "Joan mustn't be very committed to this class if she arrived late."). Though it is certainly the case that students differ in their commitment to learning, Hammer's point was that the research supports persons having general attributional styles and that these affect relationships, including the relationships between teachers and students. Bain (2004) echoed this point by noting that the best teachers are able to communicate their caring for students both as people and as learners.

Hammer's (2005) second category is *ego depletion*. Here, she pointed to the research on the energy that teaching requires, that is, delivering material successfully, keeping a group of students engaged in learning, while simultaneously engaging in behavioral restraint and emotional control. Her review of ego depletion research led her to conclude that as taxing as teaching is, and as demanding as other aspects of faculty life are, faculty must protect their time for rejuvenation and reflection "necessary to produce the high quality scholarship and teaching we were hired to do" (p. 7).

Hammer's (2005) last area of discussion is *relationship types or styles*. In this section she discussed differences within the classroom that might affect learning such as learning styles, adult attachment styles, and other personality variables that have been found to correlate with student perceptions of "master" teaching. Two of these variables are being caring and being personable (Buskist, Sikorski, Bucklet, & Saville, 2002). Hammer also discussed how introversion and extroversion as faculty traits must be addressed in preparing future faculty members for the role of teacher.

Henderson and Nash (2007) included a two page self-assessment tool in their college teaching text that is devoted entirely to relationship issues. Among the many teacher behaviors the assessment targets are the following: general communication skills; observing students in one's classes, including noting when there is tension in the class, when someone is left out, and who talks to whom; morale-building skills that include praise, showing interest in students, and upholding the rights of individual students when they are experiencing group pressure to think differently; emotional expressiveness with students; ability to face, accept, and address emotional situations; and a category entitled social relationships which addresses undesirable instructor behaviors such as competing with students, dominating students, as well as desirable behaviors such as learning to trust students and keeping one's ego in check (pp. 210–212).

Laiken (2006) advocated for education that is transformative and used Cranton's (1994) definition of transformative as "the development of revised assumptions, premises, ways of interpreting experience, or perspectives on the world by means of critical self-reflection" (Cranton, 1994, p. xii). This definition describes much of the learning process in counselor education. Furthermore, we believe that the relationship between educator and student is where much of the transformative power is situated. Based on social role modeling alone (Bandura, 1977), we know that a teacher with the power to be a reinforcing and modeling agent can make learning more efficient and effective. If this is the case in the teaching of engineering or architecture, how much more so for counseling, where interpreting experience and critical self-reflection are part and parcel of professional practice?

As we stated at the beginning of this section, relationship is central to our profession. Though this makes relationship building a strong suit, there is a corollary that counselor educators must consider. Our student body is not "average" or random by any stretch of the imagination. In many cases, their attraction to the helping profession of counseling is more complicated than they may realize and they bring these complexities into their programs of study (Celenza, 1998). Some incoming master's students have only begun to establish boundaries around their very sensitive feelings; others chose counseling through prolonged experience of enmeshment with their families of origin; still others are wounded and vulnerable and seeking to understand, if not heal, themselves (Jackson & Nuttall, 2001). These students sit in our classes along with the securely attached, the family heroes, and a host of "good girls" (reflecting the gender bias of our profession), as well as students who are seeking student-teacher relationships over cultural and sometimes linguistic divides. Where does one begin?

In this chapter we share insights gleaned from our teaching experience, from the teaching literature, and from the clinical supervision literature as it applies to classroom teaching. We make reference to navigating relationships in courses that are more content driven (e.g., teaching Assessment) versus those courses that rely more on process (e.g., teaching Group Process). We also address differences in classroom relationships between beginning students and more advanced students.

ENHANCING RELATIONSHIP IN THE CLASSROOM

Building relationships with students is not dissimilar to building rapport with clients; it is not done in a vacuum. We could argue that the topic of student-teacher relationship could interface with all other chapters in this text. What follows is our list of suggestions for teaching in a manner that is relationship enhancing.

▶ *Be appropriately welcoming as a new course begins.* We hope that students walk into our classes eager to learn and open to the experience that will follow. It is important that we do nothing to dampen that enthusiasm. Assuming that we have a well-conceived course and a clear syllabus, students will be looking for cues about our fairness, our approachability, our responses to them as individuals, and so on. It's important to balance these needs with our need to cover the "front matter" of the course. Taking time to build a sense of community within a course is more effective with greater payoff to the long-term atmosphere within the course than grinding out each requirement in great detail.

We would argue that learning student names is a critical welcoming gesture. This is not a problem when a class is small; it is a bit more of a challenge when a class gets large. Still, taking time to learn names and to let our students learn each other's names seems foundational for relationship-building in a counseling course. One exercise we have used is to ask students to tell us how they understand their names were chosen for them, thus providing some context that can help in learning names as well as allowing students to learn a little about each other. Finally, there are always name tags with first names written in bold letters as an aid until names are learned.

▶ **Communicate respect and concern.** Respect is communicated in many ways in the classroom. As noted by Henderson and Nash (2007), keeping eye contact when a student is speaking is perceived by students favorably. Listening to students and attempting to find the kernel of their answer that can be embellished rather than the part of the answer that one takes exception with, enhances respect. Keeping to a schedule, letting students out on time, not playing smoke and mirrors regarding assignments, all build the student-faculty relationship. Said differently, faculty must own their authority but not revel in their power by skipping breaks as they wax eloquent, or adding another requirement to a course midway through the semester because it just occurred to them.

Concern is a level beyond respect, but has nonetheless been purported to be an important dimension in student-faculty relationships (Meyers, 2009). Around midterms, we check in with students to see how they are handling the stress. We may not be able to do much about it other than demonstrate our concern and spend a little of class time talking about ways they can cope with what is on their plate. Occasionally, we *can* do something more. During a recent semester, we realized that we were giving midterms on the same night, back-to-back. Students were clearly stressing about this, as it was their first semester of graduate work. One of us, therefore, gave an early exam on slightly less material and followed it up a couple of weeks later with a quiz to cover the additional material. Students were relieved and grateful. The benefits of this gesture were capitalized on later when "concern" came in the form of feedback on final papers. By then, most students and the instructor had a fairly strong classroom working alliance; thus, they were more open to challenging feedback.

▶ **Maintain appropriate boundaries.** Students are understandably confused in some of our classes regarding ground rules and boundaries, especially those students who have complicated backgrounds around attachment. Tasks such as completing a personal reflection journal or practicing immediacy in a skills class can activate them in ways that can lead to problematic behaviors. Critiquing a journal entry based on course objectives may be viewed as a personal affront that is followed by the student responding in a highly defensive, even inappropriate, manner. In these cases, it is the instructor who must model the parameters of the student-teacher boundary. Our formula for dealing with such instances is to: acknowledge in a non-defensive manner the rupture that has occurred in the relationship based on evaluative comments attached to personal material; communicate in as sensitive a manner as possible that the contract with the student is instructional, not therapeutic; offer to explain again, if needed, the rationale for the feedback given; and resist allowing the incident to become a focus of this particular student-teacher relationship.

Though we believe the above is solid advice for all courses, we appreciate the difference between "lecture" courses and courses such as group counseling and skills development that have a more experiential quality. In these latter learning contexts, the working alliance between the student and the instructor is more central to learning than it is in larger, more content-driven courses. As relationship is one of the three prongs of the working alliance (Bordin, 1979), the instructor must be more vigilant about modeling relationship skills such as immediacy; the instructor must also be willing to address ruptures, typically outside of class in a one-on-one context.

Instruction within counselor education also requires some boundary discipline in light of supportive relationships outside of the classroom. A prime example is the involvement with students if the program has a Chi Sigma Iota chapter. A recent study (Luke & Goodrich, 2010) found that faculty involvement in CSI activities had an overall positive impact on students' professional identity development. Moving from this mentoring role back to an instructional role is a skill that counselor educators must develop. Before we leave the topic of boundaries, we want to reinforce admonitions in the literature regarding social networking (Browder & Burke, 2009). Instructors are quite comfortable (when not inundated) with emails from students and many instructors use *Blackboard* to encourage discussion among students between classes. We would, however, draw a line between these uses of technology and social networks such as *Facebook*. Being a "friend" of a student is fraught with potential problems. In our opinion, there is no good rationale for using social networking to enhance student-faculty relationships.

▶ *Remember what we have learned from clinical supervision.* The supervision literature appropriately reflects the centrality of relationship dynamics to the supervision process (Bernard, 2005). Although classroom teaching is a very different enterprise, counselor educators are enhanced as instructors by their knowledge of supervision. The supervision literature addresses ruptures in the relationship following evaluation (Burke, Goodyear, & Guzzardo, 1998); instructors have certainly felt ruptures on occasion when graded papers have been returned to students. Similarly, the kinds of micro-aggressions that are discussed in the supervision literature (Constantine & Sue, 2007) can occur in the classroom as well if instructors are insensitive or inappropriate regarding a student's cultural background, including that of our international students. Attachment issues as described in the supervision literature (Pistole & Watkins, 1995; Renfro-Michel, 2006) can play out in the classroom as well. In short, the extensive writing and research that has occurred around relationship issues in supervision make us better able to interpret some of our students' reactions in the classroom. Our responses to these will be different from the supervisors most of the time as the level of intensity is different between student-instructor and supervisee-supervisor. Still, the knowledge our supervision training affords us is an important advantage when relationship issues arise in our courses.

▶ *Facilitate a community of practice.* The student-faculty relationship frequently begins, and is either strengthened or diminished, within the larger classroom context. As such, in addition to considering their relationships with individual students, faculty need to attend to the relationship they foster with the class as a whole, as well as how they facilitate relationships between students (Anderson & Carta-Falsa, 2002). Wenger (1998) conceived of three necessary elements within a community of practice, including, (a) a shared domain of common interest; (b) a community wherein members engage in shared activities, help each other, and exchange information to learn; and (c) a shared repertoire of resources and practices. Accordingly, much like a group leader approaches group work, faculty can structure curricular experiences to build group cohesion and common goals, encourage active engagement and meaningful interactions across class members, as well as co-construct a communal product.

▶ *Be careful not to privilege one counseling track.* One criticism we have heard from students is that some instructors seem to be teaching only to school counseling students or only to mental health counseling students, and so on. This often happens because the faculty member identifies herself or himself with a particular track and has a plethora of examples from that track to underscore the point being made. This privileging of one group of students can stimulate a host of in-group/out-group relationship issues that are unintended by the instructor. Similarly, instructors need to be careful not to privilege cultural groups, students whom they have taught in previous courses, and so on.

▶ *Know your interpersonal strengths and weaknesses and address these in your teaching.* Bain (2004) found that although faculty personality itself did not appear to determine good teaching, a core pattern of interpersonal "beliefs, attitudes, conceptions, and perceptions" (p. 137) did. In discussing the interpersonal strengths of exemplary teachers, Bain highlighted the particular importance of relational openness, an ability to communicate trust in students, and the creation of an interactive atmosphere. Although not investigated within a counselor education context, we cannot help but wonder about the potential for additional impact on student skill development when faculty members model these behaviors within the classroom, as well as when they do not.

As instructors, we can address some of our own tendencies and invite students to call us on behavior that is distracting. For example, an instructor may want to be playful with her students only to learn later that some students felt put off by her humor. Another instructor is aware that he can be blunt at times and that this makes it difficult for students to hear his feedback. Whether the "problem" is the instructor's style or the student's sensitivity, it is good classroom practice to address the obvious that teaching is fundamentally an interpersonal enterprise. Therefore, addressing interpersonal behaviors within a classroom context in a proactive manner is absolutely appropriate and can provide invaluable modeling of how to process stylistic differences. Related, instructors need to be prepared to address tension within the class. Tension can be caused, for example, by careless comments made by either an instructor or a student. It can be very important that a respectful discussion ensue to deconstruct the class atmosphere. These attempts are most often welcomed by students and give counselor educators added opportunities to model attending to process, a key counseling skill.

▶ *Adjust relationship as appropriate throughout a student's graduate training.* Most counselor educators subscribe to at least some of the tenets that focus on counselor development (e.g., Stoltenberg & McNeill, 2010). As students develop, some aspects of the student-faculty relationship can change in ways that affirm the students' development. During a previous semester, one of us was teaching a master's internship class and another course that is taken earlier in the curriculum. The latter was causing some challenges, as the group was reticent to engage in discussion. So, I took the opportunity to consult with my internship group. I shared my struggle and asked them to reflect on their experience in the same course, to speculate what might be going on, and to share some of their thoughts. The consultation was moderately helpful to me with the challenging course; however, I believe it enhanced the atmosphere in the internship class exponentially. This incident clearly moved my relationship with my internship students to a new level. However, it should also be noted that students in internship have had more time in graduate training; therefore, they have had more time to reflect on their own professional development. This professional maturity relative to students in the beginning of their graduate programs allows for different student-faculty interactions. Similar to what is reflected in individual and family developmental models, student-faculty relationships across stages of a graduate program can and should be "stage appropriate."

Many counselor educators are familiar with adjusting relationships if they work with both doctoral students and master's students. The teacher-student boundary can be more permeable when working with doctoral students, yet needs to be there nonetheless. Additionally, faculty can help doctoral students negotiate their own boundaries with master's students, as doctoral students often are teaching assistants in master's courses or serve as individual supervisors to master's students.

CASE EXAMPLE

Illustrating how the student-faculty relationship can manifest within the counselor education classroom, we share a simulated case example drawn from our teaching experiences. As a 10 year counselor educator, Dr. T has a strong record of positive student evaluations and is frequently sought by students for consultation and advice. She was, therefore, eager to teach a small enrollment course entitled "Counselor in the Schools," particularly because she knew all 12 of the students enrolled. As such, on the first night of class, Dr. T moved from syllabus review to an activity requiring students' intra and interpersonal openness. She was surprised when students seemed reluctant to participate. Throughout the next few classes, students were actively engaged during didactic instruction, but participation dissipated as soon as they were expected to interact with one another. When Dr. T challenged the group, students voiced situational attributions, saying that they were uncertain of her expectations or of the discussion topic, were feeling tired, or had already contributed and didn't want to monopolize the discussion. One student, Ryan, responded to Dr. T's confrontation with irritation. Dr. T was especially perplexed by Ryan's behavior, as she could not identify the root of the interpersonal tension between them. Despite pedagogical attempts to increase student participation in class, the pattern continued. That is, until Dr. T attended a conference session in which presenters conducted an experiential demonstration. Dr. T observed what she hypothesized were unevenly developed relationships across the presenters that appeared to influence the delivery of the presentation. This led to an epiphany about her class.

When class met next, Dr. T shared her conference experience, as well as her hypothesis that she had inadvertently contributed to something similar happening "in this room." Dr. T acknowledged how she had perhaps confused her teacher-student relationships with individual students in the class as being the same as class members' relationships with one another. Dr. T's revelation released a flood gate of disclosure from students in which they confirmed that, although they had ongoing relationships with Dr. T outside of the class, they did not know one another well and felt both insecure and irritated as a result of what Dr. T was asking. Students expressed frustration and disappointment in Dr. T for not being attuned to their experience, thus adding to their resistance. Dr. T was able to acknowledge students' phenomenological experience, as well as acknowledge how her insensitivity to them as a group impacted the teacher-student relationships. As a result, the class as a whole appeared to shift to a new level of development, wherein students explored how their attempts to protect themselves interfered with their engagement, with the material, and with one another. Moreover, students were able to identify a need for more class time devoted to their here and now experiences with Dr. T as well as with one another, something they had resisted until this point. In short, Dr. T's intervention changed the class dynamics and allowed her to achieve her initial goals of getting students to share more freely with each other and with her.

In summary, although she did not know it at the time, Dr. T was successfully enhancing relationships in the counselor education classroom using a number of the means outlined in this chapter: attending to boundaries, attending to what we know from clinical supervision related to relationship rupture, facilitating a community of practice, as well as adjusting the relationship based on development and context. End of semester course evaluations identified the attention to relationships as one of the most significant learning experiences in class. One student commented, "Dr. T *showed* us how important the relationship is within a counseling context."

EVALUATION

Despite longstanding recognition of the importance of formal evaluation in measuring and monitoring higher educational outcomes (Education Commission of the States, 1995), there has been little systematic focus on how or where the student-faculty relationship fits into the overall equation (Pascarella, 2001). Nonetheless, we argue that exemplary teaching across all levels of education has always incorporated a variety of means to assess the quality of teacher-student relationship. For example, Bain (2004) identified a number of strategies exemplary college teachers undertook to evaluate and then refine their work with students, including the assessment of teacher-student rapport. We believe that both the practice and processes of collecting feedback from students have the potential to positively influence the student-faculty relationship. That said, although the therapeutic alliance and working relationship are constructs commonly examined in our field, we were unable to locate any standardized measure that assessed the parallel between faculty and student. We believe this is an area worthy of future exploration.

What follows are various procedures that can be engaged to solicit feedback on the student-faculty relationship. Although any of the ideas can be used in isolation, as with all data collection, use of multiple procedures strengthens the ultimate knowledge claim. As such, we encourage counselor education faculty to intentionally combine two or more of the identified procedures to get a more comprehensive understanding of their student-faculty relationships.

▶ *Utilize summative feedback.* Although most higher education institutions require course evaluations, these do not always include student perception of the student-faculty relationship. If not already doing so, counselor education faculty should directly inquire about this. A quantitative Likert-type scale can be used, enabling students to respond with how much they endorse statements like, "Instructor was responsive to student questions," or "Professor developed a positive classroom environment." Qualitative assessment can be accomplished with open ended prompts such as "Discuss the instructor's interpersonal strengths and weaknesses" or "How would you describe this instructor and the atmosphere within his or her class to a peer?"

▶ *Collect formative feedback.* While summative, semester-end assessment is useful, it can be equally instructive to gather such information over the course of the semester. As such, we encourage faculty to build in formative opportunities for students to comment upon the student-faculty relationship using prompts similar to those used for summative feedback.

▶ *Conduct a time/task analysis.* Much like a food or finance diary that records the type and amount of related activity, a time/task analysis can document the type and frequency of activities related to the student-faculty relationship in a given period (e.g., day, week). Although this analysis will not provide information about the effects of each activity, it can provide detailed information about one's efforts related to establishing, developing, maintaining, and repairing the student-faculty relationship.

▶ *Examine student-faculty interaction.* Faculty can track in-class student-faculty interactions as potential reflection of the quality of the student-faculty relationship. Further, in situations when instructors are aware of a potential challenge to the student-faculty relationship, they should resist any desire to limit contact and instead be more intentional with regard to increasing helpful interactions with the identified student, tracking the results.

We surmise that student contact with faculty out of class may also reflect their perception of the strength of the student-faculty relationship. For example, the frequency and content of student-initiated email can easily be tracked and analyzed for patterns, as might the use of office hours or requests for meetings. Such student contact could be examined collectively or parceled out by type of contact (e.g., emails, meetings during office hours). Accordingly, we have anecdotally observed a positive relationship between those students requesting letters of reference and our perceptions of a positive student-faculty relationship. Although we are not suggesting that student-faculty interaction is a perfect correlate for the student-faculty relationship, in light of Bain's (2004) review of the related literature, we believe that in many instances it can serve as a meaningful proxy.

▶ *Observation.* Formal observation can be accomplished in different ways. Faculty may review a video-recorded class or gain feedback from a trusted colleague following a class observation. In either case, the direct observation can provide important information about the student-faculty relationship, enabling an added level of specificity in feedback. When we have employed these strategies, we found it particularly helpful to identify not only how various behaviors functioned, but to also explore what we were thinking and feeling in those moments, as well as to generate ideas for additional ways of responding to a variety of classroom teacher-student interactions.

CONCLUSION

Excellent teaching requires the integration of several skill sets. One of these, the ability to create positive student-teacher relationships, has a variety of positive documented outcomes for students that range from increasing motivation for learning to enhancing professional development (Christensen & Menzel, 1998; Luke & Goodrich, 2010; Wilson & Taylor, 2001). Many of the skills endemic to counseling are used to enhance student-teacher relationships. Furthermore, as in other counseling roles, the maintenance of appropriate boundaries, modeling appropriate behavior, challenging without rancor, and careful use of self-disclosure are highly relevant to the goal of creating and maintaining a positive learning environment. As Bain (2004) noted, the best instructors use their power to communicate their investment in their students. When our students know that we care about their learning and their success in our courses, they tend to care as well!

REFERENCES

Anderson, L. E., & Carta-Falsa, J. (2002). Factors that make faculty and student relationships effective. *College Teaching, 50*(4), 134–138. doi: 10.1080/87567550209595894

Bain, K. (2004). *What the best college teachers do.* Cambridge, MA: Harvard University Press.

Bandura, A. (1977). *Social learning theory.* Englewood Cliffs, NJ: Prentice-Hall.

Bernard, J. M. (2005). Tracing the development of clinical supervision. *The Clinical Supervisor, 24*, 3–21.

Bordin, E. S. (1979). The generalizability of the psychodynamic concept of the working alliance. *Psychotherapy: Theory, Research, and Practice, 16*, 252–260.

Browder, A. J., & Burke, C. (2009, August). *We can't be friends? Student-faculty multiple relationships on Facebook.* American Psychological Association Convention. Toronto, ON.

Burke, W., Goodyear, R. K., & Guzzardo, C. (1998). A multiple-case study of weakening and repairs in supervisory alliances. *American Journal of Psychotherapy, 52*, 450–462.

Buskist, W., Sikorski, J., Bucklet, T., & Saville, B. K. (2002). Elements of master teaching. In S. F. Davis & W. Buskist (Eds.), *The teaching of psychology: Essays in honor of Wilbert J. McKeachie and Charles L. Brewer* (pp. 27–39). Mahwah, NJ: Erlbaum.

Celenza, A. (1998). Precursors to therapist sexual misconduct: Preliminary findings. *Psychoanalytic Psychology, 15*, 378–395.

Christensen, L. J., & Menzel, K. E. (1998). The linear relationship between student reports of teacher immediacy behaviors and perceptions of state motivation, and of cognitive, affective, and behavioral learning. *Communication Education, 47*, 82–90.

Constantine, M. G., & Sue, D. W. (2007). Perceptions of racial microaggressions among Black supervisees in cross-racial dyads. *Journal of Counseling Psychology, 54*, 142–153.

Cranton, P. (1994). *Understanding and promoting transformative learning.* San Francisco, CA: Jossey-Bass.

Education Commission of the States. (1995). *Making quality count in undergraduate education: A report for the ECS Chairman's 'Quality Counts' agenda in higher education.* Education Commission of the States.

Hammer, E. Y. (2005). From the laboratory to the classroom and back: The science of interpersonal relationships informs teaching. *Journal of Social and Clinical Psychology, 24,* 3-10.

Henderson, G., & Nash, S. S. (2007). *Excellence in college teaching and learning.* Springfield, IL: Charles C. Thomas.

Jackson, H., & Nuttall, R. L. (2001). A relationship between childhood sexual abuse and professional sexual misconduct. *Professional Psychology: Research and Practice, 32,* 200–204.

Keiter, M. H. (2000). An analysis of the nature of the relationship between faculty social interest and students' perceptions of teaching effectiveness. *Dissertation Abstracts International, 60*(08A), 2827.

Kolbert, J. B., Morgan, B., & Brendel, J. M. (2002). Faculty and student perceptions of dual relationships within counselor education: A qualitative analysis. *Counselor Education and Supervision, 41,* 193–206.

Kress, V. E., & Dixon, A. (2007). Consensual student-faculty sexual relationships in counselor education: Recommendations for counselor educators' decision making. *Counselor Education and Supervision, 47,* 110–122.

Laiken, M. (2006). Authentic graduate education for personal and workplace transformation. In A. Herrington & J. Herrington (Eds.), *Authentic learning environments in higher education* (pp. 15–33). Hershey, PA: Information Science Publishing.

Luke, M., & Goodrich, K. M. (2010). Chi Sigma Iota chapter leadership and professional identity development in early career counselors. *Counselor Education and Supervision, 50,* 56–78.

Magolda, M. B. (1987). The affective dimension of learning: Student-faculty relationships that enhance intellectual development. *College Student Development, 21,* 46–58.

McKeachie, W. J., & Svinicki, M. (2006). *McKeachie's teaching tips: Strategies, research, and theory for college and university teachers, 12th edition.* Boston, MA: Houghton Mifflin.

Meyers, S. A. (2009). Do your students care whether you care about them? *College Teaching, 57*(4), 205–210.

Pascarella, E. (2001). Using student self-reported gains to estimate college impact: A cautionary tale. *Journal of College Student Development, 42*(5), 488–492.

Pistole, M. C., & Watkins, C. E. (1995). Attachment theory, counseling process, and supervision. *The Counseling Psychologist, 23,* 457–478.

Renfro-Michel, E. L. (2006). *The relationship between counseling supervisee attachment orientation and supervision working alliance.* Unpublished doctoral dissertation, Mississippi State University. Retrieved from http://sun.library.msstate.edu/ETD-db/theses/available/etd-04-102006-111609/

Stoltenberg, C. D., & McNeill, B. W. (2010). *IDM: An integrated developmental model for supervising counselors and therapists* (3rd ed.). New York, NY: Routledge.

Wenger, E. (1998). *Communities of practice: Learning, meaning, and identity.* Cambridge, UK: Cambridge University Press.

Wilson, J. H., & Taylor, K. W. (2001). Professor immediacy as behaviors associated with liking students. *Teaching of Psychology, 28,* 136–138. http://www.rbs2.com/fiduciary.pdf

CHAPTER 11

Using Solution Focused Evaluation to Engage Students in the Learning Process

LORETTA J. BRADLEY

JANET FROESCHLE

GERALD PARR

BRET HENDRICKS

You will come to a place where the streets are not marked.
Some windows are lighted. But mostly they are darked. A
place you could sprain both your elbow and chin! Do you dare
to stay out? Do you dare to go in? How much can you lose?
How much can you win?

—Dr. Seuss

The above quote is from a book, *Oh, the Places You'll Go!* (Seuss, 1990). While the quote was first given at a graduation speech and later expanded into a book, it was originally written to help the graduates consider the future. Despite its focus on graduates, the quote can equally apply to teacher and student evaluations.

Since evaluation has been described as an essential component of teaching (Bain, 2004; Forsyth, 2004; Palmer, 1997a, 1997b), the teacher might ponder, "How much can I produce a win-win situation from the evaluation?" The teacher might also inquire, "Do I dare stay out (remain inactive) or do I dare go in (become more active in the evaluation process)?" Answers to these questions often depend on whether the teacher perceives evaluation as friend or foe (hooks, 1994; Nylund & Tilsen, 2006; Palmer, 1997b) as active or inactive (Pare & Tarragona, 2006; Roth, 1997).

During the settling of the West, the stagecoach was a major means of transportation. In purchasing a seat on the stagecoach, the passenger selected from three different tickets: first-class, second-class, and third-class. With a first-class ticket, the passenger was provided with a permanent seat on the stagecoach until the destination was reached. Even if a wheel fell from the stagecoach or the stagecoach was stuck in the mud, the passenger could remain in his or her seat because the purchased ticket was first-class.

A second-class ticket meant the passenger had a seat unless a problem occurred. If a problem occurred (e.g., wheel fell off, seat broke), the passenger must exit the stagecoach and wait until the problem was solved. The passenger did not have to be involved in solving the problem. Instead, the passenger could wait beside the road until the problem was solved. After the problem was fixed, the passenger returned to his or her seat. In contrast, a third-class ticket meant the passenger had a seat only if a problem did not occur. If a problem occurred, the passenger must be active in solving this problem. This could involve the passenger helping to remove and repair a wheel or pushing the stagecoach out of a ditch. After the problem was solved, the passenger could again be seated.

Similar to having the stagecoach in "good working condition" is the expectation that classroom teaching is in "good working condition." One means to know if teaching is successful is in the information given to and obtained from students during the evaluation process (Cohen, 2005; Pietrzak, Duncan, & Korcuska, 2008; Wong & Fitzsimmons, 2008). As a teacher in the classroom, which ticket will you purchase? It is the hope of the authors that as a teacher, you will purchase a third-class ticket for it is the third-class ticket that will insist that the teacher be active. It is built on the premise that a good teacher should not only present cognitive information but, in addition, should teach via a process that engages the student in both learning and evaluation. Given that good teaching is dependent on honest evaluation, this chapter is written not only to illustrate the importance of evaluations but, in addition, to focus on how to actively involve the student in the evaluation process.

Counselor educators share a common and primary goal of providing instruction and incorporating assessments that meet the needs of students and society. According to the American Counseling Association Code of Ethics (2005), counselor educators should conduct counselor education and training programs in an ethical manner and serve as role models for professional behavior (ACA, 2005, F.6.a). Furthermore, counselor educators must be fair, accurate, and honest in their assessment of counselors in training (ACA, 2005, Sec. F). Thus, counselor educators have an obligation to utilize meaningful methods of student evaluation so learning experiences are maximized and professional behaviors instilled.

With this in mind, counselor educators must use assessments as foundations upon which they build increasingly effective teaching strategies and, at the same time, provide documented evidence as to the effectiveness of their teaching.

Use of specific assessment instruments (e.g., tests, examinations, essays) is important when evaluating student performance and documenting teaching effectiveness (Bain, 2004; Forsyth, 2004). At the same time, use of these instruments may not be enough to engage students in the learning process. In fact, some of the most important factors regarding success and learning depend on the establishment of relationships with professors, mentors, and peers (Tinto, 1987). Engaging students in assessment and learning, therefore, depends on the counselor educator's ability to connect with students on personal and intellectual levels. Paris and Cross (1983) believed student success is also dependent on instilling skills and creating a desire to learn. As a result, this chapter focuses on an assessment method and techniques aimed at developing relationships with students while also engaging and, therefore, motivating students to increase performance levels. Integrating the premises and techniques found within Solution Focused Brief Therapy with counseling curriculum offers a unique method for engaging, evaluating, responding to, and promoting the welfare of students (Cade, 2007). Specific strategies for using this method are described in more detail later in the chapter.

EVALUATION AND WELFARE OF THE STUDENT

Client welfare is a primary responsibility for professional counselors, including counselor educators. Thus, evaluation of student progress is a profound element in the learning and growth process; namely, that students are to be viewed with the same professionalism and care that professional counselors exhibit with clients. Therefore, just as in the counseling relationship, positive rapport, active engagement, and informed communication are integral to the counselor training experience. These conditions cannot be ignored in the classroom setting.

Counselor educators have an ethical duty to provide effective teaching. Although it is an accepted fact that counselor educators are expected to be effective professors, it is difficult to ascertain the definition of "effective." In spite of the collegiality that exists in counselor education, professors most often work alone in classrooms, thereby, creating a vulnerability to use ineffective teaching strategies, which do not meet the needs of students. Furthermore, professors may be unaware they are using ineffective strategies in the classroom. For example, when assessing their own teaching performance, professors most often report personal effectiveness in the classroom (Davis, Chang, & McGlothlin, 2005; Skoog & Johnson, 1998). Additionally, counselor education students report a disconnect between course relevance, course requirements, and professional goals (Davis et al., 2005). Active engagement in evaluation is one method whereby students can become important players in their own learning, understand the relevance of course requirements and content, and create an environment where learning occurs.

SELF-ASSESSMENT AND ACTIVE ENGAGEMENT IN EVALUATION

Self-assessment places students at the center of their own learning and requires active engagement. Further, self-assessment enables students to create relevance and additional coherence in their learning experiences as well as to critically examine and understand their own learning. Consequently, students take charge of personal improvement while utilizing Bloom's higher levels of thinking via the evaluation process (Forsyth, 2004).

Multidimensional evaluation methods are preferable over uni-dimensional evaluation in higher education courses and elicit student self-assessment and engagement. Bain (2004) contended that student performance should be assessed using a 5-point scale instead of the usual 4-point Likert scale. The 5-point scale, according to Bain, provides a greater degree of definition and clarity thereby allowing a deeper and more meaningful level of evaluation. In the following sections of this chapter, we examine the application of Solution Focused Brief Therapy, which uses a 10-point scale of measurement (an even more thorough and in-depth assessment measure) as well as additional techniques to more effectively engage students in the learning process.

RATIONALE FOR STRENGTHS BASED EVALUATION

Counseling is a profession grounded in strengths-based interventions (Corey, 2005). In order to establish a positive learning environment focusing on student growth, counselor educators must first create a positive learning environment. Just as counselors provide a relationship in which clients may safely and freely engage in self-examination, counselor educators, according to the ACA Code of Ethics (2005), must establish a relationship with students in which they are encouraged to engage in self growth and self disclosure as part of the training process (ACA, 2005, F.7.a.). Many counseling theories provide information on ways to do this; however, in this chapter, we focus on Solution Focused Brief Therapy constructs.

RATIONALE FOR THE INCLUSION OF SOLUTION FOCUSED TECHNIQUES

Research offers credence regarding the efficacy of Solution Focused Brief Therapy with regard to client change and growth in the counseling setting (Cade, 2007;

Froeschle, Smith, & Ricard, 2007). Solution Focused Brief Therapy contends that clients are the experts with regard to their lives (De Jong & Berg, 2002; de Shazer, 1988). The use of Solution Focused Brief Therapy in the classroom, therefore, requires a partnership between the counselor educator and the student with regard to evaluation, learning, and strategy for improvement. Students, rather than counselor educators, become experts on their own learning and consequently, provide input on classroom evaluation. Specific methods of evaluation as derived from Solution Focused Brief Therapy enable student engagement in learning, while at the same time offering a model of professionalism and respect.

DESCRIPTION AND USE OF SOLUTION FOCUSED EVALUATION

Solution Focused Brief Therapy has been used in many different settings with diverse individuals and groups (Cade, 2007; De Jong & Berg, 2002; Froeschle et al., 2007). In teaching, solution focused techniques personalize learning and consequently, merge with student assessment such that each student can learn regardless of their level of development. The following section draws upon solution focused skills that have been successfully used and describes a practical use for engaging and evaluating student performance. Skills such as (a) complimenting, (b) exception finding, (c) scaling, (d) coping questions, and (e) feedback (as taken from Solution Focused Brief Therapy) are described and illustrated so they can be practically used to improve student engagement in the evaluation process.

▶ *Complimenting.* The first skill used to successfully engage students in the evaluation process is de Shazer's (1988) and De Jong and Berg's (2002) complimenting. Complimenting entails pointing out personal qualities and strengths that may be drawn upon to resolve difficulties and create future successes (De Jong & Berg, 2002). Complimenting can create a positive environment such that students are comfortable sharing not only strengths, but weaknesses as well. This positive classroom environment leads to a collaborative non-fearful relationship between professor and students and becomes a catalyst for student engagement in personal evaluation. Examples follow to illustrate how this technique might be used to create positive classroom relationships leading to student engagement.

- The counseling professor comments on a student's written work in a manner that illustrates the student's personal qualities and strengths. Student fear and confusion are reduced leading to improved probabilities the student will assume ownership in the evaluation process and seek assistance from the professor. Positive comments can help students overcome confusion and fear that impedes engagement and personal growth (Walter & Peller, 1992).
- For example, complimenting is helpful when evaluating a student's presentation during an assessment or theories course. A student who presents on a

particular assessment instrument or counseling theory is complimented by the professor who points out important components contained in the presentation (i.e., reliability, validity, or cost when analyzing an assessment; or a cognitive, affective, directive, or nondirective approach in a theories presentation). Since individuals are receptive to compliments and will repeat a positive behavior once it is drawn to their attention (De Jong & Berg, 2002; Froeschle et al., 2007; Walter & Peller, 1992), it is likely the presenting student as well as others in the class will focus on these important components in future theory and instrument analysis.

- Complimenting can also help students overcome weaknesses. The professor might have students analyze theories or assessment instruments in a small group discussion. The professor listens to the discussion and interjects only when complimenting reinforces an important point or when inaccurate assumptions are challenged. For example, should a student inaccurately evaluate a theory or assessment instrument as being superior (despite research evidence to the contrary), the professor might compliment other students using research to debate the issue. Without commenting on the inaccurate student's view, the professor might say to other debating students, "You have the ability to think critically. This helps you find accurate research and use it to make good decisions." In this way complimenting positively corrects inaccurate assumptions and replaces what might be an embarrassing correction aimed at a particular student.

- Students can become engaged in their own evaluation and assist one another through complimenting. Once the professor points out positive components in an assessment or theories presentation, students are also encouraged to compliment one another on the inclusion of important details. In this way, students become engaged in the evaluation process and improved analysis of assessment instruments or theoretical concepts becomes the result.

Keep in mind compliments are not simply intended to be kind to students. Rather, they are used to reinforce student strengths that may be drawn upon to overcome weaknesses and obstacles. When used appropriately, compliments validate what students are doing well and offer confidence (De Jong & Berg, 2002). It is important to remember, however, that compliments must be authentic. Inauthentic compliments are not helpful and may actually diminish a student's self-efficacy (Franklin & Hopson, 2009; Green, Lee, Trask, & Rheinscheld, 2005). Consequently, much thought should be put into compliments so they illustrate actual strengths that students possess. Compliments can be used alone or alongside other skills described below.

▶ **Exceptions.** Counselors using Solution Focused Brief Therapy employ questioning to illustrate times when problems are less severe or nonexistent (De Jong & Berg, 2002). Focus is given to past successful behaviors. Consequently, this means clients take ownership of and create personal strategies for success (De Jong & Berg, 2002; Froeschle et al., 2007; Walter & Peller, 1992).

Use of exceptions easily transfers to the counseling classroom and promotes active engagement in evaluation. Students are asked to think of times when personal performance was better and to apply past actions to current situations. For example:

- Contract grading is a concept whereby students are given a list of assignments to perform varying in difficulty and number as based on grade desired in the course. For example, students wishing to receive an "A" in a course might have to complete a 10 page term paper accompanied by a presentation whereby those satisfied with a "B" might only need to complete the paper. Students must perform the assignment at the level corresponding to the grade desired. Having used this in recent classes, it is often helpful to let students know up front that any assignment that does not express the desired level of quality must be redone. Exception finding and complimenting assist confused students who must rewrite these assignments. For example, the counseling professor can first address what is done well in the assignment and follow up by asking questions that lead to better performance. Complimenting ensures that adequate parts of the assignment remain and are extended. Exception questions such as, "I wonder how you could enhance this so it looks more like the paper you turned in last month?" can be used to assist students in revising inadequate papers.

The use of exceptions can be a helpful skill when trying to engage students in their own evaluation process. The very nature of exceptions requires students to address methods of improvement based on past successes and focuses on processes that work for each individual (De Jong & Berg, 2002; Froeschle & Nix, 2009; Froeschle et al., 2007).

▶ *Scaling.* It is important to have students evaluate their own progress. One technique conducive to this concept is scaling (De Jong & Berg, 2002). For example, in a counseling techniques course students might be asked to evaluate their own work by rating it on a numeric scale numbered from 1 to 10. Several examples follow.

- After a student shows a counseling role play via video, professors ask, "On a scale from 1 to 10 with the number 1 meaning there were few things done well in this video to the number 10 meaning everything was done well, where would you rate your performance in this video?" Students choose a number and justify their own performance evaluation with examples taken from the video.
- A follow up of the aforementioned scaling of a video performance might entail asking the student, "What would you need to do to improve your performance by one number?" Students should give specific examples of ways to improve the counseling performance.
- If students cannot think of ways to improve, professors can ask scaling questions about specific skills (e.g., questioning). For example, suppose a student

rates their counseling video quite high and the professor disagrees. The professor might say, "Let's watch this again and I would like you to evaluate yourself on number of questions asked during this video." After watching the video again, the student would scale himself or herself based on only questioning skills. If a student continues to overrate the video, the professor might ask an exception question such as, "I noticed during your last video, you asked few questions. What do you think could be done to reduce the number of questions you asked in this video so it appears more like your last video?"

As illustrated in the previous examples, scaling offers a concrete method whereby students become the center of their own evaluations. Not only are students actively involved in determining levels of success, they also take control in suggesting personal improvements.

▶ *Coping questions.* Coping questions have been successfully used in the counseling setting with individuals exhibiting hopelessness as a result of an inability to see problem improvement (De Jong & Berg, 2002). Occasionally, students feel overwhelmed and frustrated about completing assignments. This may be a time for professors to instill hope via coping questions. Counseling professors can use coping questions in the classroom to aid discouraged students and offer encouragement. For example:

- A student is quite confused about an assignment and has done a poor job on it. When asked to give feedback on ways to improve, the student is ready to give up and becomes quite frustrated. The professor might use a combination of complimenting followed by a coping question thus, "It is quite encouraging that despite the fact you were unsure how to proceed, you had enough determination and skill that you turned something in. This determination and skill tells me you are going to be able to do this. How is it that you remained determined and submitted your work?" By combining a compliment with a coping question, the student is given encouragement to continue persevering. Further, the question engages the student so they can respond and offer personal thoughts on ways to proceed. Feedback, as described in the next section, can also help students engage in the evaluation process and focus on personal areas of growth.

▶ *Feedback.* Often, a student is unable to determine personal areas of growth without feedback from the professor. Students who recognize a need for change are more likely to experience growth (Franklin & Hopson, 2009). For this reason, it is important to phrase feedback in a manner such that students agree that changes are needed. Feedback is broken into three separate and distinct parts (compliment, bridge, task; De Jong & Berg, 2002; Walter & Peller, 1992). First, a compliment is given as a strength that will aid in the change process. Next, a bridge statement is given tying the compliment to the upcoming task. Finally, a task is given to complete (De Jong & Berg, 2002). The following scenarios illustrate how feedback can be used in the counseling classroom such that students become engaged in the evaluation process.

- A counseling student has written a paper that is not at the level expected by the professor. Despite using complimenting and exceptions, the student does not agree that the paper is deficient. The professor might say, "You are a good writer and you put much thought into everything you do (compliment). I agree with you that many of the ideas in this paper have merit (bridge). Given your talent, I am thinking this paper could be turned into something meaningful (bridge). I am thinking it might be helpful for you to read a few sample papers and determine some things you might add to make your paper better (task). Once you have read those papers, we can meet again and discuss areas you think you should change (task)." Although the professor in this scenario has made it clear changes are needed, the student is still involved in the evaluation and a respectful environment is instilled. As a result, it is more likely actual learning and growth will occur (Marchiondo, Marchiondo, & Lassiter, 2010).
- Suppose the student above comes back with inadequate correctness in the paper. The professor would give a compliment, bridge and task that might sound like this, "I appreciate that you were open minded enough to put so much thought into this task. You did not give up and your perseverance is going to get you through the assignment and this class (compliment). I agree with you there are things that need to be changed in this paper (bridge). I would like you to pretend for a moment that this is a better paper (task). You and I can brainstorm a list of things together that might make this an improved paper (task)." The professor has now structured the evaluation so hope is instilled within the student. Ownership in the changes is still in the hands of the student.

The aforementioned techniques involve students in their own evaluation while offering assistance, and avoiding criticism.

EVALUATING STUDENT FOCUSED EVALUATIONS

Recently, we used solution focused evaluation techniques in a classroom. We found students were more comfortable approaching the professor, asked more questions, and gave better course evaluations when using a solution focused approach. The following comments (as written on course evaluations) indicate increased feelings of support and rapport between professor and students, feelings of competence, and perceptions of improved learning:

- "The best part of the class was the professor. I've never felt this kind of support."
- "This professor is very interested in students as individuals and respectful and encouraging of our unique input and perspectives."

- "I almost gave up this profession before this class. The professor was extremely helpful in helping me improve."
- "I wish I had taken this class earlier. I feel better prepared now."
- "This is the best class I ever took. I learned more than in other classes."

While these comments lend credence to solution focused evaluation techniques, the idea of using course evaluations to ensure success may be suspect. Will solution focused evaluation influence students' evaluation of educators? Are these methods valid for determining the efficacy of solution focused evaluation?

Students' Evaluation of Educators

Student Evaluations of Teaching (SETs) in higher education can be used as a feedback mechanism for the improvement of teaching (a formative function); as a source of information for personnel decisions about tenure, promotion, and merit pay (a summative function); or as a way to better understand pedagogy and the conditions that affect learning. Critics of SETs indicate a lack of agreement on what constitutes effective teaching (Marques, Lane, & Dorfman, 1979; Orenstein, 1990) while advocates argue that if evaluation instruments are adequately developed, student ratings are valuable, reliable, and valid (Marsh & Roche, 1997; Marsh & Ware, 1982; Murray, 1983). This position was well articulated by Wilbert McKeachie (1990, p. 195) who wrote that "despite faculty doubts about the ability of students to appreciate good teaching, the research evidence indicates that students are generally good judges." Further, Marsh and Roche (1997, p. 1188) reviewed the reliability and generalizability of SETs and concluded that the "reliability of class-average SETs compares favorably with that of the best objective tests." Validity studies demonstrate that SETs reflect students' learning (Marsh, 1987; Marsh & Dunkin, 1992). Added evidence that SETs are valid is found in studies that show SETs are "significantly and consistently related to ratings of former students, students' achievement in multisection validity studies, teachers' self-evaluation, and extensive observations of trained observers on specific processes such as a teachers' clarity" (Marsh & Roche, 1997, p. 1190). It would seem, therefore, that despite the limitations of course evaluations in evaluating a professor's effectiveness as a teacher, the aforementioned comments shared by students on course evaluations are useful tools when evaluating the use of Solution Focused Brief Therapy techniques in the classroom. As this chapter has set forth, if educators approach teaching in general, and evaluation in particular, from a framework such as Solution Focused Brief Therapy, student-learning outcomes may excel and students may evaluate their teachers positively. Here, of course, lies our challenge, to extend research and discussion around pedagogical practices into counselor education.

REFERENCES

American Counseling Association (2005). *ACA Code of Ethics*. Alexandria, VA: Author.

Bain, K. (2004). *What the best college teachers do*. Cambridge, MA: Harvard University Press.

Cade, B. (2007). Springs, streams and tributaries: A history of the brief solution focused approach. In F. N Thomas & S. Thorana (Eds.), *Handbook of solution focused brief therapy: Clinical applications* (pp. 25–64). Binghamton, NY: Haworth Press.

Cohen, E. (2005). Student evaluations of course and teacher: Factor analysis and SSA approaches. *Assessment and Evaluations in Higher Education, 30*, 123–136.

Corey, G. (2005). *Theory and practice of counseling and psychotherapy* (7th ed.). Pacific Grove, CA: Brooks/Cole.

Davis, K. M., Chang, C. Y., & McGlothlin, J. M. (2005). Teaching assessment and appraisal: humanistic strategies and activities for counselor educators. *Humanistic Counseling, Education and Development, 44*, 94–101.

De Jong, P., & Berg, I. K. (2002). *Interviewing for solutions*. Pacific Grove, CA: Brooks/Cole.

de Shazer, S. (1988). *Clues: Investigating solutions in brief therapy*. New York: W. W. Norton.

Forsyth, D. R. (2004). *The professor's guide to teaching*. Washington, DC: American Psychological Association.

Franklin, C., & Hopson, L. (2009). Solution focused methods with involuntary clients in public schools. In R. H. Rooney (Ed.), *Strategies for work with involuntary clients* (pp. 322–333). New York, NY: Columbia University Press.

Froeschle, J. G., & Nix, S. (2009, February 9). A solution-focused leadership model: Examining perceptions of effective counselor leadership. *Journal of School Counseling, 7*(5). Retrieved from http://www.jsc.montana.edu/articles/v7n5.pdf

Froeschle, J., Smith, R. L., & Ricard, R. (2007). The efficacy of a systematic substance abuse program for adolescent girls. *Professional School Counseling, 10*, 498–505.

Green, G. J., Lee, M., Trask, R., & Rheinscheld, J. (2005). How to work with clients' strengths in crisis intervention: A solution focused approach. In A. R Roberts (Ed.), *Crisis intervention handbook: Assessment, treatment, & research* (pp. 64–89). New York, NY: Oxford University Press.

hooks, b. (1994). *Teaching to transgress: Education as the practice of freedom*. New York, NY: Routledge.

Marchiondo, K., Marchiondo, L. A., & Lassiter, S. (2010). Faculty incivility: Effects on program satisfaction of BSN students. *Journal of Nursing Education, 49*, 608–614.

Marques, T. E., Lane, D. M., & Dorfman, P. (1979). Toward the development of a system for instructional evaluation: Is there consensus regarding what constitutes effective teaching. *Journal of Educational Psychology, 71*(6), 840–849.

Marsh, H. W. (1987). Students' evaluations of university teaching: Research findings, methodological issues, and directions for future research. *International Journal of Educational Research, 11*(3), whole issue.

Marsh, H. W., & Dunkin, M. (1992). Students' evaluations of university teaching: A multidimensional perspective. In J. C. Smart (Ed.), *Higher Education: Handbook on Theory and Research* (Vol. 8, pp. 143–234). New York, NY: Agathon Press.

Marsh, H. W., & Roche, L. A. (1997). Making students' evaluation of teaching effectiveness effective: The critical issues of validity, bias, and utility. *American Psychologist, 52*(11), 1187–1197.

Marsh, H. W., & Ware, J. E. (1982). Effects of expressiveness, content coverage, and incentive on multidimensional student rating scales: New interpretations of Dr. Fox effect. *Journal of Educational Psychology, 74*(1), 126–134.

McKeachie, W. J. (1990). Research on college teaching: The historical background. *Journal of Educational Psychology, 82*(2), 189–200.

Murray, H. G. (1983). Low inference classroom teaching behaviors and student ratings of college effectiveness. *Journal of Educational Psychology, 75*(1), 138–149.

Nylund, D., & Tilsen, J. (2006). Pedagogy and praxis: Postmodern spirit in the classroom. *Journal of Systemic Therapies, 25*, 21–31.

Orenstein, A. C, (1990). A look at teacher effectiveness research; Theory and practice. *NASSP Bulletin, 74*(528), 78–88.

Palmer, P. J. (1997a). *The courage to teach: Exploring the inner landscape of a teacher's life.* San Francisco, CA: Jossey-Bass.

Palmer, P. J. (1997b). The heart of a teacher: Identity and integrity in teaching. *Change, 29,* 14–21.

Pare, D., & Tarragona, M. (2006). Generous pedagogy: Teaching and learning postmodern therapies. *Journal of Systemic Therapies, 25*, 1–7.

Paris, S. G., & Cross. G. R. (1983). Ordinary learning: Pragmatic connections among children's beliefs, motives, and actions. In J. Bisanz, G. Bisanz, & R. Kail (Eds.), *Learning in children* (pp. 137–170). New York, NY: Springer Verlag.

Pietrzak, D., Duncan, K., & Korcuska, J. (2008). Counseling students' decision-making regarding teaching effectiveness: A conjoint analyses. *Counselor Education and Supervision, 48,* 114–132.

Roth, J. (1997). *Inspiring teaching: Carnegie professors of the year speak.* Boston, MA: Anker.

Seuss, Dr. (1990). *Oh, the places you'll go!* New York, NY: Random House.

Skoog, G. D., & Johnson, M. (1998). *Connecting to improve methods courses.* Austin, TX: Texas State Board for Educator Certification.

Tinto, V. (1987). *Leaving college: Rethinking the causes and cures of student attrition.* Chicago, IL: University of Chicago Press.

Walter, J. L., & Peller, J. E. (1992). *Becoming solution focused in brief therapy.* Levittown, PA: Brunner/Mazel.

Wong, A., & Fitzsimmons, J. (2008). Student evaluation of faculty: An analysis of survey results. *U21 Global Working Paper Series, 3,* 1–7.

CHAPTER **12**

Broaching the Subjects of Race, Ethnicity, and Culture as a Tool for Addressing Diversity in Counselor Education Classes

NORMA L. DAY-VINES

CHERYL HOLCOMB-McCOY

iven the steady demographic shifts and future predictions of the U.S. population's increasing racial/ethnic and linguistic diversity, Sue et al. (1982) proposed a set of cross-cultural competencies that dramatically changed the way in which counselor education departments conducted their training. Over 25 years ago, the competencies explicated by Sue et al. set the stage for the Multicultural Counseling Competencies that mandated counselor education to prepare students to function and work effectively in a pluralistic and multicultural society (Sue, Arredondo, & McDavis, 1992). Later in 1996, the Association for Multicultural Counseling and Development (AMCD) added explanatory statements to the competencies, which further clarified and defined the three cultural competence domains of awareness, knowledge, and skills (Arredondo et al., 1996). In 2003, the American Counseling Association's (ACA) Governing Council unanimously passed a motion endorsing the Multicultural Counseling Competencies (Arredondo & D'Andrea, 2003). And as a result, training in multiculturalism and diversity became a prerequisite for accreditation by the Council for Accreditation of Counseling and Related Educational Programs (CACREP) and an ethical obligation set forth by ACA (ACA, 2005).

After the development of the AMCD Multicultural Counseling Competencies, multicultural counseling training (MCT) evolved and a plethora of professional activity ensued, including new MCT conceptual models (e.g., Toporek & Reza, 2001), new multicultural counseling course formats (e.g., Malott, 2010), and varied pedagogical approaches to multicultural training (e.g., Ancis & Ali, 2005). With the increasing need for effective MCT, questions emerged about the appropriate and most effective classroom and/or pedagogical strategies to cultivate growth in cultural competence. Pedagogical approaches that emphasize one or a combination of the three multicultural counseling competence domains are being developed (e.g., Buckley & Foldy, 2010) and research related to these approaches has revealed positive outcomes in Counselors-in-Training (CITs; D'Andrea, Daniels, & Heck, 1991; Neville et al., 1996). Nevertheless, there is still no general consensus as to which approaches produce the best counselor outcomes.

BROACHING RACE, ETHNICITY, AND CULTURE

Although there is general agreement that cultural factors play a significant role in the lives of clients and the counseling process, addressing culture, particularly race, presents complex challenges for not only students but also counselor educators (Tummala-Narra, 2009). Discussions about race, ethnicity, class, or any other cultural identity/dimension often produce powerful emotional responses in students that range from guilt and apathy to anger and despair (Locke & Kiselica, 1999). There have even been debates among counseling professionals (e.g., Arbuckle, 1997; Brown, 1996; Ivey & Ivey, 1997) that have further demonstrated the strong emotion and significance of discussing multicultural and diversity-related topics in graduate counseling programs.

The conceptual framework highlighted in this chapter was developed in order to help Counselors-In-Training (CITs) and counselor educators explore the extent to which not only race but any dimension of culture may influence a client's presenting concern, including but not limited to ethnicity, gender, social class, religiosity, sexual orientation, disability, English language variation, and age. Like Robinson (2005), we contend that these identity and/or cultural dimensions represent status variables in society that confer power, privilege, and dominance on those who maintain membership in higher status groups (e.g., middle class heterosexual males). By extension, those in lower status groups (e.g., poor and/or working class lesbian females) are often the target of mistreatment, derision, and structural inequality that may serve as the source of a client's concern during the counseling event. Effective counseling rests largely on the counselor's ability to process the client's concerns in a multiculturally sensitive and productive manner. Throughout the remainder of this chapter we use the terms race, ethnicity, and culture to address the inclusive nature of these identity dimensions as they arise within the context of counseling. Most of the research we cite as a rationale for the broaching continuum focuses on race as an identity dimension, primarily because race is a contentious and unresolved issue within the United States.

Day-Vines et al. (2007) developed the broaching construct to capture the CIT's orientation towards having explicit conversations about the impact of race and culture on the client's presenting concerns. Essentially during treatment, the CIT creates a safe and trusting therapeutic counseling environment within which clients can talk authentically about their race and culture-related concerns. The CIT's deliberate and intentional efforts to validate and affirm the client's sociocultural and sociopolitical realities can help alleviate psychological distress, promote empowerment, enhance resilience, stimulate more effective coping strategies, and facilitate improved decision making (Arnold, 2010; Day-Vines et al., 2007).

During the broaching process, the CIT does not define the client's race or culture as the primary source of concern, but rather considers the client in a cultural context. That is, the client and CIT work together to determine how race and culture *may* impact certain counseling related concerns and work subsequently to reduce client distress. Although every presenting concern will not be related to race, or culture, CITs have an ethical obligation to consider whether these issues warrant attention (ACA, 2005). Previous research has demonstrated that when clients have an opportunity to talk openly about their racial, ethnic, and culture-related concerns a number of benefits accrue, including but not limited to increased counselor credibility, a stronger therapeutic alliance, greater levels of client self-disclosure, higher levels of client satisfaction, and lower levels of premature termination (Fuertes, Mueller, Chauhan, Walker, & Ladany, 2002; Thompson, Worthington, & Atkinson, 1994).

Day-Vines et al. (2007) enumerated the *Continuum of Broaching Behavior* which addresses five separate categories or styles of exploring race, ethnicity, and culture during the counseling process: (a) *avoidant*, (b) *isolating*, (c) *continuing-incongruent*, (d) *integrated-congruent*, and (e) *infusing*. Each category along the continuum describes distinct approaches to examining race, ethnicity, and culture with the client. The first three categories reflect the CIT's labored and ineffective efforts to broach issues of diversity during the counseling process, and the final two categories describe the CIT's integration and synthesis of effective broaching behaviors. More recently, Day-Vines and Bryan (2011) operationalized the *Continuum of Broaching Behavior* using the *Broaching Attitudes and Behavior Scale* (BABS) and identified empirical support for four of the five broaching categories. Each of the identified subscales was labeled in accordance with the corresponding category represented along the broaching continuum. In the next section of this chapter, we describe the *Continuum of Broaching Behavior*, the revised *Multidimensional Model of Broaching Behavior*, followed by a discussion of strategies for including the broaching framework in content courses.

CONTINUUM OF BROACHING BEHAVIOR

Avoidant CIT

When issues related to race, ethnicity, and culture arise during the counseling process, the *avoidant* CIT ignores the client's culture-specific concerns (i.e., emic), opting instead to pay selective attention to universal concerns (i.e., etic) that apply broadly to all clients. Such an orientation may ignore salient aspects of the client's presenting concerns leaving the client with unmet counseling needs. In fact, the research of Pope-Davis et al. (2002) demonstrated that when clients, for whom race was salient, perceived counselors as unable to address their race-related concerns, clients met their cultural needs outside the counseling relationship within the safety and familiarity of friends and family members. Recent studies have demonstrated that higher levels of race neutral attitudes are associated with lower levels of multicultural counseling competence (Neville, Spanierman, & Doan, 2006) and lower levels of empathy (Burkard & Knox, 2004). Utsey, Gernat, and Hammar (2005) examined White European American CITs' reactions to racially provocative stimuli and concluded that participants struggled in their efforts to bring up or respond to racial and cultural issues with clients.

Isolating CIT

Unlike the avoidant CIT, the *isolating* CIT will broach racial, ethnic, and cultural concerns minimally. Soon after acknowledging the client's culture-specific concerns, the CIT may redirect the client's focus to topics that are less racially, ethnically, and culturally provocative. This superficial acknowledgement of the client's concern may suggest that the CIT has not been able to engage in multicultural case conceptualization. That is, the CIT does not consider multiple identity contexts (e.g., race, ethnicity, culture, religion, social class, sexual orientation, etc.) that may influence the client's concerns, the consequence of which may be that the client does not have her or his needs met.

Continuing-Incongruent CIT

The *continuing-incongruent* CIT maintains an openness towards broaching racial, ethnic, and cultural factors but lacks the accompanying skill set to do so. That is the CIT may broach racial, ethnic, and cultural factors in a mechanical fashion and experience difficulty translating the client's sociocultural and sociopolitical realities into effective counseling strategies and interventions. CITs with continuing-incongruent attitudes are likely to experience a sense of awkwardness as they broach and express difficulty finding the precise verbiage to communicate their intent to explore racial, ethnic, and cultural concerns with the client (Day-Vines & Bryan, 2011). The CIT's difficulty articulating conversations about race and representation with clients may reflect an unintentional form of bias during the counseling process.

Boysen (2010) cautioned about the potential for implicit biases to interfere with the counseling process. Implicit bias refers to the fact that stereotypes as well as negative attitudes and assumptions influence people's social behavior. Because implicit biases are difficult to control, people often remain unaware of how their attitudes, biases, and assumptions influence their behavior. We surmise that implicit attitudes may interfere with the CIT's ability to explore issues related race, ethnicity, and culture comfortably and objectively with the client. Boysen and Vogel (2008) examined the relationship between implicit bias and multicultural counseling competence in a sample of CITs. Their findings demonstrated that CITs who scored high on a self-reported measure of multicultural counseling competence also exhibited significant levels of implicit bias. This finding may be related to the CIT's tendency towards social desirability.

Overview of the First Three Broaching Categories

The first three categories along the broaching continuum suggest that CITs may struggle to broach racial, ethnic, and cultural concerns with their clients. Cardemil and Battle (2003) attributed this difficulty to concerns about saying something offensive, apprehensions that clients may perceive their helpers as biased, discomfort with racially charged topics, lack of personal efficacy, and limited skill sets. Additional reasons include the CIT's diminished ability to engage in cultural perspective taking, over-identification with the client, minimal exposure to people from diverse backgrounds, and the cognitive dissonance that can result from living in a racially ambivalent society (Cardemil & Battle, 2003; Day-Vines et al., 2007; Liu & Pope-Davis, 2005; Pope-Davis et al., 2002; Utsey et al., 2005). The final two categories along the continuum describe advanced broaching efforts that reflect more highly developed levels of cultural sensitivity.

Integrated-Congruent CIT

The *integrated-congruent* CIT recognizes the contextual dimensions of race, ethnicity, and culture and encourages the client to make culture-specific interpretations of their counseling concerns. As such integrated-congruent CITs can initiate and respond to racial and culturally related issues that surface during treatment without becoming anxious or defensive, redirecting the client's attention to more race or culturally neutral concerns, or minimizing the client's experience. *Integrated-congruent* CITs also recognize and accept the cultural meaning clients attach to their experience, and refrain from holding the client accountable for their encounters with racism and other forms of discrimination. Moreover, they can discuss racial, ethnic, and cultural issues without losing empathy towards the client or developing a defensive posture.

Because of the CIT's openness to cultural (e.g., racial, ethnic, gender, sexual orientation, disability) issues, *integrated-congruent* CITs can help clients explore their concerns in a meaningful way. More importantly, they do not rely on stereotypes to guide their judgment about clients. They possess self-awareness, recognize the client's sociopolitical concerns, attach importance to culture-specific knowledge, and translate their awareness and knowledge competencies into culturally relevant counseling responses. Unlike counselors operating within the first three broaching categories, *integrated-congruent* counselors can distinguish between culture-specific behavior and psychopathology (Day-Vines et al., 2007).

Zhang and Burkard (2008) examined the effects of counselor discussion of racial and cultural factors with clients. They concluded that European American counselors who addressed racial and cultural factors were deemed more credible than those who ignored racial and cultural issues.

Infusing CIT

The *infusing* CIT shares many similarities with the integrated-congruent CIT, insofar as her or his facility in exploring racial, ethnic, and cultural dynamics with clients during treatment (Day-Vines et al., 2007). The distinctive feature between *integrated-congruent* CITs and *infusing* CITs rests in the fact that *integrated-congruent* CITs relegate their broaching efforts to the counseling dyad. In marked contrast, *infusing* CITs demonstrate a commitment to eliminating oppression and promote social justice and equality. Essentially, the *infusing* CIT works both within and outside the counseling relationship to provide systemic interventions that promote client well-being (Day-Vines et al., 2007).

Whereas the *Continuum of Broaching Behavior* represents the CIT's openness or resistance towards having explicit conversations with clients about race, ethnicity, and culture, we proffer that the counselor may broach across a number of specific cultural domains or contexts. In the next section of this chapter we introduce the MultiDimensional Model of Broaching Behavior.

MULTIDIMENSIONAL MODEL OF BROACHING BEHAVIOR

The original *Continuum of Broaching Behavior* (i.e., described above) serves as a useful heuristic device for exploring racial and cultural factors with ethnic minority clients; however, in the absence of a discussion about the specific contexts in which the CIT broaches sociocultural and sociopolitical concerns, the model is limited. As presented here, the current iteration of the model is expanded to include not only the continuum of broaching behavior but also the domains or contexts under which the counselor may broach.

We proffer that the CIT may broach across a number of specific domains or contexts related to race, ethnicity, and culture which may include (a) *intra-individual* issues; (b) *intra-racial, ethnic, and cultural* issues; (c) *inter-racial, ethnic, and cultural* issues; and (d) *inter-counseling* issues and dynamics. CITs who broach *intra-individual* concerns facilitate client introspection with regard to race, ethnicity, and culture by helping the client explore the orthogonal relationship between several different identity dimensions (e.g., race, gender, social class, religious affiliation, sexual orientation, ability, English language variation, etc.) and their impact on the client. For instance, the counselor may help the client sort through what it means to be the only lesbian of color with a disability in her cohort to earn an advanced degree in a specialized area of physics. This negotiation of inner attitudes and identity states may be germane to the client's presenting problem, aid in symptom reduction, and promote psychological growth and empowerment. A sample broaching statement is as follows: "Often I ask my clients about their racial, ethnic, (and cultural) background because it helps me have a better understanding of who they are. Is that something you'd feel comfortable talking about?" (Cardemil & Battle, 2003, p. 279).

Counselors may also broach *intra-racial, ethnic, and cultural* issues that refer more to sociocultural or within group tensions that arise between the client and people with whom he or she shares a common heritage. That is, the client may have personal beliefs, value orientations, and behaviors that are at odds with values and viewpoints sanctioned by the cultural group. As an example, a young adult child of immigrants whose family of origin values collectivism may grapple with whether to honor familial expectations and reside at home until marriage or live apart from family members as so many of her or his western friends do. Value conflicts such as these can contribute to psychological distress in the client. Rather than merely focus on the client's desire to live independently, the CIT may invite the client to talk about her frustration in a cultural context. As such, the CIT may say, "It sounds like you're torn between honoring traditional cultural values and adapting more Americanized practices." The CIT's open acknowledgment of the client's cultural concern may help facilitate a discussion about the impact of differential levels of acculturation among family members on the client's well-being.

Counselors who broach *inter-racial, ethnic, and cultural* concerns help the client negotiate differences between the culture of origin and the dominant culture. This would also include efforts to help the client negotiate encounters with the sociopolitical dynamics of racism and discrimination, especially since a compelling body of research documents the fact that encounters with racism and oppression have compromised the psychological and physical well-being of people from marginalized groups during both historical and contemporary times (Bryant-Davis & Ocampo, 2005; Clark, Anderson, Clark, & Williams, 1999; Erickson & Al-Timimi, 2001). As an example, the client with a physical disability might present with concerns about work related stress that may be exacerbated by biased treatment in the workplace. A relevant broaching statement might be as follows: "It sounds like your stress is related more to the climate in the workplace and assumptions people make about your disability than it is about the actual job itself." Such a statement demonstrates CIT's recognition and willingness to discuss the client's challenges.

Inter-counseling dynamics refer to the interpersonal process that governs the counselor-client relationship. For instance, Cardemil and Battle (2003) described the counselor's effort to broach inter-counseling dynamics:

> I know that this can sometimes be a difficult topic to discuss, but I was wondering how you feel about working with someone who is from a different racial/ethnic background? I ask because although it is certainly my goal to be as helpful to you as I possibly can, I also know that there may be times when I cannot fully appreciate your experiences. I want you to know that I am always open to talking about the topics whenever they are relevant. (Cardemil & Battle, p. 281)

With appropriate training and preparation, the CIT should have the capacity to help the client explore a particular counseling concern from each of the broaching domains, as appropriate. In the next section of this chapter we identify several instructional approaches to teaching CITs to broach racial, ethnic, and cultural factors.

TEACHING STUDENTS TO BROACH RACE AND OTHER CULTURAL DIMENSIONS

Ideally, counselor educators should introduce the *Continuum of Broaching Behavior* and the *Multidimensional Model of Broaching Behavior* early during the didactic component of the counseling curriculum. As an example, the first author introduces each component of the Broaching model during the *Professional Orientation* class in order to help students recognize that the counselor's broaching behavior functions as an indispensible correlate of multicultural counseling competence by providing justification for the model. In order to provide continuity, CITs encounter the Broaching construct again during the *Counseling Techniques* course. After a short re-introduction of the Broaching model, students explore their attitudes and assumptions about broaching racial, ethnic, and cultural factors with clients in order to acknowledge both positive and negative feelings towards using this skill set. Students also have opportunities to examine case studies so that they can identify appropriate strategies for facilitating discussions of race, ethnicity, and culture with clients. Because we believe fervently that knowledge and experiential skills are inseparable, students also engage in peer interviewing activities during the *Counseling Techniques* course. As we discuss later in the chapter, one requirement of their peer interviewing activity is that they broach inter-counseling dimensions with one another.

Counselor educators may also incorporate the Broaching skill in several other courses within the counseling curriculum. For instance, during the *Counseling Theories* course, students might have opportunities to consider how a counselor would broach racial, ethnic, and cultural factors across theoretical frameworks. Students might develop a hypothetical broaching dialogue between the counselor and client using Rogerian Counseling, Cognitive Behavioral Therapy, Narrative Therapy, and so forth. During a *Career Counseling* course, students could determine how they might broach racial, ethnic, and cultural factors using Social Cognitive Career theory. During an *Assessment* course, counselor educators could administer the BABS (Day-Vines & Bryan, 2011) so that students could assess their functioning along the broaching continuum. Below, the reader will find a series of activities that counselor educators can use to introduce broaching skills. Although we have provided some recommendations, we recognize the importance of not being overly prescriptive, and we suggest that counselor educators examine their own curricula and determine how best to sequence the activities presented below.

1. Consider Own Attitudes, Biases and Assumptions
   - Administer Implicit Association Test (Greenwald, McGhee, & Schwartz, 1998)
2. Introduce Broaching Model
3. Identify Rationale for Broaching Behavior
4. Explore CIT's Attitudes towards Broaching Behavior
   - Identify positive and negative feelings about broaching racial, ethnic and cultural issues with clients (e.g., resentment, ambivalence, excitement, curiosity)
   - Normalize reactions
5. Demonstrate the counselor's broaching behavior (see sample statements listed under the *Multidimensional Model of Broaching Behavior*)
6. Use case studies and films to help students develop their multicultural case conceptualization skills. For instance, have students distinguish between emic and etic concerns; identify hypothetical counseling concerns; generate broaching stems or statements that may help the client explore the contextual dimensions of race, ethnicity, and culture. Based on the case studies and film clips, have students generate hypothetical broaching statements of counselors operating at each of the five categories of the broaching continuum (Avoidant – Infusing). Have CITs identify the contexts in which they may broach (e.g., intra-individual; intra-racial, -ethnic, and -cultural; inter-racial, -ethnic, and

-cultural; and inter-counseling dynamics); have students role play relevant broaching statements between the protagonist in the film and the CIT; have CITs acknowledge and identify their tacit assumptions about clients within the case study or film so that they can monitor their reactions.

Multicultural Interviews and Supervision

Multicultural interviewing is a course assignment that we have utilized to provide CITs an opportunity to put into practice their broaching skills. Essentially, CITs identify an individual from a culturally diverse background and conduct two, 30-minute videotaped interviews that allow them to practice their broaching efforts. Multicultural interviews differ from a counseling relationship in that they do not attempt to engage in problem definition or resolution with the interviewee, but they are designed to help the CIT explore and better understand the salient aspects of the interviewee's sociocultural and sociopolitical reality. Ladany, Inman, Constantine, and Hofheinz (1997) suggested that interviews are less threatening than a true counseling session.

During the interview, CITs ask the interviewee questions about her or his racial, ethnic, and cultural background using appropriate broaching statements that CITs generate in advance of the actual interview (e.g., cultural background; values instilled by the cultural group; what membership in racial, ethnic or cultural group means to interviewee; encounters with racism and discrimination; etc.). Once CITs broach multicultural issues they continue the interview by using the basic listening sequence to explore the interviewee's experience (e.g., rapport building, attending skills, open questions, reflection of content, and reflection of feeling as appropriate).

Upon completion of the first interview, trainees review their tapes and provide detailed written analysis of the session. This reflective paper summarizes the interview content; provides a multicultural case conceptualization of the interview; describes the CIT's thoughts, feelings, and concerns about the broaching process prior to, during, and following the interview; distinguishes between *etic* and *emic* concerns; appraises the CIT's broaching efforts; identifies related intentions associated with each broaching question or statement; and identifies possible directions for the subsequent interview. In addition, CITs identify any biases and assumptions they harbored towards the interviewee that could interfere with the interview process, and examine personal insight acquired during the interview process.

Afterwards, CITs convene for triadic supervision. Each CIT presents a five-minute taped segment of her or his broaching efforts for peer review and constructive feedback from the instructor. During supervision, CITs discuss their broaching experience relative to what they anticipated the experience would be like, identify statements used during the interview to enhance or inhibit their broaching efforts, examine the effectiveness of those efforts, identify intentions associated with their broaching behavior, and generate follow-up questions for the final 30-minute session. Triadic supervision affords students the opportunity to make mistakes and to speak openly and honestly about their fears, revel in their accomplishments, and build efficacy levels surrounding their ability to broach racial, ethnic, and cultural factors.

Using feedback gleaned from the initial supervision session, CITs conduct a second interview and continue to explore and examine the interviewee's experiences within the context of their race, ethnicity, and culture. Additionally, CITs ask the interviewee to explore what it was like to discuss racial and cultural factors and they elicit constructive feedback regarding the interview. Following the second broaching interview, students participate in the triadic supervision process again. During supervision, the instructor can address process issues with CITs: "Is broaching (the technique) more difficult depending on the cultural dimension? For instance, is it more difficult to broach the topic of race than it is to broach gender with clients?" "What was your initial reaction to the concept of broaching?" "What is your main barrier to ever broaching sexual orientation with a client?" "What impact did your broaching behavior have on your ability to connect with the interviewee?"

EVALUATION OF BROACHING SKILLS

Teaching CITs to broach race, ethnicity, or a specific cultural dimension with a client is a complex phenomenon, and one can assume that several factors act synergistically. Surely, factors at the level of both student (e.g., motivation, racial background, prior beliefs, anxiety about topic) and instructor (e.g., rapport, teaching alliance, immediacy skills) may have the potential to influence skill development and teaching effectiveness. Consequently, the use of a teaching evaluation may be contaminated by multiple factors and not provide an accurate evaluation of the effectiveness of the broaching practice activities described in this chapter. Given the limits of assessing effectiveness with a standard teaching evaluation, we recommend that instructors measure the effectiveness of the broaching exercises and students' understanding of the broaching concept by utilizing a variety of performance-based assessments and self-report measures. Comments that follow describe strategies for evaluating students' broaching skill set.

Performance-Based Assessments

Performance-based assessments require that instructors are explicit in explaining what they will be assessing and these guidelines are communicated to the student prior to the assessment. One of the simplest measures of skill development is to construct and communicate detailed guidelines or criteria for successful completion of the skill. Instructors can use the multicultural interviews to assess whether CITs have mastered the skill of broaching. Weeks before the interview, instructors should enumerate the rubric or grading criteria that will guide the assessment. See below for an example of a grading rubric for assessing the CITs broaching effectiveness. Through live observations and/or evaluating recordings, an instructor can assess a student's broaching competence.

Performance-Based Rating Scale

4 = Outstanding Mastery of Broaching Skills: Strong mastery of skills evident
3 = Mastered Basic Broaching Skills: Understanding of broaching skills evident
2 = Developing: Minor skill errors in broaching; in process of developing
1 = Needs Improvement: Significant remediation needed; deficits in broaching skills
Note: Scores of 3 and 4 indicate performing well for developmental level

FIGURE 12.1. Broaching Rubric

When constructing a performance-based assessment of broaching behavior, instructors should consider separating cognitive understanding of broaching from performance-based understanding of broaching. Cognitive understanding of broaching can be assessed by self-report measures, examinations, and/or journaling, whereas using a performance-based measure best assesses skill development.

Self-Report Measures

Counselor educators may administer the *Broaching Attitudes and Behavior Scale* (BABS; Day-Vines & Bryan, 2011) as a self-assessment tool to help CITs reflect on and guide their broaching behavior. The BABS operationalizes the Continuum of Broaching Behavior and assesses counselors' attitudes towards having explicit discussions about race, ethnicity, and culture with clients. Instructors can use this instrument as a pre-post measure that permits CITs to estimate their self-perceived broaching behaviors prior to and directly following the multicultural interviews. We recommend that the instrument be used strictly as a diagnostic tool that provides instructors with insight for continued training and preparation of CITs and not as a tool to evaluate student competency attainment.

After teaching the broaching model, instructors should also take time to reflect on their experiences, their challenges, and their feelings about the teaching strategy. Below is a list of sample questions that instructors may ask of themselves:

1. Did I provide a safe classroom environment for students to practice the skill of broaching?

2. Did I provide a safe classroom environment where students felt open enough to discuss their beliefs about multiculturalism, diversity, and so forth?
3. Did the broaching concept/activities make a difference in students' engagement in the course?
4. Did I leave enough time for students to share their feelings and reactions to the broaching concept?

CONCLUSION

The need for MCT strategies that have evidence of effectiveness remains an urgent priority in counselor education given the increasingly diverse client caseloads of counselors. The broaching model, as described in this chapter, is an example of a new strategy for teaching CITs to integrate the sociopolitical experiences of their clients' concerns into the counseling process. Our experiences teaching multicultural counseling and using the broaching framework have been overwhelmingly positive. Students, via formal and informal feedback, have found the broaching framework to be useful in their development of multicultural counseling competence as well as their own personal growth and understanding of race, ethnicity, and culture.

REFERENCES

American Counseling Association. (2005). *American Counseling Association Code of Ethics*. Alexandria, VA: Author.

Ancis, J. R., & Ali, S. (2005). Multicultural counseling training approaches: Implications for pedagogy. In C. Enns, A. L. Sinacore, C. Enns, & A. L. Sinacore (Eds.), *Teaching and social justice: Integrating multicultural and feminist theories in the classroom* (pp. 85–97). Washington, DC: American Psychological Association.

Arbuckle, D. (1997, Fall). *Arbuckle's response*. ACES Spectrum, pp. 4–5.

Arnold, K. (2010). *A qualitative examination of African American counselors' experiences of addressing issues of race, ethnicity, and culture with clients of color*. Unpublished doctoral dissertation, Virginia Tech.

Arredondo, P., & D'Andrea, M. (2003, May). Honoring the divinity of our children. *Counseling Today*, p. 36.

Arredondo, P., Toporek, R., Brown, S., Jones, J., Locke, D., Sanchez, J., & Stadler, H. (1996). Operationalization of the multicultural counseling competencies. *Journal of Multicultural Counseling and Development, 24*, 42–78.

Boysen, G. A. (2010). Integrating implicit bias into counselor education. *Counselor Education and Supervision, 49*, 210–227.

Boysen, G. A., & Vogel, D. L. (2008). The relationship between level of training, implicit bias, and multicultural competency among counselor trainees. *Training and Education in Professional Psychology, 2*, 103, 110.

Brown, D. (1996, Fall). *Reply to Derald Wing Sue*. ACES Spectrum, pp. 3–4.

Bryant-Davis, T., & Ocampo, C. (2005). The trauma of racism: Implications for counseling, research, and education. *Counseling Psychologist, 33*, 574–578.

Buckley, T. R., & Foldy, E. (2010). A pedagogical model for increasing race-related multicultural counseling competency. *The Counseling Psychologist, 38*(5), 691–713.

Burkard, A. W., & Knox, S. (2004). Effect of therapist color-blindness on empathy and attributions in cross-cultural counseling. *Journal of Counseling Psychology, 51*, 387–397.

Cardemil, E., & Battle, C. (2003). Guess who's coming to therapy? Getting comfortable with conversations about race and ethnicity in therapy. *Professional Psychology: Research and Practice, 34*, 278–286.

Clark, R., Anderson, N. B., Clark, V. R., & Williams, D. R. (1999). Racism as a stressor for African Americans. *American Psychologist, 54*(10), 805–816.

D'Andrea, M., Daniels, J., & Heck, R. (1991). Evaluating the impact of multicultural counseling training. *Journal of Counseling & Development, 70*(1), 143–150.

Day-Vines, N., & Bryan, J. (2011). *The Broaching Attitudes and Behavior Scale (BABS): An exploratory assessment of its dimensionality.* Unpublished manuscript.

Day-Vines, N. L., Wood, S. M., Grothaus, T., Craigen, L., Holman, A., Dotson-Blake, K., & Douglass, M. J. (2007). Broaching the subjects of race, ethnicity, and culture during the counseling process. *Journal of Counseling & Development, 85*(4), 401–409.

Erickson, C., & Al-Timimi, N. (2001). Providing mental health services to Arab Americans: Recommendations and considerations. *Cultural Diversity and Ethnic Minority Psychology, 7*, 308–327.

Fuertes, J., Mueller, L., Chauhan, R., Walker, J., & Ladany, N. (2002). An investigation of European American therapists' approach to counseling African American clients. *The Counseling Psychologist, 30*, 763–768.

Greenwald, A. G., McGhee, D. E., & Schwartz, J. L. K. (1998). Measuring individual differences in implicit cognition: The Implicit Association Test. *Journal of Personality and Social Psychology, 74*, 1464–1480.

Ivey, A. E., & Ivey, M. B. (1997, Winter). *White privilege and the need for collaboration: Reflections from New Hampshire.* ACES Spectrum, pp. 10–12.

Ladany, N., Inman, A. G., Constantine, M. G., & Hofheinz, E. W. (1997). Supervisee multicultural case conceptualization ability and self-reported multicultural competence as functions of supervisee racial identity and supervisor focus. *Journal of Counseling Psychology, 44*, 284–293.

Liu, W. M., & Pope-Davis, D. B. (2005). The working alliance, therapy ruptures and impasses, and counseling competence: Implications for counselor training and education. In R. T. Carter (Ed.), *Handbook of racial-cultural psychology and counseling: Training and practice* (Vol. 2, pp. 148–167). Hoboken, NJ: John Wiley and Sons.

Locke, D. C., & Kiselica, M. S. (1999). Pedagogy of possibilities: Teaching about racism in multicultural counseling courses. *Journal of Counseling and Development, 77*, 80–86.

Malott, K. M. (2010). Multicultural counselor training in a single course: Review of research. *Journal of Multicultural Counseling and Development, 38*(1), 51–63.

Neville, H., Spanierman, L., & Doan, B. (2006). Exploring the association between color-blind racial ideology and multicultural counseling competence. *Cultural Diversity and Ethnic Minority Psychology, 12*, 275–290.

Neville, H. A., Heppner, M., Louie, C., Thompson, C., Brooks, L., & Baker, C. (1996). The impact of multicultural training on White racial identity attitudes and counseling competencies. *Professional Psychology: Research and Practice, 27*, 83–89.

Pope-Davis, D. B., Toporek, R. L., Ortega-Villalobos, L., Ligiero, D., Brittan-Powell, C., Liu, W. M., . . . Liang, C. T. (2002). Client perspectives of multicultural counseling competence: A qualitative examination. *Counseling Psychologist, 30,* 355–393.

Robinson, T. L. (2005). *The convergence of race, ethnicity, and gender: Multiple identities in counseling* (2nd ed.). Columbus, OH: Prentice Hall.

Sue, D. W., Arredondo, P., & McDavis, R. J. (1992). Multicultural counseling competencies and standards: A call to the profession. *Journal of Multicultural Counseling and Development, 20*(2), 64–88.

Sue, D. W., Bernier, J. E., Durran, A., Feinberg, L., Pederson, P., Smith, E., & Vasquez-Nuttall, E. (1982). Position paper: Cross-cultural counseling competencies. *The Counseling Psychologist, 10*(2), 45–52.

Thompson, C. E., Worthington, R., & Atkinson, D. R. (1994). Counselor content orientation, counselor race, and Black women's cultural mistrust and self-disclosures. *Journal of Counseling Psychology, 41,* 155–161.

Toporek, R. L., & Reza, J. V. (2001). Context as a critical dimension of multicultural counseling: Articulating personal, professional, and institutional competence. *Journal of Multicultural Counseling and Development, 29*(1), 13–30.

Tummala-Narra, P. (2009). Teaching on diversity: The mutual influence of students and instructors. *Psychoanalytic Psychology, 26,* 322–334.

Utsey, S. O., Gernat, C. A., & Hammar, L. (2005). Examining White counselor trainee's reactions to racial issues in counseling and supervision dyads. *The Counseling Psychologist, 33,* 449–478.

Zhang, H., & Burkard, A. W. (2008). Client and counselor discussions of racial and ethnic differences in counseling: An exploratory investigation. *Journal of Multicultural Counseling and Development, 36,* 77–87.

CHAPTER 13

Epilogue: Teaching in Counselor Education

DONALD L. BUBENZER

JOHN D. WEST

JANE A. COX

JASON MCGLOTHLIN

O ur engagement in this writing and editing process has heightened our appreciation for the complexities of teaching. As we reflected on our teaching, and corresponded and discussed issues with the chapter authors, we were reminded of lessons we had learned (about teaching) and how we had been introduced to new ideas and practices. Our discussions about teaching methods and materials, students as learners, and educational atmospheres that motivate learning, grew in complexity and breadth. Above all we became even more aware of the personhood of engaged teachers; teachers who are shrouded with patience, passion, compassion, courage, kindness, generosity, accountability, curiosity, wisdom, and the knowledge that education is a process.

As the project moved forward, there were a number of areas about teaching and the engagement of students in learning that were drawn to our awareness. Three areas were particularly poignant to us: preparation, learning as a communal and on-going activity, and the personhood of the teacher.

PREPARATION

Looking across the authors' writings on teaching methods, we were struck by the immense amount of preparation that precedes stepping into the classroom. Palmer

(2004), writing to a slightly different context, termed this preparation "the work before the work" (p. 104). Many of us have listened to how people chose to get into teaching and even more specifically into counselor education. On occasion, teaching was a role they chose in childhood play. And at times folks may have recalled their interest in counseling as being linked with sensitivity to the pain of a family member or resident of the community, and may remember the desire to use counseling or educational means to lessen that pain. In some ways, many of us might say, "Much of life has been in preparation for the actual engagement of teaching."

No matter the activity with which we are involved, a part of our mind might easily be on teaching, upon the teaching-learning related puzzles that are lodged there. A good deal of what we read or discuss or observe or recall has application to these puzzles that are seeking solutions. These reflections and thoughts about teaching seem to sally-forth from our involvements, perhaps because we live a teaching-learning lifestyle. Even while writing about these reflections, ideas and quotations from Annie Dillard's, *Pilgrim at Tinker Creek* (1974) come to mind. From her chapter titled, *Seeing,* she notes there are two kinds of folks who can truly see: "lovers" and "the knowledgeable" (p. 18). Upon visiting an aunt in Wyoming she was feeling a bit useless in assisting with the chores of the ranch. She came upon the idea of contributing to the ambiance of the occasion by offering what she thought were her drawing skills and by creating a picture of a horse. When she passed her drawing down the table, her nieces and nephews, lovers of horses, each picked up a pencil and drew his or her version of a horse. Annie wrote, "When the paper came back it looked as though five shining real quarter horses had been corralled by mistake with a papier-mâché moose. . . ." Further, "Everyone in that family, including my cousins, could draw a horse. Beautifully" (p. 18). Her point was that the lover has developed special eyes for seeing the object of his or her love. Later she spoke of the knowledgeable by writing, "The herpetologist asks the native, 'Are there snakes in the ravine?' 'Nosir.' And the herpetologist comes home with yessir, three bags full" (pp. 18-19).

In reviewing these chapters we were captured by the love for teaching and the knowledge of teaching that the authors hold and the desire they have for engaging students in learning. A key seems to be in the preparation they make in order to further develop their love and knowledge of teaching. For them, and we suspect all good teachers, preparation appears to be an intentional and continual activity. Their reading, research, and scholarship seem to contain a scan for an application to teaching. As counselor educators, we have the good fortune that whether attending a movie or taking a break at our favorite coffee shop, we may encounter and see an illustration or idea that can nudge our teaching and classroom conversations towards meaningful exchanges. For knowledgeable teachers who love their work, all of life offers an opportunity to engage in the "work before the work" (Palmer, 2004, p. 104). Part of the work before the work might include engaging in what

Gergen (1999) termed "self-reflexivity" (p. 162) or questioning of one's assumptions and positions, that is, the letting go of firm positions in favor of identifying and probing our assumptions. Gergen indicated such a practice provides opportunity for new and transforming conversations. The following is a small sample of questions that may illustrate thinking about the practice of preparation.

- In preparing for a particular classroom session, what elements do I include in my effort?
- In preparing for a particular classroom session, what elements do I not include that might assist in engaging students in learning?
- In preparing for today's class, in what ways have I built on previous classroom sessions?
- In what ways does my preparation for teaching consider the content to be covered, as well as my readiness to respond to learning that lies beyond the focus of today's class?

KNOWLEDGE AS CONTINUALLY EVOLVING COMMUNAL PROCESS

Included in the myriad of ideas that came to mind and stuck, as we engaged in this project, was the thought that teaching and learning, the pursuit and transmission of knowledge, is a continually evolving and communal process. The idea that "knowledge" is evolving and community driven is obviously not a new idea. That which we call knowledge or truth, particularly in the social science-education arena, is always "historically and culturally located" (Gergen, 1999, p. 93). So even that which is presented as truth, is really a contribution to a conversation, and when that conversation takes place, it may alter the very truth that was just pronounced. Stated another way, Palmer (2004) wrote, "Truth [knowledge] is an eternal conversation about things that matter, conducted with passion and discipline" (p. 127).

The implication is that what we call knowledge is really a continual community dialogue that becomes the soul of the term "education." The continual journey of knowledge creation cannot be taken alone. It is a dialogical journey as witnessed by the authors of these chapters. The vast majority of these chapters on teaching were written communally. Even those written solely were derived communally. The ideas presented were the result of contact with other authors via readings—see Shulman's (1999) comments on drawing from the "scholarship of others" (p. 15)—and through experiences and dialogues with students, colleagues, and members of the larger society. The outcomes of these dialogues, even if research based, remains our best hunch (knowledge) about life, counseling, education, engaging students in learning, and so forth, and these hunches are seen as ever evolving.

The authors, singularly or in groups, have shared and explored ideas about using particular instructional methods (e.g., lectures, small group activities, etc.)

to engage students in this pilgrimage of knowledge. They have discussed ways in which we can encourage ourselves and others to enter a journey into a profession (counselor education) with an identifiable people (students, colleagues). In each instance they have left us as teachers with ideas about some ways in which they and others have assisted in the communal exploration of ideas. As teachers, the contributions of these authors also raise questions in our minds about how to provide opportunities for students to engage in this knowledge seeking pilgrimage. Palmer (2004) indicated that the search for truth (knowledge) usually does not come from debate, a process that results in winners and losers, but from discussion. He further noted that one way an atmosphere of discussion can be created is by cultivating an environment that provides for a "community of solitudes" (p. 54), a place in which each person can reflect on who he or she is, and what he or she thinks, and ways in which we are part of a community. How do we as teachers provide such a learning environment and encourage the internal and external reflection implied in a "community of solitudes?" We would hope the following questions might exemplify such a reflective examination.

- Who do I avoid including in my community of learning and what might I gain/lose as a teacher by seeking them out?
- How does my commitment to specific communities and traditions of knowledge, for example, theories, research methodologies, and teaching practices, enhance and/or diminish my growth as a teacher?
- What does engaging students in the communal process of knowledge creation mean and not mean to me?

PERSONHOOD OF THE TEACHER

A third theme that runs through the chapters related to teaching methodologies could be termed the personhood of the teacher. Parker Palmer (2007) wrote, "the things I teach are things I care about—and what I care about helps define my selfhood" (p. 17). Palmer also noted that, "good teachers share one trait: a strong sense of personal identity infuses their teaching" (p. 11). Examples of one's identity as a teacher are, of course, endless but might include "enthusiasm for . . . [one's] subject" (p. 11), demonstrations of a "quiet and confident" manner (p. 15), sensitivity for societal concerns and integrating them into teaching, and/or talent for introducing stories and possible humor into teaching. Obviously, faculty can also infuse other identities into teaching that, for example, may represent a distancing between the teacher, subject, and student (p. 11), a "critical and judgmental" stance (p. 15), a peer relationship with students where boundaries seem unclear, and/or an effort at establishing a paternal/maternal mentoring relationship.

It is also thought worthwhile to remember another of Palmer's (2007) perspectives on identity and teaching, "I can choose the place within myself from which my teaching will come. . . . I need not teach from a fearful place: I can teach from curiosity or hope or empathy or honesty, places that are as real within me as are my fears" (Palmer, 2007, p. 58). This would seem to speak to a plurality of possibilities, from which a counselor educator can recognize potential and promising identities as a teacher. Along these lines, Gergen and Warhus (2001) noted that "there . . . [has been] the traditional ideal of a self whose mental world is coherent, integrated and unified" (p. 108); however, they went on to mention that, "With the emergence of constructionist consciousness, these traditional romances with unity are placed in question. The argument for multiple constructions of the real . . . renders the concept of the 'single, coherent truth' both parochial and potentially oppressive" (p. 108). Gergen (2009) wrote of "critical reflexivity" or what we consider to be reflective thinking and mentioned that it was "the attempt to place one's premises into question, to suspend the 'obvious', to listen to alternative framings of reality, and to grapple with the comparative outcomes of multiple standpoints" (p. 12). It would seem to be just this type of reflective effort that is needed if counselor educators are to consider the identity or self they wish to infuse into their teaching; for example, counselor educators might ask themselves:

- What preferred personhoods (identities) are in my narrative about teaching?
- What is unhelpful about my preferred personhoods (identities) and how might this influence the engagement of students in learning?
- What is useful or beneficial about my preferred personhoods (identities) and how might this influence the engagement of students in learning?
- What additional personhoods (identities) might be useful in the engagement of students in learning?

At its best, education, including counselor education, would seem to be responsive to the puzzles of the time and offer avenues for attending to them. With an awareness of the multicultural nature of the world in which we live, and the potential for both conflict and hope, we sense in education the need for thoughtfulness and preparation, for significant collaboration, and for teachers who in their personhood recognize the need for inclusive and respectful conversations. We are grateful to those who have dedicated themselves to teaching, for they have worked to influence the future of the counseling profession.

REFERENCES

Dillard, A. (1974). *Pilgrim at Tinker Creek*. New York, NY: Harper & Row.

Gergen, K. J. (1999). *An invitation to social construction*. Thousand Oaks, CA: Sage.

Gergen, K. J. (2009). *An invitation to social construction* (2nd ed.). Thousand Oaks, CA: Sage.

Gergen, K. J., & Warhus, L. (2001). Therapy as social construction. In K. J. Gergen (Ed.), *Social construction in context* (pp. 96-114). Thousand Oaks, CA: Sage.

Palmer, P. J. (2004). *A hidden wholeness: The journey toward an undivided life.* San Francisco, CA: Jossey-Bass.

Palmer, P. J. (2007). *The courage to teach: Exploring the inner landscape of a teacher's life* (10th ed.). San Francisco, CA: John Wiley & Sons.

Shulman, L. S. (1999, July/August). Taking learning seriously. *Change, 31,* 11–17.

Index

Figures are indicated by f following the page number.

reflection's role in, 53–54, 55–56
simulations as, 57
types of, 56–59
written journals and, 61
Experiments, 52, 56–57

F

Facebook, 88, 125, 130
Faculty. *See* Instructors
Fairy tales and storytelling, 31
Family therapy, 59–60
Feedback
 in distance learning, 110
 in evaluations, 146–147
 on homework, 73–74
 for multicultural interviews, 161
 solution focused evaluations and, 146–147
 student–teacher relationships and, 134–135
 as teaching mechanism, xiv
Fink, L. D., 17–18
Finlay, W., 105
Fisch, Richard, xiii
Fitzmaurice, M., 2–3
Flowers, S. K., 106
Focus groups, 60
Formative feedback, 135
Forsyth, H., 103
Fouts, J. T., 81
Friesen, M., 6, 8
Froeschle, Janet, xx, 139

G

Gee, Gordon, 1
George, Kelsey, xix, 67
Gergen, Kenneth, xiii, 6, 169, 171
Gergen, Mary, 6
Gernat, C. A., 154
Gestalt learning theory, 30
Getz, H., 82
Ginsberg, S. M., 2
Goals
 syllabus reflection of, 20
 in teaching philosophy statement, 7–8
Goodman, A., 31
Google+, 88
Grades. *See* Evaluations
Granello, P. F., 110
Griffin, P., 32

Griffith, E. M., 108
Group counseling courses, 61
Group dynamics
 in-group/out-group relationship issues, 131
 in seminars, 41
Gu, X., 104

H

Haberstroh, S., 103
Hammar, L., 154
Hammer, E. Y., 126, 127
Harnish, R. J., 14
Harrawood, L. K., 60
Hash tags, 85
Hastings, J. K., 106
Hativa, N., 3
Hawthorne, K., 106
Hazler, Richard J., xviii, 37
Henderson, G., 127, 129
Hendricks, Bret, xx, 139
Herron, J. F., 4
Hill, N. R., 1
Hinkle, Michelle S. Gimenez, 1
Hofheinz, E. W., 160
Hohenshil, T. H., 100
Holcomb-McCoy, Cheryl, xx, 151
Holland, J. L., 32
Homework, xix, 67–79
 accreditation standards and, 73
 class discussions on, 76
 critical thinking and, 73
 evaluating effectiveness of, 76–77
 feedback on, 73–74
 instructor's implementation of, 71–74
 instructor's investment in, 77
 instructor's rationale for, 67–70
 licensure requirements and, 73
 peer reviews of, 76
 purpose for, 71–72
 student evaluations of, 76
 student implementation of, 74–75
 student investment in, 77
 student rationale for, 70–71
 student's sense of responsibility and, 72–73
 therapeutic role of, 67–68
Hong, E., 75
Houston, H., 106